Lord Mountbatten

Admiral Rickover

Six Men Out of the Ordinary

Lord Zuckerman

Six Men Out of the Ordinary

With a Foreword by
HRH The Duke of Edinburgh

PETER OWEN · LONDON

PETER OWEN PUBLISHERS
73 Kenway Road London SW5 0RE

First published in Great Britain 1992
© Lord Zuckerman 1992

A catalogue record for this book is
available from the British Library

ISBN 0–7206–0854–6

Printed in Great Britain by Billings of Worcester

Contents

*   *   *

Two Nuclear Scientists

Patrick Blackett   13
Isidor I. Rabi   39

Two Air Chiefs

Marshal of the RAF, Lord Tedder   65
General Carl A. Spaatz   99

Two Admirals

Admiral Earl Mountbatten of Burma   131
Admiral Hyman G. Rickover   169

Index   198

Foreword

*   *   *

It takes an extraordinary man to write about out-of-the-ordinary men. If Lord Zuckerman had not been the author of this book, he would certainly have qualified to be included. It says a lot for the diversity of his interests and occupations that he was able to become so intimately acquainted with six men, such remarkable men, from such different backgrounds. What makes his accounts so particularly interesting is that he was associated with them during the dramatic days of the Second World War and the issues they were handling were crucial to the conduct of that war.

It was an unlikely fate for someone who started life in South Africa and who made his first contribution to science through the study of monkeys and apes. Life is pretty uncertain anyway, but the second round of the great European conflict which commenced in 1939 changed or formed the lives of everyone involved. Much depended on your age and what you happened to be doing or chose to do when the war broke out. Lord Zuckerman chose to study the effects of bomb blasts on people and buildings and from there one thing led to another until he found himself Scientific Adviser to the Ministry of Defence. The six men of this book, among many great, eccentric and flamboyant characters, came into his life on the way from one to the other. I am sure that he would class them as the pearls of his vast collection of interesting human specimens that he has come to know during his long and very active life.

Balmoral Castle
1991

Preface

*   *   *

My professional life has been spent in the pursuit of science and in public service, with the result that I have had the good fortune to enjoy friendships with many men who, although not politicians, exerted a significant influence on the course that national and international affairs have taken over the past fifty years. In this book I have tried to contrast the personalities of three British and three American men belonging to three different callings, who, if they themselves did not set the course of history, certainly helped it along the path it has taken. There are others about whom I might have chosen to write, but I decided, somewhat arbitrarily, to contrast two nuclear physicists, Patrick (Lord) Blackett and I.I. Rabi; two admirals, Lord Mountbatten of Burma and Admiral Hyman Rickover; and two airmen, Lord Tedder and General Carl Spaatz.

My purpose is not to add to the formal biographies that have been written about some of these men, and on which I have drawn when painting the brief biographical sketches that follow. What I have tried to do is provide a picture of them as I knew them, and to show what they were like and what it was like to work with them. All were widely known – some more so than others – and I hope that these brief sketches will help put off the day when their memories are relegated to the place where those of so many great men lie buried. The reason why I open my mini-biographical anthology with the story of two scientist friends is not because, I, too, am a scientist, but because what they did to a large extent conditioned what the other four, all military figures, were able to achieve – and because the repercussions of the work they did will never fade.

S.Z.

Acknowledgements

*   *   *

I should like to record my thanks to the following who helped me clarify certain factual matters.

Lord Blackett: Professor Margaret Gowing, the official historian of the UK's nuclear programme; Professor Sir Bernard Lovell, the author of the Royal Society's biographical memoir on Blackett.

Lord Tedder: Lord Scarman, who was the Air Chief Marshal's principal private secretary during the time I was his chief planning adviser.

General Spaatz: Mrs Katherine Bell, the General's daughter; William Walton, a mutual friend of the General, Mrs Bell and myself; and Dr Tami Davis, who searched for and found such papers as exist relating to Spaatz and Tedder informally taking the first steps that transformed the UK into the US's unsinkable aircraft-carrier.

Lord Mountbatten: Gérard André, one-time Minister in the French Embassy in London, for checking my story of Lord Mountbatten's London meeting in 1945 with the French Ambassador.

Admiral Rickover: Dr Norman Polmar, the author of an unauthorized biography; Dr Francis Duncan, an official historian of the US Department of Energy; Dr Frank Panton, a one-time member of my staff, and at the same time the UK liaison officer in Washington for nuclear affairs; and B.T. Price, a nuclear physicist and also a one-time member of my staff.

My thanks are also due to the following, who have provided me with photographs of my subjects: Mrs Katherine Bell, daughter of General Spaatz; Mrs Giovanna Bloor, daughter of Lord Blackett; Lord Brabourne, for the photograph of Lord Mountbatten; David Longstreath, US Navy, for the photograph of Admiral Rickover; and the Zoological Society of London for the photograph of Lord Mountbatten with the author.

Finally, I should like to express my gratitude to my archivist, Deirdre Sharp, for unearthing such papers as I needed to refresh my memory, and to Gillian Booth for her critical and unstinting assistance in helping me through successive drafts of my text to the point where I was satisfied that it could bear the light of day.

S.Z.

TWO NUCLEAR PHYSICISTS

*   *   *

Isidor I. Rabi

Patrick Blackett

Patrick Blackett

1897–1974

The Father of Operational Research

* * *

Patrick Blackett, like Isidor Rabi, with whom I have chosen to contrast him, was a Nobel Laureate and one of the pioneers of nuclear physics. Like Rabi, too, he became prominent in the world of defence science and a powerful crusader for the growth and exploitation of science for the betterment of society. There was another characteristic they shared. Both were passionately outspoken about their *bêtes noires*. Rabi's main one was Edward Teller, the arch-priest of the American nuclear establishment. Blackett's was Professor F.A. Lindemann, later to become Lord Cherwell, and widely known as 'the Prof', Winston Churchill's personal defence and economic adviser. There any immediate resemblance between the two ended.

In background, appearance and personality they could not have been less alike. Blackett belonged to an upper-middle-class English family and was brought up to follow a naval career. Where Rabi was anything but an outdoor type, Patrick was particularly keen on sailing and loved the countryside. He used part of his Nobel Prize money to buy a boat in which he sailed, with friends as crew, and sometimes for a month at a time, either to France or to Ireland, putting in here and there, as inclination or need dictated. He also had a cottage near the Welsh coast, not far from where some other intellectuals, among them Bertrand Russell, lived. He was a tall and strikingly handsome man in the film-star mould, in contrast to the stocky Rabi, whom few would have described as good-looking but whose face had an attractiveness and alertness of its own, ready as he always was either for conversation, a joke or an impassioned speech. The Blackett I knew was more measured, less immediately forthcoming. He often wore a look as though all the cares of the world were on his shoulders.

From the circumstances of my first meeting with Patrick Blackett, I should have expected him to be the more light-hearted of the two. It was about 1930, some four or five years after I had arrived in England from South Africa in order, ostensibly, to qualify in medicine and then embark on the life of a medical practitioner. Instead, I had become beguiled by the social and cultural life of London. Living as I did on the fringes of Bloomsbury, I had made friends with Adrian and Karin Stephen, who it turned out also knew Patrick. Adrian was the younger brother of Virginia Woolf and had studied law at Cambridge. Karin was a stepdaughter of Bernard Berenson, the celebrated art historian. She had been a pupil of Bertrand Russell at Cambridge and then a Fellow of Newnham, and had written a book, her only book, with the title, *The Misuse of Mind*. Both Stephens had switched their interests and qualified in medicine in order to become professional psychoanalysts. They lived in Gordon Square, the centre of the Bloomsbury world, and also owned a primitive country cottage, a converted inn in the minute village of Thorpe-le-Soken on the banks of a small east coast estuary, where I was often their guest. When the tide was in we bathed or sailed in a small boat. When it was out we could examine the debris that littered the muddy bed of the estuary.

On my arrival one weekend I found that there were two other guests: Patrick and his wife, Pat. How the Stephens had first met the Blacketts I do not know. During the twenties Patrick had emerged as one of the rising stars of the Cavendish Laboratory in Cambridge, where, my hosts told me, he was an expert on cosmic rays, those high-energy subatomic particles that bombard the earth from outer space. I hadn't the slightest idea what this meant, any more than I imagine that Patrick appreciated what I was hoping to achieve by enquiring into the hormonal control of the 'family' structure of monkeys and apes. I remember feeling somewhat in awe of him, but none the less enjoyed the weekend immensely. After that we occasionally ran into each other, although I do not recall doing so in Bloomsbury society. In those days Patrick and Pat moved in a different Bohemian orbit, mostly in Cambridge.

We met at the dinners of the Tots and Quots, a small dining club of scientists and economists that I had helped found in 1931, and whose name derived from the Latin tag *quot homines, tot sententiae*, to indicate the wide spectrum of views, often conflicting, that our company reflected. The first phase of the club's existence lasted no more than about three years. The second began in 1938 as war loomed, and for some three to four years the club met frequently to consider how best scientists could assist in the war effort – the discussion at one of our dinners became the basis of an influential early Penguin, published anonymously under the title *Science in War*. During that phase of the club's life Patrick usually attended, and his interventions were always to the point, warning us that there was a war to be won before we became too grandiose in our ambitions about the place of science in the post-war world. He was already far more deeply involved in defence matters than the rest of us. It was then, too, that he came to a view about nuclear weapons that was contrary to the one which Rabi had first entertained. Once he had got over a feeling that nuclear physics should not be used to devise weapons of mass destruction, Rabi had not hesitated to help Robert Oppenheimer in the Manhattan Project, and then in the preparation of the ill-fated Acheson/Lilienthal plan for the control of the 'atom' by the United Nations. For his part, Patrick had been a member of the small and highly secret so-called MAUD Committee that was formed early in the war to advise the British Government whether to set about the development of an atom bomb in the UK. He had been the odd man out in opposing the proposed project. After Hiroshima and Nagasaki, he published a short book in which he declared that the belief that atomic bombs could be effective in wars between Great Powers, 'appears to have been based on a superficial appreciation', and in his view 'almost irretrievable harm has resulted from this error', for which American atomic scientists, among whom I suppose he had in mind Rabi, were mainly responsible. Strangely enough, I do not recall Rabi ever saying anything nice about Patrick, whose views, however, years later seemed to me to be no different from his own.

The Sailor

On his paternal side, Patrick's background was ecclesiastical. His father had, however, broken with the family tradition and become a stockbroker, but one with literary tastes. His maternal background was military, and according to Sir Bernard Lovell, the author of the biographical memoir of Patrick that was published by the Royal Society, it was that which determined his start in the Navy and the interest he subsequently developed in defence policy and in Indian affairs.

Patrick was born in London in 1897. After three years at a preparatory school in Guildford, where his hobbies were building model aircraft and crystal radio sets, he entered the Royal Naval College, Osborne, at the age of twelve. As was the custom in those days, he moved after two years to Dartmouth, which he left, 'top of his term', on the outbreak of war in 1914. He was straight away posted as a midshipman to a cruiser in which, a few months later and soon after his seventeenth birthday, he saw action off the Falklands in the engagement in which the German armoured cruisers *Scharnhorst* and *Gneisenau* as well as the light cruisers *Nürnberg* and *Leipzig* were sunk. He was then moved to the flagship of a battle squadron which in 1916 suffered severe damage in the Battle of Jutland. With his interest in flying, Patrick then sought, but was refused, permission to transfer to the Royal Naval Air Service – naval officers as highly trained as he was could not be spared for such novelties. After two more years at sea, during which he took part in several further actions, Patrick ended the war with the rank of lieutenant.

By then he had decided to leave the Navy, and if possible, to embark on an academic career. His chance came when in January of 1919 he was one of a group of four hundred naval officers – which included Lord Mountbatten – who were sent to Cambridge for a six-month stay. He soon resigned his commission and embarked on the career that was to make him one of the leading physicists of the day and, in due course, President of the Royal Society.

The Physicist

The college which he joined was Magdalene, where, so he said, he immediately and for the first time found himself participating in intellectual conversation. He read mathematics, from which he switched to physics, in which he gained a first class degree in 1921. The college then appointed him to a Bye Fellowship. This made it possible for him to continue to work in the Cavendish Laboratory, which under Rutherford's direction was at the time becoming the foremost centre in the world for the experimental study of the structure of the atom.

Not long before Patrick became a member of his team, Rutherford had carried out an experiment in which he had 'split' the nitrogen atom – he was the first scientist to show that atomic fission could be made to occur in the laboratory. It was already known that it occurred naturally in a few heavy elements, with the consequent release of radioactive subatomic particles. Using what was called the cloud chamber technique which had been developed at the Cavendish by C.T.R. Wilson, Patrick was set to work to help elucidate exactly what happened when the nitrogen atom disintegrated. His work was fruitful, and within three years, having modified the Wilson cloud chamber, he provided at least part of the answer to the question that he had been put by Rutherford.

By this time Patrick had been elected to a Fellowship of King's College. But before settling down in his new college he decided to spend a year in James Franck's laboratory in Göttingen, familiarizing himself with the work that was being done there in the effort to provide an experimental foundation to quantum theory – Patrick wanted to know about the nature of the atom as a whole, not just that of its nucleus, which was Rutherford's main concern.[1] On his return to Cambridge Patrick changed the focus of

---

1. Patrick was not to know that twenty years later his views on nuclear weaponry

his research and turned to the study of cosmic rays, always demonstrating, as Bernard Lovell has written, a 'remarkable facility . . . of thinking most deeply when he was working with his hands'. Above all, Patrick was a practical experimentalist.

In 1933 he was elected a Fellow of the Royal Society, and in the same year he left Cambridge to become head of the Department of Physics at Birkbeck College in London. There, in charge of his own ship, he remained until 1937, when he moved to the more important chair in Manchester University that Rutherford had once filled. He quickly transformed his new department into a centre for the study of cosmic rays, to which scholars were attracted from far and wide. He was outstanding not only as a researcher and teacher but as a university administrator. He remained Langworthy Professor of Physics in Manchester for twenty years, that is to say until 1953, when he accepted an invitation to become head of the Department of Physics at Imperial College in London where, as in Manchester, his abilities as an organizer and administrator were allowed full play in the phase of university expansion that had started at the end of the Second World War. It was in large measure due to his influence that Imperial College grew in size and eminence until it ranked not just as part of the University of London, but as an institution equivalent to a university on its own.

Patrick's transformation from a young naval officer who had been under fire into a university man whose scientific genius immediately became apparent was, I should say, unique. I certainly do not know of any similar case in the academic history of Great Britain. But the transformation did not erase from him all those traits that characterize the man who has been brought up from boyhood within a military system that trains men to command and to obey. What was remarkable was how far the transformation went.

To the best of my knowledge, and unlike Rabi, Patrick had never concerned himself with politics, national or international, before he entered Cambridge. But in the atmosphere of the university of the twenties he gradually drifted to the left, in the same way as Mountbatten is said to

---

were to be close to those of Franck, who was then a refugee physicist working in Chicago in a division of the Manhattan Project. Franck had been asked to chair a small committee to consider the social and political implications of nuclear weapons. The report which he produced argued against the use of the 'bomb' against Japan, and warned about the dangers of a post-war nuclear arms race with the USSR. In the words of Ronald Clark, it was 'a sober and prescient forecast of what would happen if certain mistakes were made by America in revealing the almost unimaginable power which she now commanded'. (*The Greatest Power on Earth*, London: Sidgwick & Jackson, 1980, p. 189.)

have done. In 1924 he married Constanza Bayon, a beautiful Italian girl, better known as Pat, and the two are said to have led a highly sociable life, keeping open house at least once a week, and according to the obituary published in the *King's College Gazette*, cultivating 'semi-bohemian and left wing' company. A friend who knew them in those days says that she remembers Pat doing things like sitting on the steps leading up from the street to their front door, shelling peas while singing Italian songs.

As today's 'spy writers' have revealed, King's was the home of the Apostles, the secret intellectual and nonconformist club that had had among its members the notorious pair Burgess and Maclean who, after joining the Foreign Service, spied for the Soviet Union. Even though he may not have recognized them as such, Patrick must have run across a few Apostles, but he was certainly not one of their number. I should imagine that the Apostles, who were then strongly inclined to the left, must have been wary of an ex-naval officer who, despite his Bohemian life, was on the way to becoming a highly prominent scientist. None the less, as the wave of fascism started to spread across Europe towards the end of the twenties, Patrick was undoubtedly regarded by most people who knew him, or knew of him, as belonging to the left, although certainly not as far to the left as were those of his Cambridge contemporaries who became members of the Communist Party.

The Tizard Committee

Patrick's political sympathies did not, however, prove a bar to his being invited at the end of 1934 to join a committee on air defence which the Air Ministry had asked Sir Henry Tizard to set up, and whose deliberations led to the development of the early-warning radar chain that was to prove so critical to the RAF's victory in the Battle of Britain, and years later to the dramatic story that C.P. Snow told in his celebrated Godkin Lectures about the disputes which plagued the committee. Tizard was at the time the Rector of Imperial College, and also Chairman of the Government's Aeronautical Research Committee. His new committee included two other independent scientists: A.V. Hill, a neurophysiologist and Nobel Laureate, and Patrick, for whom the committee was an introduction to Whitehall – and a stormy one too. The fifth member of the committee was H.E. Wimperis, an old friend of Tizard, and an engineer who had joined the Air Ministry as Director of Research, a post that Tizard had declined when it was offered to him in 1924.[2]

2. Tizard was an Oxford physicist who had served in the Royal Flying Corps during

As the Air Ministry's chief scientist, Wimperis had been having to deal with all kinds of suggestions about how to defend the UK against air attack, and it was for that reason that it was agreed that he could call in a few independent scientists to help in setting priorities for the R&D (Research and Development) work that would be needed in pursuing those ideas that looked promising. Both Tizard and Hill had been concerned with aeronautical R&D problems during the First World War and were obvious choices as members of the committee. Patrick's qualifications were that he had been a naval officer throughout that war and was now an expert on cosmic rays. He was also a friend of A.V. Hill and, despite his left-wing sympathies, belonged to the same breed of Englishmen as did the Air Ministry's other two 'independents'.

For the first six months of 1935 the committee met frequently and worked harmoniously, throwing its considerable weight behind the exploitation of the concept of the radio-direction finding (RDF) of aircraft, the practicality of which Sir Robert Watson-Watt of the Government's Radio Research Station demonstrated at Wimperis's request shortly after the committee's first meeting.

The committee was not, however, the only governmental body concerned with the problem of air defence. The subject had stimulated widespread public concern and was a matter of major interest to the Government's Committee of Imperial Defence. This body – the CID – dealt with all service problems, and partly as a result of pressure that was being exerted by Winston Churchill, was considering the setting up of its own Air Defence Research subcommittee. Churchill was not at the time in the Government, but he was much in the public eye because of the campaign he was waging to speed up the UK's rearmament programme. He was being advised by Professor F.A. Lindemann, then head of the Oxford Department of Physics, who, when told that the Air Ministry had already set up a committee under Tizard, declined an invitation to become one of

---

the First World War. When it ended he returned to Oxford to resume his career as a physicist, leaving in 1920 to become the full-time Executive Secretary of the Government's Department of Scientific and Industrial Research. He resigned this appointment in 1929 to become Rector of Imperial College of London University, a post from which he retired in 1942, when for a few years he served as President of Magdalen College, Oxford. He returned to full-time public service in 1946 to become Chairman of both the Government's Advisory Council on Scientific Policy and Defence Research Policy Committee. In 1945, when Air Chief Marshal Tedder, the Chief of the Air Staff, wanted me to abandon academic life and become his scientific adviser, Tizard warned me that were I to accept the invitation, which I did not, he feared that I would never again return to academic life. He did not tell me that he had declined the equivalent position when it was offered him twenty years before.

its members. It had been proffered mainly in order to prevent the creation of a parallel and possibly rival body. Lindemann was always suspicious of departmental committees that were managed by civil servants. What he wanted was a committee that had more political clout, one supported by big political guns.

Some six months after the committee had begun its work, and after it had been arranged that it should be answerable to the CID as well as to the Air Ministry, he did, however, agree to join. Trouble started almost immediately. Lindemann took it upon himself to go behind Tizard's back to report on the committee's deliberations – usually unfavourably – both to Churchill and to his other powerful political friends, his main complaint being that the wrong R&D priorities were being set. He agreed that radio-direction finding, soon to be called radar, was a valuable early-warning device against daylight intruders, but he thought that it was being accorded too much emphasis. What he felt was needed was defence against night bombers. In particular he favoured the laying of aerial minefields, and the development of thermopile devices that could detect at night the infra-red radiation of the heat emitted by aircraft engines.

Lindemann and Tizard had once been friends, and indeed it was Tizard who in 1923 had been instrumental in seeing that his friend was elected to the Oxford Chair of Physics. Like Tizard, Lindemann had also been involved in aeronautical problems during the First World War. But all that was in the past. They now lived in different social worlds. Lindemann, the son of a wealthy Alsatian who had assumed British nationality after settling in England, was a rich, highly conservative bachelor who, when outside Oxford, and despite his own austere habits – he never drank, smoked or ate meat – enjoyed a luxurious life in country-house circles, particularly those where the views of his friend Winston Churchill found an echo. The only time I ever saw him at a loss for words was at a large weekend party. Among the other guests were the Prof and a Baroness Budberg – also known as the Bedbug – who was H.G. Wells's mistress at the time, and a woman much loved in social and intellectual circles. After dinner on the Saturday a few of us had got together in our host's study, among them the Bedbug, who was a liberal drinker, and the Prof, whom she set about teasing because of his austere habits. 'Come on, Prof,' she said, 'when did you last sleep with a woman?' The Prof simply did not know how to counter the tease. He could be immensely kind, but his urbane exterior and soft tongue also belied a determination to put down anyone who got in his way. Whether he had ever had any dealings with Patrick Blackett before they met on Tizard's committee I do not know, but I cannot imagine any two people less likely to trust or like each other – Patrick straightforward, a leftish 'Bohemian' and unconventional, the Prof high-Tory, enigmatic and 'grand'. A.V. Hill was also, I should say, instinctively antipathetic to him. (I remember his telling me once that the Prof was a menace and that I had to join with those who were trying to reduce his influence in Whitehall.) Lindemann was not of their breed, and the only thing in which the three were alike, apart from being leading members of the scientific establishment, was that they were all over six feet tall. But there they now were, independent scientists brought together to advise on matters that were vital to the security of the State.

With Lindemann a member, the committee lasted only one more year. He continued to intrigue behind the backs of his colleagues, constantly complaining about their failure to pay sufficient attention to his views, and decrying theirs.[3] Without consulting Tizard, he also arranged that Watson-Watt should see Churchill, and paradoxically encouraged him to express his dissatisfaction with the speed with which radar was being developed. Hill and Patrick were as incensed by his behaviour as was Tizard, who wrote to the Minister for Air to let him know what he thought about Lindemann 'playing his own game', and about his failure to work as a member of a team. A stormy meeting in July of 1936 broke up in disorder, and Hill and Patrick promptly resigned.

There was nothing the Air Ministry could then do except formally dissolve the committee. About a month later, however, it was reconvened, minus Lindemann, and with the addition of Edward Appleton, also a scientific bigwig, and the authority on the physics of the ionosphere, the zone above the atmosphere from which radio waves are reflected on to suitable receivers on earth. Harmony then reigned in the committee until the outbreak of war three years later. In the interval Lindemann, having failed to win a seat as an MP, continued to promulgate his views under the shadow of Churchill. He did not reappear on the Whitehall scene until war broke out, when the Prime Minister, Neville Chamberlain, made the Prof's powerful friend a member of the Cabinet in the post of First Lord of the Admiralty. When Chamberlain resigned a year later Churchill became Prime Minister and, not long after, the Prof was brought into the Government, in the titular post of Paymaster-General, at the same time being ennobled with the title Viscount Cherwell.

The Prof's return to Whitehall meant a resurgence of trouble for Tizard and his colleagues. Before then, however, they had enjoyed the satisfaction of overseeing the transformation of radar into an operational early-

---

3. The most reliable and complete account of the story of the Committee is given by Ronald Clark in his biography of Tizard (London: Methuen, 1964). C.P. Snow's Godkin Lectures, in which he gave a dramatic account of the dispute between Tizard and Lindemann, were published before Clark's book appeared.

warning system, and of setting in train work that was to lead to the invention of the cavity magnetron, and so to airborne radar. Tizard had by then accepted the position of scientific adviser to the Chief of the Air Staff, but with Lindemann back, and operating from the power-base of 10 Downing Street, life in Whitehall became impossible for him. In 1942, he accepted the office of President of Magdalen College, Oxford.

Operational Research

On the outbreak of war, Patrick had attached himself to the Royal Aircraft Establishment, where he directed his energies mainly towards the improvement of bomb-sights. After a year there, and at the instigation of A.V. Hill, he transferred to Anti-Aircraft Command where, as scientific adviser to its chief, General Sir Frederick Pile, he brought together a group of young scientists as an operational research team in order to analyse the successes and failures of the anti-aircraft batteries in relation to the tactics they were pursuing. This work was immediately fruitful, and news soon spread about the improvement in the ratio of 'shots per bird' that operational research had achieved in the 'ack-ack' world.

RAF Coastal Command then called for Patrick to apply the same methods to help them in the battle against German submarines. Once again simple analysis soon led Patrick and a new team of young scientists to recommend valuable changes in tactics, even in such straightforward matters as the depth-setting of the mines that were dropped in the path of submerged submarines, and in having Coastal Command's aircraft painted white in order to make their detection by surfaced boats more difficult. The Navy was of course co-operating closely with Coastal Command in the anti-U-boat war, and in January 1942, after three months with the airmen, Patrick was asked to transfer to the Admiralty. This he did, at the same time leaving behind in Coastal Command a highly efficient team of operational researchers to carry on the work he had started, in the same way as he had left a team in AA Command. Patrick had become the father of wartime operational research.

He was now back with the service for which he had been trained as a boy, and in which he had seen action twenty years before. It must have been a curious experience for him to be working once again with naval officers, some of whom must have been of his Dartmouth vintage, and many of whom were now admirals. He duly became Director of Naval Operational Research, and once again his analytical work quickly yielded practical results; for example, in the organization of the transatlantic convoy system. He was also responsible for introducing changes in naval tactics in the anti-U-boat campaign, which resulted in significant reductions in the number of ships sunk, and increases in the number of U-boats destroyed. But the Admiralty also brought him once again into the orbit of Lindemann, with whom he was soon at odds over general strategic policy, and in a way which, when added to his undisguised sympathies with the left, in the end made him suspect in the higher councils of war.

Patrick had moved to the Admiralty at a time when the war was going very badly for the Allies, with the German armies still on the ascendant in Russia, as U-boats were in the Atlantic, and when the battle in the Western Desert had not yet been turned. Lindemann had got it into his head that the only way Hitler could be defeated was by bombing, and early in 1942 had arranged with the Ministry of Home Security, which was responsible for civil defence, for a rapid study to be made of what the Luftwaffe had achieved by bombing Birmingham and Hull in relation to the effort it had cost. Desmond Bernal, Britain's leading crystallographer and a man with a very wide-ranging mind, and I, both friends of Patrick, and both then attached to the Ministry of Home Security, were in charge of the study, for which large staffs were quickly recruited in order to obtain as detailed a picture as was possible in the time that we were set. Our task was to get a measure of the amount of physical destruction that had been caused, of the numbers of casualties, of industrial production lost, of effects on morale, and so on. Without waiting for our full report, but using some of our preliminary figures for which his staff had called, Cherwell (as I shall from now on call him) sent Churchill in March of 1942 a minute in which our conclusions had, by omission, been misused, and which ended with the claim that, given the forecast figures for the production of heavy bombers, the RAF could destroy all German cities with a population of more than a hundred thousand – then said to number fifty-eight – with, as he claimed, 'little doubt that this would break the spirit of the [German] people'. The War Cabinet accepted Cherwell's argument and endorsed the policy that his paper advocated. RAF Bomber Command then became committed to the strategy of the 'area bombing' of German cities.

I did not see Cherwell's minute when it was circulated, nor to the best of my knowledge did Bernal. Tizard and Patrick did, Tizard still being chief scientific adviser to the Chief of the Air Staff, and Patrick in his capacity as the Admiralty's Director of Operational Research. Neither disavowed the principle behind the proposed bombing policy, that is to say the bombing of cities, which was surprising, for as Lovell indicates in his biographical memoir, Patrick was instinctively opposed to the idea of attacking civilian populations. What the two did was contest Cherwell's sums. Taking into account the rate at which aircraft could be produced, together with anticipated operational losses and bombing accuracy, Patrick concluded that Cherwell's 'estimate of what can be achieved was at least 600% too high'. Tizard was equally sceptical. Their attack on Cherwell's claims became known in higher circles, but to no avail. The fact was that the way in which figures were being bandied around was certain to mislead, for the report that Bernal and I produced explicitly stated that we had found no evidence that the German attacks had got anywhere near breaking 'the spirit' of the inhabitants of the two cities which were the subject of our study. Bernal and I later discussed our final report with Tizard, and Bernal may also have done so with Blackett. Neither of us could have known how many bomber sorties against cities would have been needed to break the spirit of the German people. It was not the number of bombs it took to destroy so many square miles of built-up area that mattered. As events were to reveal, what was far more critical as a target system was the communication network by which towns and cities were linked. But for the rest of the war, area bombing continued to be the main strategy pursued by RAF Bomber Command.

Tizard retired to Oxford not long after the dispute over the new bombing policy. Patrick continued at the Admiralty, but he was now marked as someone opposed to 'strategic bombing'. Early in 1943, a paper he had written was tabled by the Admiralty for one of the fortnightly meetings of an Anti-U-Boat Committee over which Churchill presided. It argued that the campaign against German submarines in the Bay of Biscay could be decisively won were Coastal Command to be provided with an additional 260 aircraft, of which 190 heavy bombers would have had to be diverted from Bomber Command. The paper had not been cleared with RAF Coastal Command before it was submitted, and its C-in-C, Air Chief Marshal Sir John Slessor, reacted strongly against the proposal, stating that while he was all in favour of operational research, he was not going to allow 'strategy to be determined by slide-rule'. Not surprisingly, the Admiralty paper was quashed. In due course the number of aircraft in Coastal Command was increased, but only by a third of the figure that Patrick had proposed. Unfortunately, however, Slessor then put it around that Patrick had not been giving the objective advice that would be expected of a scientist, and that his views were coloured by an aversion to the bomber offensive against the German homeland, which, to Slessor, was an essential element of Air Force policy. Inadvertently, Patrick had also provoked an inter-service dispute about the allocation of resources. The top brass did not mind him opposing politicians, as he had done when he was a member of the Tizard committee. It was a different matter to provoke a quarrel with a top commander in a service to which he did not belong. The Air Force cry, as I too was to learn, was 'Tell us what you want done, but don't tell us how to do it. That's our job.' Patrick was not only up against Slessor in this dispute. Cherwell was also a member of the Anti-U-Boat Committee, and it probably gave him satisfaction to see Patrick put down.

When I returned from the Mediterranean theatre at the beginning of 1944 as strategic air adviser to Air Chief Marshal Sir Arthur Tedder, the Deputy Supreme Commander in the planning of *Overlord*, the code-name for the projected invasion of France, I ran into Patrick only occasionally. Although he was around, he was not present at the inter-service planning meetings I attended at Eisenhower's and the naval headquarters at Portsmouth. I had been warned not to talk to him about the matters in which I was involved and, when I enquired, was told that he was now being denied access to the War Room. It was all inexplicable to me.

Blackett and the Bomb

In addition to his involvement in the problems of air defence, Patrick was brought into the initial discussions about the making of atom bombs. In March 1940 Tizard had received from Professor Mark Oliphant of Birmingham University a short paper, now known as the Peierls/Frisch Memorandum, which set out for the first time how an atom bomb, about which there had been much speculation, could actually be made. Although he himself was sceptical, Tizard set up a small committee of physicists, among them Patrick, to consider the document. The group was given the code-name *MAUD*, and put under the aegis of the Ministry of Aircraft Production. In July of the following year, after a great deal of hectic work and consultation, it recommended to the Government that what Peierls and Frisch had set out in their memorandum made enough sense for the UK to embark on the production of atom bombs, at the same time as work was set in hand to produce nuclear power for civil purposes.

Patrick did not doubt that what was being proposed was sound in theory, but, unlike the other members of the committee, he did not believe that a bomb could be produced in the two to three years that had been estimated. There were too many unknowns in what would be involved, and far more urgent things to do. He accordingly submitted a minority report, in which he strongly expressed his doubts about the likelihood of a bomb being produced in time to be of any use in the war, and urging that the US, with all the scientific, technical and industrial resources that it commanded, and with whose nuclear experts the MAUD Committee had been in close touch, should be entrusted with the task. Tizard agreed with him, but initially not Cherwell. None the less, it was Patrick's view that was followed by the Cabinet.

I do not know whether Patrick was then kept informed about the progress of the Manhattan Project, or whether he was forewarned about its success before the destruction of Hiroshima and Nagasaki. Nor do I know whether Niels Bohr, the highly distinguished Danish nuclear physicist, whom the British Government got to England via Sweden in 1943, ever discussed with Patrick his views about the dangers of keeping the Russians in the dark about the development of atom bombs, and about the likelihood that doing so would stimulate a post-war nuclear arms race, views that he managed to press all the way up to the American President and Winston Churchill.

Although he had been Deputy Prime Minister in the wartime coalition government, Attlee knew nothing at all about the Manhattan Project before he took Churchill's place as Prime Minister at the end of the war. To help him decide what the UK should now do, he accordingly set up a small 'advisory committee on atomic energy', but having no political colleague who knew any more than he did about the subject, he placed it under Sir John Anderson,[4] a Conservative member of Churchill's Coalition Cabinet who had carried the responsibility for atomic affairs during the war years. Patrick was appointed to the committee, but once again found himself the odd man out in strongly opposing the committee's recommendation that the UK should straight away set about making atom bombs. He argued his objections, which were essentially strategic in nature, not only round the table but in two separate minutes he sent the Prime Minister. This time he lost. The inner Cabinet which Attlee had appointed to deal with nuclear secrets accepted the majority recommendation. As soon as possible after the committee was dissolved, he made his objections public in a small book that appeared in 1948 under the title *Military and Political Consequences of Atomic Energy*.

I was seeing a lot of him in those days – we were both members of another high-level advisory committee and had much to talk about. He and Pat also had the use of my London flat at weekends, and he sometimes stayed with my wife and me in Birmingham, either alone or with Pat. Soon after the atomic energy committee was dissolved, he sent me copies of the two minutes he had submitted to the Prime Minister, and followed them up with the proofs of his book, on which he wanted my comments. I sent him many – several pages, most of them trivial, but some highly critical of the view he held that the whole strategic bombing campaign of the war had been a waste of resources. In acknowledging what I sent him, he wrote that he had taken account of most of my comments in his final text.

4. Lord Waverley, as he became.

What I had mainly tried to get him to do was to tone down his scathing condemnation of RAF Bomber Command's offensive – he called it the worst strategic mistake of the war – but rereading the book today I can see that on this point I had had little success. His argument was that it was futile to suppose that wars could be won by bombing the enemy's home-land over the heads of battling armies, that the advent of the atomic bomb had not changed the situation, and that the new weapon did not presage a fundamental change in the nature of war. At the time he seemed to regard atom bombs as just another kind of armament, and while he supposed that they might have a use as 'tactical weapons', they would fail, so he contended, in the same way as had conventional bombs in justifying the Trenchard/Douhet air force doctrine of strategic bombing. Were a new war with the Soviet Union to break out, the United States alone would have the bomb, and he pulled no punches in condemning the motives he discerned behind the American use of the bomb in Japan. The destruction of Hiroshima and Nagasaki he regarded as a political act, so timed as to dispense with any need for the USSR to enter the war against Japan, and thus having a say in any future political settlement in the Pacific theatre. Dropping the bombs 'was not so much the last military act of the Second World War', so he wrote, but 'the first act of the cold diplomatic war with Russia'. And the Acheson-Lilienthal plan for the international control of atomic energy, as amended by Baruch, he regarded as a subterfuge which, if accepted, would not only assure the maintenance by the US of a military nuclear monopoly but which would deny the Russians the opportunity of developing nuclear energy even for civil purposes.

What was curious was that at the time Patrick failed to realize the possibility that future technical developments might undermine his cen-tral thesis that the emergence of atom bombs had not made any basic change in the nature of warfare – particularly surprising, since hydrogen bombs were already being spoken about in the US, and with long-range rocketry already a reality. What was also surprising was that, in his condemnation of US policy, Patrick seemed to lump all Americans together. He made no mention of the fact that several American nuclear physicists, many of them more in the know than he was – for example, Oppenheimer and Rabi – had fought against Baruch's corruption of the Acheson-Lilienthal plan, and had also publicly opposed the idea of pro-ceeding to the development of more powerful nuclear weaponry. When I raised Patrick's name with Rabi many years later, he discounted him as politically naïve. But Rabi's views about the dangers of the nuclear arms race, like those of many other of America's leading scientists, were in fact no different from Patrick's.

Quoting Margaret Gowing, Lovell says that Patrick advocated 'a neutralist policy for the UK both in atomic energy and in foreign and defence policy', a view which the Government dismissed as dangerous nonsense. He also writes that Patrick's insistent and publicized opposition to government policy, marked him as 'unreliable' – in the same way as Oppenheimer was to become in the United States. Until Harold Wilson became Prime Minister in 1964, Patrick was accordingly never invited to become a member of any further top-level governmental advisory committees. For some years he was also excluded from the United States, which was one of the main reasons why, as the Government's chief scientific adviser, I was later unable to associate him with my discussions of nuclear matters with my American opposite numbers.

The rejection by the authorities of Patrick's far-seeing views did not mean that on his return to the laboratory he ceased writing about the subject. On the contrary, he sought every opportunity he could to express his discordant opinions. 'During twenty years of my lifetime of sixty years I have been either training for war, fighting wars, or studying or thinking about them' were the opening words of a radio broadcast he made in 1958 entitled *Atomic Heretic*. But apart from rejecting the concept of strategic bombing as a militarily futile idea, his mind was not shut. As soon as the Russians demonstrated that they, too, knew 'the secret' of the bomb, he accepted that he had been wrong in not realizing that the advent of nuclear weapons had created a fundamental change in the conduct of war, and from that moment on he adjusted his views in step with the changing nuclear scene. In the Lees Knowles Lectures, which he delivered in Cambridge in 1956,[5] he provided a fresh synthesis of his views, beginning with the proposition that a state of atomic parity had developed between East and West (which, I myself would add, it continued to do regardless of all the technological developments made by the two sides over the past thirty-five years in the effort to outbid each other, and despite all attempts to devise a defence against a nuclear assault). In contrast to the polemics that characterized his first book, Patrick used the occasion of the lectures to consider calmly – although he was still forthright in his criticisms when touching on decisions and views with which he disagreed – how the arms race had reached a point where military superiority of either West or East had ceased to have any meaning, and when nuclear war was unthinkable to any rational man. 'Strategical atomic weapons have not only cancelled themselves out and so made all-out total war exceedingly unlikely,' he declared, 'but have finally abolished the possibility of victory by air power alone against a great power. . . .' In drawing his final lecture to a close, he declared that 'we should act as if atomic and hydrogen bombs had abo-

5. Published in 1957.

lished total war and concentrate our efforts on working out how few atomic bombs and their carriers are required to keep it abolished'.

Had he known that that objective would be precisely the purpose of East-West negotiations some thirty years later, Patrick would no doubt have been amazed. The trouble was not that he was ahead of his time in what he was proclaiming. It was that he neither appreciated the strength of the opposition to his views, nor the political power of the interests which on both sides were concerned to further the arms race. Nor did he seek to ally himself with the many prominent American scientists, and the smaller number of British scientists, who were also battling against the prevailing trend. He was a one-man army fighting for reason. Rabi would have been a natural ally, but somehow the paths they were pursuing never seemed to merge. So far as I can discover, Patrick never involved himself in Rabi's Atoms for Peace movement, nor did he concern himself with the affairs of CERN, to which I shall refer later on in the present book.

Needless to say, Patrick became regarded in England as 'the leading military scientist of the left', and his forthright denunciation of the nuclear policy of the Western powers was used to help provide an intellectual justification for the anti-nuclear movements that crystallized in the Campaign for Nuclear Disarmament. Patrick was in fact present at the party at which it is said that the CND movement was born. It was given by Kingsley Martin, the Editor of the *New Statesman*, for George Kennan, the ex-State Department 'head of plans' who was then in London delivering the celebrated radio lectures in which he condemned America's foreign and nuclear policies. Patrick had been a friend of Kingsley Martin ever since his first night in Cambridge in 1919, and Martin must have been at least partly responsible for steering his political sympathies to the left.

Patrick was never associated publicly with CND as were many intellectuals, most prominently Bertrand Russell, but his opposition to US and UK nuclear policy was constantly reinforced by his voracious reading of the ever-increasing volume of writing on the subject. He must have spent hours studying, and occasionally writing, critical reviews of the outpourings of academic armchair strategists who applied 'games theory' to scenarios of nuclear war, and who pontificated on so-called 'deterrence theory'. He must have felt that it was his duty to keep himself informed about the exotic elaborations of presumed operational research. In doing so he displayed much more patience than did Rabi, who soon came to dismiss the offerings of the new breed of strategists, however well dressed in numerical terms, as being beyond the reach of rational discussion. To Rabi the numbers were people, not abstractions. Patrick thought the same way, but he felt impelled to say so. As he put it in an article published in

Encounter in 1961, 'many of the most important decisions of war have necessarily to rest on rough calculations', and operational researchers had a duty to try to improve on them without, however, 'decking out what is essentially only a hunch with a pseudo-scientific backing'. But none the less he felt an obligation to meet the new academic strategists 'on the methodological ground of their own choosing', necessarily having to adopt their methods and terminology. In doing so he apologized in advance 'for the nauseating inhumanity of much of what I will have to say'. He asked me to comment on the draft of his *Encounter* paper, and in my reply I suggested that he had not gone far enough in his condemnation.

Science Policy

One of the reasons why Patrick had opposed the MAUD Committee's recommendation that the UK should embark on the production of an atom bomb was that it had become apparent from the start of the war that there was a considerable shortage of scientists and engineers in the UK, and that there were more immediate and important tasks for those who were available. The post-war advisory committee of which he and I were members had been set up by Attlee not many weeks after his committee on atomic energy had begun its work. It was chaired by Sir Alan Barlow, the Second Secretary of the Treasury, and its remit was to consider what should be done to remedy the country's lack of scientific manpower. Apart from Patrick and myself, it had four other 'independent' members. Two 'assessors' sat in for the Civil Service – one of them C.P. Snow, who was then a member of the governmental body responsible for recruiting members for the scientific classes of the Civil Service. I was the youngest member of Barlow's committee – today I am its only survivor – and it was not long before Patrick and I were regarded as its two radicals.

The best estimate that we were then able to obtain indicated that at the outbreak of the war there had been no more than about 50,000 full-time university students in the whole country, with an annual output of some 2,500 science graduates, plus a further 1,000 or so of professional engineers (today the figures are respectively about 11,000 and 9,000). Between them Oxford and Cambridge then accounted for about one-fifth of the total. Both Patrick and I regarded the low proportion of an age group that went into higher education – then something like 0.1 per cent – as a deplorable sign of the country's class structure, and both of us argued forcibly that all the talent that was needed was available in order to increase the proportion significantly. After taking evidence from far and wide, the committee recommended that resources should be provided to double the annual output of trained scientists and engineers, suggesting at the same time that it would take five to ten years for that goal to be reached. It took only four.

That part of our work took six months. The committee then went on to consider the need for a permanent advisory body to help the Government in formulating a 'science policy'. But before we had made much progress, the Chiefs of Staff, mainly for reasons of security, were given permission to set up their own Defence Research Policy Committee. Achieving a unanimous recommendation on civil science then proved difficult. The representative of the Royal Society on the Barlow committee felt that a Cabinet Office advisory council on scientific policy smacked too much of central planning and would threaten the liberty of the individual scientist to follow his own bent. Correspondingly, the representative of the Government's Research Councils feared that a Cabinet scientific advisory committee would threaten their autonomy. Since the exploitation of new knowledge was critical to the country's well-being, Patrick and I fought hard to get our colleagues to appreciate that there was nothing dangerous in the idea of a central body that would be in a position to monitor the whole field of scientific endeavour. He was much less in awe than I was of the two pillars of the scientific establishment on the committee, nor did he appear to like Sir Alan Barlow, who on one occasion turned up some fifteen minutes late for a meeting. Most of us just chatted away while we waited, but Patrick became more and more irritated. When Barlow came in, clearly in a happy mood after a bibulous lunch, he threw off the morning coat he was wearing and said: 'Well, where do we start?' Patrick was still seething with anger when the two of us left the meeting. It was as though he felt that Barlow, as the officer in charge, should be reprimanded by higher authority for a misdemeanour.

The best we managed to achieve was agreement that a central advisory council on science policy should be appointed, but without executive power, or indeed much authority. This recommendation was accepted by the Cabinet without, so far as I knew, any discussion.

Not many weeks later I received an invitation to become one of the members of the new council. For a number of reasons I was dubious about accepting, and decided to explain my misgivings to Max Nicholson, the civil servant who now had the responsibility of setting up the committee. He brushed aside my fear that it would be an ineffective body, and showed me the names of all who were being invited to serve, at the same time telling me that Tizard was likely to become the chairman of both the new civil and defence councils. I was appalled when I saw that Patrick's name was not on the list, but Nicholson refused to tell me the reason for his omission. Only about a year later, after Patrick had sent me copies of the minutes he had submitted to the Prime Minister, and in which he had set out his reasons for opposing the proposal that the UK should proceed to make atom bombs, did I realize why he had been blacklisted for service on central advisory committees. I felt very isolated but, knowing Tizard, I decided that all was not lost, and after further reflection accepted.

Being a realist, Patrick must have appreciated that the firm stand he was taking on nuclear and foreign policy would have made him *persona non grata* to the Government and to the higher Civil Service. The upshot was that while he and I continued to meet and to discuss the problems that were involved in strengthening the UK's scientific and technological resources, nearly twenty years were to pass before we again sat together at a Whitehall council table. I was not the only one who missed him. During the few years that Tizard remained chairman of both bodies, he too felt Patrick's absence, and at one moment he and Nicholson suggested that I should resurrect the Tots and Quots dining club so as to provide an informal forum where Patrick could help in our deliberations. I wrote to Patrick but otherwise did not pursue the idea. Like him, I had more than enough on my hands at the time. We both had to play our separate parts in helping implement the recommendation that the university output of scientists should be doubled in as short a time as possible.

Away from Whitehall

If anything, Patrick's ostracism by the Attlee government and the Whitehall machine impelled him to become far more actively political as a socialist than he had been previously. Before the war the furthest that he had gone was to associate himself with a short-lived scientific advisory committee of the Trades Union Congress. Now he not only cultivated but was sought out by the more radical elements of the Labour Party, and in particular by those who wanted to see socialist principles transformed into government policy more rapidly than the members of Attlee's government thought possible. But, although divorced from Whitehall advisory committees that dealt with 'policy', he was appointed a member of a National Research Development Corporation, which the Government set up to help inventors who had realistic ideas that were not being followed up by industry. Here he was most useful through the contacts he was able to provide the corporation with university departments, for, as the Corporation's chief executive soon discovered, Patrick in fact knew little about the way manufacturing industry worked. He was also appointed to the Governmental Research Council which in those days was styled the Department of Scientific and Industrial Research, and as head of its Research

32

Grants Committee he worked hard to steer funds to university departments where work was going on that looked as though it might result in
some practical development. Whenever opportunity offered, and in whatever way he could, he made known his conviction that it was a lack of
trained manpower which was responsible for the weakness of British
manufacturing industry and, *ipso facto*, of the British economy. As an
academic, he differed in this respect from Rabi, whose philosophy leant
more in the direction of encouraging the growth of basic knowledge and
then leaving it to the initiative of others to see whether what was discovered had any practical value. On the other hand, if one judged both men
purely as university professors, one could see that Patrick's endeavours
were as successful as were Rabi's at Columbia, particularly in the way that
Patrick built up his Department of Physics in Manchester, and later the
corresponding department in Imperial College in London. His own scientific interests had also widened, and he had become fascinated by the
problem of how 'continental drift' had broken the earth's crust into conti-
nents, a problem he studied by focusing on the magnetic characteristics of
rocks. In both universities his influence spread far beyond his own specific
domain, and without him I am sure that neither could have grown into the
formidable institutions that they are today.

Patrick and the Labour Party

During the thirteen years of Conservative rule that followed Attlee's defeat at
the polls in 1951, Patrick, in addition to his academic work and his
anti-nuclear polemicizing, became prominent among informal discussion
groups whose concern was to formulate plans whereby a future Labour
government could improve the efficiency of British industry. His firm
belief that the viability of manufacturing concerns depended critically on
the number of trained technical people who were employed, and on the
amount that was spent on R&D, led him to doubt whether small undertakings could ever survive, given the way that industry was growing in other
countries. He soon became one of the prominent advisers of the Labour
Party who were calling for central planning and governmental interven-
tion in industry.

His leanings were clearly to the left of the party. Hugh Gaitskell, its
leader for the better part of the thirteen years it was in opposition, had set
up an advisory group of scientists in 1956, but, as Philip Williams, his
biographer, writes, Gaitskell never felt at ease with them and did not trust
their political judgements – 'partly no doubt because so many of them',
including Patrick, he regarded as 'left-wing unilateralists'.[6] Things

changed when Harold Wilson became leader on Gaitskell's death in January 1963. Patrick now became probably the most forceful and outspoken member of the group which Wilson charged his colleague Richard Crossman to get together in order to formulate a science and technology policy for a Labour government. In mid-1963, according to Geoffrey Goodman, Patrick produced a memorandum calling for the formation of a super-Ministry for Industry, one 'that would be responsible for the development of science and technology throughout the private sector'.[7] Lovell writes that Patrick also told Wilson that 'the best hope for the Labour Party to make a definite impact on the technological competence of manufacturing industry, would be to create, immediately on taking office, a new and small *Ministry of Technology*'. This is an idea that Wilson may already have had in mind, for in his *Personal Record*[8] he writes that he had long felt that such a department was wanted, on the one hand to serve as a ministry that sponsored industries in need of modernization and restructuring, and on the other, to take charge of the technological 'as opposed to the pure scientific work previously presided over by the Lord President of the Council'. But Wilson also saw the department he had in mind as absorbing the aircraft production section of the existing Ministry of Aviation. What he was planning was enormously ambitious, something he saw as presaging a 'white-hot technological revolution' that would revitalize British industry and restore the country's battered fortunes.

The reality was to prove very different.

One of the first things that Wilson did after taking office was to appoint Frank Cousins, the trade-union leader, as the department's first ministerial head. Rumour then had it that Patrick was to be made a peer in order to enter the Government as one of the new department's subordinate ministers. Whether he was ever formally invited, I do not know. Some newspapers took it upon themselves to say that Patrick was regarded by Whitehall as a security risk,[9] and no more was heard of the suggestion. Instead Patrick became the department's chief scientific adviser, only to discover that setting up a new department was not as easy in practice as it was on paper. Neither he nor any of the others in Crossman's discussion group had any idea of what would be entailed in creating new and major administrative machinery to implement the plans they had laid, or what the repercussions would be on existing departments of state. One of

---

6. P.M. Williams, *Hugh Gaitskell* (Oxford: OUP, 1982), p. 449.
7. G. Goodman, *The Awkward Warrior* (London: David Poynter, 1979), p. 371.
8. H. Wilson, *The Labour Government 1964–1970: A Personal Record* (London: Weidenfeld & Nicolson and Michael Joseph, 1971), p. 8.
9. Goodman, op. cit., p. 406.

Patrick's unrealistic ideas was that the work of the new ministry would be guided by a central council that would formulate policy, which would then be implemented by executive departments, in the same way as the Chiefs of Staff organization was supposed to control the work of the service departments.

Although I was ignorant, except for what I had read in the newspapers, about the plans that Harold Wilson's advisers had put to him before he won the 1964 election, it was to me, the outgoing government's chief scientific adviser whom he had inherited and reappointed, that he sent Frank Cousins to help him spell out specific terms of reference for his new department. When Cousins had explained what he believed to be his responsibilities, it took me no more than an hour or so to draft three or four paragraphs on a single sheet of paper. What was more important was that I was able to suggest the name of the best man for whom I thought Cousins should ask to be the department's Permanent Secretary, that is to say, its chief civil servant. Not all the mandarins whom I knew would have liked the job. Maurice Dean, whom I had known well for some twenty years, did, and he and I had many exchanges during that first week before he was satisfied that he had a document on the basis of which he could proceed.

Whatever he may have thought about the way the ministry was being launched, Patrick threw himself enthusiastically into the new job of being its chief scientific adviser. His belief that central planning and governmental participation in industry were essential meant that the department needed a powerful intelligence service in order to be knowledgeable about what was going on in manufacturing industry. It also meant a readiness to help firms with R&D and finance. On this latter point, according to Wedgwood Benn,[10] who in 1966 succeeded Cousins as the ministerial head of the department, Patrick was more successful than in his efforts to create an intelligence organization. Patrick was soon involved in helping establish an Industrial Reorganisation Corporation, a governmental body whose main purpose was to help manufacturing firms that were in financial and management difficulties.[11] But nothing proved easy. Above all, the department had little if any influence over 'defence industry', which was consuming half the total resources provided by the Exchequer for all industrial R&D. Patrick's ideas about what it would take to make the British computer industry, in which he had a particular

10. Tony Benn, *Out of the Wilderness: Diaries 1963–1967* (London: Hutchinson, 1987), p. 479.
11. The idea was first suggested by Mr Ben Cant, an industrialist, and was taken up by Sir Maurice Dean, Frank Cousins's first Permanent Secretary (Goodman, op. cit., p. 454).

interest, internationally competitive were also hopelessly unrealistic. A proposal that the Government should make something like £5 million available for computer R&D was considered at a ministerial meeting over which Wilson presided, and which was attended by a large number of advisers. With the knowledge I had gained during the previous four to five years in trying to exercise an oversight over defence R&D, I had to say, when asked for my views, that if the Government agreed the proposal it would be 'money down the drain'. The amount that was being suggested was totally inadequate when contrasted with the vastly greater resources, both financial and technical, that our competitors overseas were already committing to computer development.

The meetings of the new department's Advisory Council, of which the Minister was Chairman and Patrick Deputy-Chairman, were at first enthusiastic gatherings, full of hope. But the vision of a new Jerusalem started to recede as the department assumed increasingly onerous executive responsibilities, especially when it absorbed the old Ministry of Aviation and as it departed from the shape that Patrick had hoped it was going to assume. It was not long before he became disillusioned. The steam for which he had been so noted seemed to be going out of him.

This was not so apparent in a Cabinet Office Central Advisory Council on Science and Technology, which was answerable directly to the Prime Minister. The remit of this body affected the responsibilities of all government departments, and at first Patrick contributed significantly to its deliberations. When his statutory term as a member of the Council expired, I as Chairman wanted him to continue, since his membership provided him with the freedom to speak his mind without worrying about his departmental loyalties. When Wedgwood Benn became Minister, the Central Council spent a lot of time considering a proposal that the Department of Technology should transform itself into industry's major contract research organization. Benn appeared twice before the Council to argue his case, but the Council thought the idea impractical. Patrick never spoke up in support of his minister's plan.

The 1947 All-India Scientific Congress had made Patrick very interested in what was happening in India. It was at this meeting that he met Jawaharlal Nehru, with whom a close friendship developed. Nehru first asked Patrick how long it would take to 'Indianize' the armed forces. Patrick's quick answer to this very general question led to his being invited back to advise on the organization of Indian military R&D. Soon, however, he became more interested in questions relating to the state of science in the country, and how science could help in the elimination of poverty and in economic growth. This, of course, found him many friends in India's scientific community, among them Homi Bhabha, the driving force behind

India's work in the nuclear field. I have, however, found no record that Patrick and Bhabha ever discussed the latter's interest in military matters. Indeed, the fact that Patrick played so little, if indeed any, part in the Atoms for Peace movement in which Bhabha and Rabi were so prominent might well have been because the members of the advisory committee which had been charged by the UN to organize the international meetings on the subject were governmental nominees, and Patrick was at the time *persona non grata* in Whitehall.

Patrick always saw science and education as basic to the problem of eliminating poverty in the Third World. What I find surprising is that in his many addresses on the subject, he rarely referred to the need to curb the rate of growth of population. Compared with Rabi's main focus on nuclear matters, the canvas that Patrick tried to cover was much too vast, and his brush-strokes too sweeping, for him to end up with a convincing picture.

His appointment in 1965 as President of the Royal Society provided a much more favourable opportunity than did Whitehall for him to get things moving the way he wanted. Whitehall for Patrick had not proved a responsive instrument. The Royal Society did. He soon got that ancient institution to concern itself with matters that previously it had been content to leave to others. Bernard Lovell quotes Sir William Mansfield Cooper, who was the Vice-Chancellor of Manchester University for much of the time that Patrick was its Langworthy Professor, as saying:

'A problem – of any kind – fired his imagination and he found the hunt for a solution irresistible. . . . If one remembered not to meet his latest idea with hostility all would be well. One might dislike it but to reject it, scorn it, or declare it impossible in the first round was to harden his attitude and temporarily to close his mind. If he felt you were prepared to give an idea a run for its money then his attitude was quite different – one could torpedo it in the end without incurring his enmity – but he tended to judge sharply in the first phase of any operation. His approach was always positive and he had much distrust of the negative approach.'[12]

That, I feel, sums up Patrick's character very nicely. He was brought up more to give orders than to seek counsel. He was precise and made up his mind quickly. And he expected the plans that he drew up to be implemented as soon as they had been formulated. Rabi's views on social

12. Sir Bernard Lovell, 'Patrick Maynard Stuart Blackett, Baron Blackett, of Chelsea', *Biographical Memoirs of Fellows of the Royal Society*, Vol. 21 (1975).

and political matters, as he admitted to his biographer, derived more from hunches and from an intuitive sense that he could not explain. Patrick was not intuitive. He was always explicit and expected others to be. That is how I knew him, a man to whom thought and action were the same. After his term of office as President of the Royal Society came to an end, he faded from public view, subsiding gently into old age and dying two years later. He had made his mark and, once removed from the world of action, there was no more for him to do.

Isidor I. Rabi

1899–1988

Nuclear Physicist, Nobel Laureate and International Statesman

* * *

Isidor Rabi, like Patrick Blackett, was, as I have said, a Nobel Laureate who belonged to the small band of scholars which, in the years before the Second World War, created the science of nuclear physics. Like him, he also had political interests, but whereas Blackett focused more on domestic and Third World affairs, Rabi was mainly concerned with post-war East/West relations. He was to reveal himself as a statesman who, as much as anyone I knew, had a realistic view of what scientists could do in the promotion of international understanding and world peace. He was the progenitor of the Atoms for Peace movement which President Eisenhower launched in 1955, and also the man who sowed the seeds that blossomed into the international high-energy physics institution near Geneva known as CERN.

Rabi and I first met in 1958, at the opening meeting of the scientific committee that had been established by the Nato powers for the purpose of stimulating the growth of Western science. He was the representative of the US, and I of the UK, and since representatives at meetings of official international organizations are placed alphabetically round the table in accordance with the first initial of the countries they represent, my UK chair was next to his US one. While we were milling around talking before the meeting started, Rabi's deputy, Bob Robertson, a Caltech cosmologist whom I had got to know well during the war years when he was a key figure in the field of military scientific intelligence, came over and introduced us. I do not know what Rabi had been told about me, but as he looked me up and down, his opening words were: 'So you're the redoubtable Solly Zuckerman.' I laughed and said something like 'Clearly not as redoubtable as you'. From that moment a friendship started that grew in warmth and understanding until his death at the age of eighty-nine.

Rabi had one of the most powerful minds it was my good fortune ever to enjoy, and from which to learn, for although his field of professional scientific enquiry was remote from mine, we never encountered any barriers to intellectual discourse. He 'thought big' and was fearless in expressing his views, often with a passion that belied his small stature. He was generous in his comments about those whom he admired, and forthright in his criticism of others from whom he differed, or in his condemnation of the few whose views he despised. Sometimes he was overimpatient in argument. More often, his sense of humour and feeling for the absurd would make him break into a burst of high-pitched laughter.

The Child and the Scientist

Isidor Rabi was born in 1898 in a small town in what is now Poland into a poor and strictly Orthodox Jewish family that emigrated to the United States before he was a year old.[1] His formal education started in a small Hebrew school in New York where, as he told John Rigden, his biographer, he started to question Jewish orthodoxy without abandoning a sense of religious belief, of 'the mystery and the philosophy' of the Creation. He was a precocious reader. The Copernican solar system, about which he learnt from a small book on astronomy in a local public library, came as a revelation that eliminated his need to believe in a God whose job it was to make the sun rise and set every day. At his next elementary school, he read about socialism and Marxism, which he soon realized did not provide the integrated view of society he was seeking, for by the age of thirteen he already felt that there had to be some overriding conceptual scheme into which could be fitted the disparate events of both the past and the present.

The high school where he spent his next four years was a craft school, chosen as a way for him to escape from his otherwise narrow environment. He left it 'street-wise and self-educated' – street-wise because he had to learn to avoid the gangs that set upon small Jewish boys on their way to and from school; self-educated, because the school left him all the time in the world for his own reading. A scholarship took him to Cornell, which he entered as a student of electrical engineering. He quickly switched to chemistry, and continued the process of self-education through avid reading of whatever caught his fancy. He told his biographer that the

1. According to John S. Rigden (*Rabi: Scientist and Citizen*, New York: Basic Books, 1987), the names he was given at birth were Israel Isaac. When he was enrolled at his public school, by a misunderstanding the Israel became Isidor, the name to which Rabi stuck. Rigden's book is based on wide reading, on interviews with more than a score of scientists who worked with Rabi, and, most important, on extensive talks with Rabi and his wife.

atmosphere of Cornell in those days was so anti-Semitic that he never got to know a single faculty member during his four undergraduate years. Nor, after he graduated in chemistry in 1919, were there any jobs in the academic world or in industry either for him or for any of his Jewish classmates. But unlike Admiral Rickover, the father of the American nuclear navy about whom I tell later in the book, he was in no way scarred by the prevailing anti-Semitism. He took it all for granted.

The Pioneering Physicist

Rabi spent the next three years under the parental roof in New York, moving from one odd job to another, visiting museums, discovering music, continuing with his reading and enjoying the close company of three Cornell friends who had also graduated with distinction, but who were now also unemployed.

This aimless period ended when he decided to return to Cornell as a graduate student, with his interest now in physics. But having failed to secure a fellowship with which to pay his way, he returned to New York and entered Columbia University. His return made it easier for him to go on seeing Helen Newmark, whom he had first met at Cornell and whom he married in 1927. A part-time tutorship at City College provided him with a slight measure of financial security. The subject of his thesis for the Ph.D., which he was awarded in 1926, was the magnetic susceptibilities of crystals, a problem that turned his attention to quantum mechanics. Only what was then called the 'new physics' could explain why different atoms have different chemical properties.

A fellowship that he was awarded in 1927 then allowed him and Helen to embark on a tour of the European centres where the new phase of physics was flourishing. In Munich he ran into other American scholars who had set out on the same pilgrimage. He met young European theoretical nuclear physicists, among them Hans Bethe and Rudolf Peierls. He moved to Niels Bohr in Copenhagen, and then to Wolfgang Pauli in Hamburg. Here he stayed, doing brilliant work in a stimulating intellectual environment. For a short time he studied with Werner Heisenberg in Leipzig, where he met both Robert Oppenheimer and Edward Teller. His final port of call was Zurich, to which Pauli had moved from Hamburg, and where he ran into still more of the pioneers of the new physics, including Leo Szilard and two other Hungarian scholars, Eugene Wigner and John von Neumann. After some three months there, he returned in 1929 to Columbia, where he had been appointed to a lectureship. In the two years that he had been away, he had met most of the top scientists with whom he was later to become associated in the wartime project to produce an atom bomb.

He had been given his appointment at Columbia on the basis of his reputation as a theoretical physicist, and on the understanding that he would introduce quantum mechanics into the physics curriculum. But Rabi the theorist soon became Rabi the experimentalist. He explored the properties of atomic nuclei by developments of the molecular-beam technique that he had learnt in Stern's laboratory in Hamburg. The researches that he and his post-graduate students at Columbia completed during the few years that preceded the Second World War were so outstanding that they were acknowledged internationally when in 1944 he was awarded the Nobel Prize for Physics. Later his work was memorialized in a schematic picture of a tree which, as it grows, throws out powerful branches from which hang an ever-increasing number of basic scientific discoveries. The Rabi tree takes the story of his impact on the development of nuclear physics only to the end of the fifties. By then it already recorded the names of twenty Nobel Laureates in addition to his own – including a few who had been his pupils. In a tribute to Rabi on his eightieth birthday, it was justly said that he had not only greatly enriched the cultural and intellectual life of Columbia but had helped to establish the university as a 'foremost center of scientific teaching and research'.[2]

The War Years

In June 1940, that is to say about a year and a half before the US entered the Second World War following the Japanese attack on Pearl Harbor, President Roosevelt had set up a National Defense Research Committee 'to expedite and coordinate' all military research that was held to be relevant to American security. Some weeks before this happened, Sir Henry Tizard, the scientific adviser to the British Air Ministry, had arranged that Professor A.V. Hill, the prominent neurophysiologist and Nobel Laureate to whom I have already referred, should be attached to the British Embassy in Washington, in order, as he put it, to use his considerable influence to bring American scientists into the war ahead of their government. Hill was an impressive figure and he quickly succeeded in capturing the attention of the many anglophile US scientists with whom he made contact. The next step that he and Tizard took was to persuade a cautious British Government that it was in the UK's interest to reveal to the

2. *Celebration of the Fiftieth Anniversary of the Pupin Laboratories* (New York: Columbia University Press, 1979).

President's new scientific committee all the secret military technical projects on which British scientists were then working. Permission having been granted, Tizard, with Sir John Cockcroft, another nuclear physicist and Nobel Laureate, as his deputy, led a select team of British scientists to the US, accompanied by a number of military men with whom they had worked, and carrying with them a 'black box' that contained 'samples, blueprints and reports of all new British war devices',[3] one of which, the cavity magnetron valve, a device that was capable of generating very high-powered radio-waves on a wavelength of 10 centimetres, was later described by an American writer as 'the most valuable cargo ever brought to our shores.'

Rabi was more than ready to turn his creative talents to any scientific enquiry that might help in the war against Hitler, and was one of the American scientists who were invited to meet the British team. Of all the items that Tizard demonstrated, the one that made the greatest impression was the cavity-magnetron valve; its ability to produce high power in the centimetre waveband was essential for airborne radar interception systems. Rabi was so impressed that he immediately offered to join two other physicists, Lee DuBridge and Wheeler Loomis – the latter already head of a microwave panel that had been set up by the President's Research Committee – in establishing and directing what became the famous Radiation Laboratory at the Massachusetts Institute of Technology in Cambridge, Mass. The job that they were given was to improve radar techniques, and in particular to develop airborne radar.

The principle of radar was known long before the outbreak of the Second World War. Hertz, the discoverer of electromagnetic waves, had shown that beams of electromagnetic energy bounce back from objects that lie in their path, and that the reflected echoes can be registered on a receiver such as a cathode-ray tube – precursor of the familiar TV screen of today. A patent for a very primitive kind of radar had been taken out by a German called Hulsmeyer as far back as 1904. But it was not until 1935 that Sir Robert Watson-Watt, the head of the British Government's Radio Research Station, in responding to a request from H.E. Wimperis and Sir Henry Tizard to see whether there was anything in the idea of a death-ray, discovered that while such a ray was an impossibility – today this is not the case – electromagnetic waves could be used to discern the presence of aircraft well out of visual range. By measuring the time interval between the transmission of electromagnetic beams or 'pulses' that strike something in their path, and the echoes that they make when they bounce back

3. P.M.S. Blackett, *Studies in War* (Edinburgh and London: Oliver & Boyd, 1964), p. 107.

to be registered as signals on a radar screen, it was possible to determine not only the presence of an object somewhere 'out there', but its range and the direction in which it was moving, as well as its height and speed.

All three of the British armed services had a few primitive radar sets in operation by the beginning of the war, but at the time only the one that had been developed for the RAF had any significant practical value. Tizard had recognized from the start that it was necessary to devise a system in which radar could become operationally effective, with ground controllers – at first many of them scientists – manning the radar screens, and in radio contact with the pilots whose job it was to shoot down enemy intruders whose paths had been followed on the screens.

The first RAF ground radar stations were furnished with relatively enormous aerials and massive power sources, but the range at which they could pick up approaching enemy aircraft was limited. Unfortunately, too, the 'lengths' of the electromagnetic waves which they transmitted – then at best several metres – was nowhere near what was operationally desirable. It was obvious that shorter wavelengths would enable narrower beams of radar waves to be transmitted without increasing the size of the aerials, and that it would then be more likely that the presence of two or more aircraft flying together would be signalled as separate as opposed to registering as a single blip on a radar screen.

The problem was solved by a young physicist, John Randall by name, who had been drafted to Mark Oliphant's department of physics in the University of Birmingham, to join a team that was working there on radar. Within the space of little more than four months, and helped by Harry Boot, a technical assistant, Randall invented a relatively small piece of equipment that generated microwaves with enormous power on a wavelength of about 10 centimetres. The two men had succeeded by combining two lines of thought which different physicists had until then been pursuing separately. The magnetron that they devised, working on a wavelength of 10 centimetres, enabled a powerful, narrow beam of radiation to be transmitted from an antenna small enough to be carried by a fighter plane. Randall's device became the foundation of the MIT Radiation Laboratory's work.

Rabi took over the device as his special responsibility, and quickly became the intellectual leader of the whole MIT group. The first problem that had to be solved was to develop a system with a single antenna that would scan the sky in front of the fighter and at the same time detect the considerably weaker echoes of the electromagnetic beams which were reflected when they impinged on a target. In this way ground controllers could be eliminated from the chain of command, with the pilots themselves responding to the blips that were made on their radar screens by hostile aircraft. A solution was soon found and, in parallel with similar work that was going on in the UK, and where, indeed, the problem had already been solved (work for which Rabi told me he had the highest admiration), it was not long before airborne and seaborne radar sets were developed that were able to detect enemy aircraft, ships and surfaced submarines at a considerable distance. Rabi and his group then went on to develop 3 centimetre and 1.5 centimetre magnetrons, so increasing still further the power of radar to discriminate the echoes from objects on which the radar beams struck. Centimetric radar also made it possible to develop airborne sets that were able to provide a somewhat crude picture of the configuration of a harbour or a town, so that aiming-points could be roughly picked out for bombers – a real advance on blind bombing through cloud, and a technique that had already been developed by Bernard Lovell in England.[4]

While radar was Rabi's main concern, he also became involved in the atomic bomb project. Robert Oppenheimer, who early in 1943 had been put in charge of the scientific effort to develop the 'bomb', had wanted him to become his deputy in setting up and directing what became the vast Manhattan Project laboratory at Los Alamos in New Mexico. Rabi had, however, become so involved and excited by the work of the 'Rad Lab' at MIT that he declined the invitation. He did, however, help Oppenheimer recruit some key personnel, and remained Oppenheimer's chief adviser and consultant throughout the war, visiting Los Alamos whenever he could. He was present at the bomb test that took place on 16 July 1945 at Alamogordo in the New Mexican desert. Oppenheimer, and those senior scientists who knew all the details of the construction of the test bomb, had speculated about its possible success – or failure – and had laid bets on what its 'yield' (that is to say, explosive power) would be, given that the device worked. Rabi provided the closest estimate, and as Robert Bacher, one of Oppenheimer's chief scientific colleagues in the project, recorded, 'won the pot hands down'.

4. After his successes with the magnetron, Rabi took charge of an Advanced Development Division of the whole laboratory. Since the war, developments in radar have of course made much more possible than was conceivable at the time. Today the size of a small object orbiting in space can be measured, and by its shape or 'signature' its nature can be diagnosed; for example, a fragment of the casing of a rocket that has carried a communications satellite into space.

The Early Post-war Years

After the war, Rabi returned to Columbia to take charge of and rebuild the Physics Department, which soon became an academic power-house as research students were attracted from far and wide. MIT and Los Alamos had, however, brought him into the public arena of science, and had added a new dimension to his interests. Strengthening American science in general became a major concern of his. He helped to bring about the transformation of the powerful Office of Naval Research into an institution that was not only responsible for the scientific and technological work that the US Navy wanted done, but one that supported scientific research in universities throughout the United States – and, indeed, abroad as well. He was among those who campaigned hard for the establishment of the National Science Foundation that Vannevar Bush, the Chairman of the President's wartime Office of Scientific Research and Development, had wanted to see created. He and his close colleague Norman Ramsey then took the lead in establishing the vast inter-university, high-energy laboratory at Brookhaven on Long Island. Soon he was in demand everywhere. The Atomic Energy Act that became law in 1946 not only called for the setting up of an Atomic Energy Commission but specified that it should be assisted by a General Advisory Committee. Oppenheimer was appointed its chairman and Rabi one of its members – succeeding Oppenheimer as chairman in 1952.

Rabi and the International Control of Nuclear Energy

At the outset, Rabi had implicitly accepted the notion that nuclear weapons had a military utility. He also shared the fear that German physicists were trying to devise an atom bomb. Like Oppenheimer, he had realized that once Hiroshima and Nagasaki had demonstrated to the whole world that an atom bomb could be made, and that it had enormous destructive power, other nations would want to follow in the USA's footsteps. Like many others they realized that it would be safer for all were 'the atom' to be placed under international control in order to avoid a nuclear arms race.

This at first was also President Truman's view. James Byrnes, his Secretary of State, had accordingly instructed Dean Acheson, the Under-Secretary, together with a board of consultants chaired by David Lilienthal, the head of the Tennessee Valley Authority, to prepare a paper for submission to the fledgling United Nations to show how the President's idea could be implemented. As Acheson relates in his memoirs, their main mentor in the exercise was Oppenheimer, who had been appointed a member of Lilienthal's board. He in turn kept in close touch with Rabi, who years later told me that some of the drafting for which Oppenheimer was responsible was carried out in the very room in his apartment where we were then talking.

When completed, Truman handed over Acheson's paper to Bernard Baruch, the financier who had made himself an indispensable adviser to presidents. Baruch added his own ideas, one of which called for the abolition of the Security Council's power of veto where nuclear matters were concerned. Acheson, Lilienthal, Oppenheimer and Rabi knew that such a condition would make certain that the President's plan – now the Baruch plan – would be rejected by the Russians, which Patrick Blackett cynically believed was the goal of American policy. This was Rabi's first experience of frustration about the way a critical matter in the nuclear field had been handled politically. His second related to the decision to develop the hydrogen bomb, or 'super'.

The Super

In 1949, when the US learnt that the USSR had successfully tested its first atomic bomb, heavy pressure was brought to bear on President Truman to give the go-ahead for the development of the more powerful 'super'. Oppenheimer's committee unanimously advised against this move. In their view, fission bombs were powerful enough to serve as a deterrent to war. Rabi, together with Enrico Fermi, another member of the committee, went one further, and in a minority report urged the President to call an international meeting to seek world-wide agreement that no country would ever embark on the development of the 'super', a weapon which, they warned, could have unlimited destructive power. As they put it, the H-bomb 'is necessarily an evil thing considered in any light'.[5] Truman decided otherwise, and Los Alamos was given the order to press on vigorously. As a member of the General Advisory Committee, Rabi, like Oppenheimer and Fermi, continued to be kept in touch with the progress of the work, without, however, being directly involved.

The controversy that the H-bomb issue generated was, however, to bring Rabi into public conflict with Edward Teller, the theoretical physicist whom he had first met in Leipzig in 1928, and who, during 1939, had worked in his laboratory at Columbia before joining the staff of the Los

5. Richard Rhodes, *The Making of the Atom Bomb* (New York: Simon & Schuster, 1986), p. 769.

Alamos laboratory. Almost from the moment that he had become one of its members, Teller had been at odds with Oppenheimer, and when the war ended had started to lobby and intrigue in hawkish quarters for a more vigorous nuclear-weapons programme than Oppenheimer thought wise, particularly in view of the fact that the President and Congress were still undecided about what the future of the Manhattan Project should be. Teller had from the start been in the vanguard of those who were urging the development of the hydrogen bomb. Three years after authorization for its development had been given, the manoeuvrings and intrigues in which he had been engaged came to a head when he indirectly instigated inquiries about Oppenheimer as a security risk.

It was the era of McCarthy. The FBI started to dig into Oppenheimer's pre-war connections with anti-fascist organizations, with the result that he was publicly arraigned by the Atomic Energy Commission – then headed by Teller's friend Lewis Strauss. Teller was among those who testified against Oppenheimer, stating that while he had 'always assumed' that Oppenheimer was loyal to the United States, he would 'like to see the vital interests' of the United States 'in hands which I understand better and therefore trust more'.[6] Teller also tabled a written statement which, had it not been for the statute of limitations, would have amounted to a criminal charge against Oppenheimer 'for having lied to a security person'. Teller had made it plain to an official of the AEC that whatever the outcome of the hearings, he wanted Oppenheimer 'unfrocked', as he put it, because otherwise, so he claimed, scientists 'would lose their enthusiasm for the program' to develop a hydrogen bomb.

To those like Teller who instinctively believed that greater destructive power automatically meant greater military strength, anyone who opposed the super was an enemy of the State and was not to be trusted. Whatever his wartime and post-war achievements, to them Oppenheimer was, therefore, necessarily a security risk. In the face of all the prejudice, an abundance of distinguished and powerful testimony on Oppenheimer's behalf proved impotent. His public career had been doomed from the moment that the AEC decided to bring the action.

Rabi was one of the prominent scientists who testified powerfully on Oppenheimer's behalf. Whatever left-wing political contacts Oppenheimer may have had during the years that led up to the war, however arrogant Teller and some others thought him, it was nonsense, so Rabi said, to brand him as a security risk. Like most other scientists who had been involved in the Manhattan Project, Rabi was also contemptuous of Teller

6. S.A. Blumberg and G. Owens, *Energy and Conflict: The Life and Times of Edward Teller* (New York: Putnam, 1976), pp. 361–2.

for the part, both direct and indirect, that he had played in precipitating the action. Rabi was later to say that he had never known Teller to 'take a position where there was the slightest chance in the interest of peace. I think he is an enemy of humanity'.[7] Rabi's outright condemnation of Teller led to the latter's virtual ostracism by the vast majority of America's scientific community. Years later I attended a small meeting in Sicily where I expected to meet Rabi. He was not there, and I wrote to express my disappointment, but telling him that the meeting had provided me with an opportunity of arguing with Teller face to face, and that Wigner, whom Rabi had first met during his stay in Europe in the late twenties, was also there, but was now 'an old man with a major preoccupation with nuclear war – fed by ignorance'. Rabi replied that he had thought of going but 'the idea of a serious meeting, with Teller and Wigner present, was too preposterous'.

CERN and Atoms for Peace

Any sense of failure that Rabi might have felt at having been on the losing side over the Baruch plan and the hydrogen bomb was more than offset by his successes in helping to bring about international co-operation in non-military nuclear matters. As a member of the US delegation to the 1950 Florence meeting of the General Assembly of Unesco, he put forward a proposal that a research centre should be established in Europe in order 'to increase and make more fruitful the international collaboration of scientists in the search of new knowledge'. The conference agreed, and the Director-General of Unesco was asked 'to assist and encourage the formation and organization of regional research centres and laboratories in order to increase and make more fruitful the international collaboration of scientists in the search of new knowledge in fields where the effort of any one country in the region is insufficient for the task' – the very words that Rabi used at the meeting. The proposal was taken a formal step further in 1952, and not long after led to the formation of CERN (Centre Européen des Recherches Nucléaires).

Rabi's second major success in helping to bring about international co-operation in nuclear matters came about as a result of an initiative taken by President Eisenhower.

When his post as Allied Supreme Commander during the Second World War came to an end, Eisenhower had been appointed President of Columbia University, an office he held until he succeeded Truman as US

7. Ibid., p. 407.

President in 1953.[8] The US was then engaged in a vigorous arms race with the USSR, with considerable emphasis on nuclear weaponry. At Potsdam in 1945 Eisenhower had, however, expressed misgivings about the use of such destructive armament. He was also opposed to attempts to find military solutions to political problems. About a year after becoming President, he accordingly decided to deliver a speech to the United Nations in order to proclaim the view that there were uses for nuclear power other than the making of bombs, and that what was wanted was an International Atomic Energy Agency, which would 'devise methods whereby fissionable material would be allocated to serve the peaceful pursuits of mankind' – as opposed to its destruction.

The speech was widely acclaimed, and the President then instructed the Atomic Energy Commission to formulate a plan to further his proposal. They in turn asked their General Advisory Committee for its views. Rabi, now its chairman, leapt at the challenge, and suggested that the first step had to be the convening of a non-political international conference to discuss 'the peaceful uses of atomic energy'. The proposal was accepted, and he was then charged with the task of planning the meeting. He travelled to gain the support of scientists in other countries, at the same time as the President instructed Foster Dulles, his Secretary of State, to put the idea of a conference as a specific US proposal to the 1954 UN General Assembly. It was accepted, and in the following year the first international conference on the peaceful uses of atomic energy duly took place in Geneva, under the presidency of the Indian physicist, Homi Bhabha, and with the full participation of the Soviet Union, which, encouraged by the declassification that Rabi had urged of secret American data, came forward with some of its own secret information.

The conference was an enormous success. When in 1957 the UN set up the International Atomic Energy Authority, Rabi was, not surprisingly, appointed a member of its Scientific Advisory Committee, remaining one for all of fifteen years.

---

8. In 1950 he was given leave of absence to serve a two-year stint as Nato's first Supreme Commander. It used to please me to think that as adviser during the war on strategic air operations to his deputy, Sir Arthur Tedder, I was probably the first academic scientist with whom Eisenhower had had dealings, and that Rabi had now become one of his trusted advisers. Shortly before Eisenhower left Columbia University to assume the presidency of the United States, I called on him to pay my respects, but unfortunately that was before Rabi and I had met. It would have been good to have met him first with the President.

Scientific Advice at the Centre

The controversy about the hydrogen bomb had broken out shortly before the start of the Korean war in 1950, by which time the resources that the federal government was devoting to science and technology had become so considerable that neither the President's executive office nor Congress could keep proper track of what was going on, either from the point of view of priorities or from that of financial control. What was missing in the R&D field was a central advisory body that could help bridge the gap between the presidency and the executive departments of state on the one hand, and on the other, the congressional committees that decided what resources should be provided the President for the proper discharge of his duties – a responsibility that implied a reasonable understanding on both sides of the programmes for which the funds were required and voted. In an effort to remedy the situation, President Truman therefore established a Scientific Advisory Committee to help the institution then known as the Office of Defense Mobilization (ODM) in deciding the merits of the demands that the armed services were making for R&D resources. It was, however, only a part-time body and lacked any real authority. From 1952 onwards, under Rabi's chairmanship, the committee had accordingly begun to use its own initiative in considering problems of national security, including questions that related to air defence and rocketry.

The situation remained unchanged until 1957, when the launch of the first sputnik by the Russians led to widespread concern that the Soviet Union was winning the arms race. Eisenhower was now in power and was having to deal with an ever-increasing avalanche of demands for new and exotic weaponry. He decided to call both on Rabi's ODM committee and on the National Academy of Sciences for advice about what needed to be done so that order could be restored to the R&D scene. Rabi, who had known the President during the time he was at Columbia, urged him to appoint a personal science adviser, 'a man whom he liked who would be available full-time to work with him right in his office, to help by clarifying the scientific and technological aspects of decisions which must be made from time to time.' He would, so Rabi declared, have to become 'part of the President's mind-set'.[9] Eisenhower unhesitatingly accepted the suggestion, and appointed James Killian, then the President of MIT, to the office, establishing at the same time a President's Science Advisory Committee (PSAC) to help him discharge his responsibilities. Rabi became one of its leading figures.

9. William T. Golden (ed), *Science Advice to the President* (Oxford: Pergamon Press, 1980), p. 16.

Western Scientific Co-operation

The creation of PSAC coincided with the setting up of the Nato Science Committee. The need for that body was one of the recommendations of a committee of four European politicians – styled the 'four wise men' – who had been charged by the Nato Council of Ministers in 1957 to propose measures to strengthen the Western Alliance. The job of saying how a science committee should work and of providing it with terms of reference was handed over to a small 'task force' of scientists chaired by Joe Koepfli, a Caltech professor of chemistry who was then serving as scientific adviser to the State Department. I was appointed the UK member of his small group, which acted swiftly enough for the proposed committee, helped by a full-time secretariat, to start its work the following year.

The committee was not, however, set up to deal with military matters, but in so far as it had to establish itself within a military organization whose war plans predicated the use of nuclear weapons, its full-time chairman, although directly answerable to the Secretary-General of Nato, and not to the organization's military chief, had at the start necessarily to be an American who was 'cleared' to deal with nuclear matters. An impossible situation would have been created had a veil of secrecy separated him not only from another scientific unit in the Nato headquarters which served as a source of technical advice for the Supreme Commander and his staff, but from other US technical personnel who were always around in those days, busily trying to arrange co-operation in defence R&D. Norman Ramsey, Rabi's colleague in Columbia, who had been on Oppenheimer's staff at Los Alamos, was the first chairman – and an excellent chairman he was.

It was inevitable that Rabi, with all his experience in the organization of international co-operation in nuclear matters, and with the prominent part that he had played in the establishment of PSAC, should be called upon to serve as the US representative on the committee – which he remained, again for some fifteen years. During the first ten he was still head of the Department of Physics in Columbia, and after his retirement in 1967 his status was that of university professor. I served for only eight. Two years after the committee started its work I had accepted the post of chief scientific adviser to the UK Ministry of Defence, without, however, surrendering charge of my large Department of Anatomy in Birmingham University, where I was able to continue my academic researches with the help of colleagues and students. But I gradually discovered that two full-time jobs left little time for additional activities, and in 1966 I arranged to be replaced on the Nato committee. I did so reluctantly, for its quarterly meetings in Paris, then the headquarters of Nato, more than anything else meant regular contact with Rabi, with whom, in addition to talk about the strengthening of Western science, I found a great deal else to discuss, particularly those aspects of my governmental work that overlapped with the concerns of PSAC, with which Rabi soon brought me into contact.

The fact that Rabi and I had had more experience of working with our respective governments than had any of our committee colleagues at that time – all of them distinguished scientists – and that we had both been involved in military or military/political affairs, meant that at the start we were expected to give a lead in the committee's discussions. But the widespread belief that a special US/UK relationship existed also meant that we had to be careful not to give the impression that we were ganging up on the others in order to get them to follow our lead. So as to prevent this impression from taking root, we evolved a technique of occasionally opposing each other, even when we wanted a discussion to reach a goal on which we had both agreed. Rabi constantly warned me that it was a mistake to give the impression that there was a 'special relationship' between the US and the UK. He often said that in the end it would be a disaster if the UK did not realize that its future lay in Europe, not the US.[10]

The committee, which still survives after well over thirty years, has certainly been a power for good, and it can legitimately be claimed, as some do, that from a practical point of view it has been a more effective organization than has any other institution that has been set up to achieve international co-operation in science. Whether it justifies a comment of Rabi's that it was also the best thing that Nato ever did is another matter. What the committee first helped do was encourage the countries that were members of Nato to increase the proportion of their gross national products that they devoted to the furtherance of science. Co-operative research funds and a system of studentships were also set up. But probably the committee's most successful achievement was the establishment of a continuous series of summer study schools for scientists engaged in particular areas of enquiry. Doing this had been one of the recommendations of the 'four wise men', but the successful launch of the scheme was very largely due to Rabi's advocacy. In 1978, at a celebration to mark the twentieth anniversary of the foundation of the committee, there were on display scores of volumes that recorded the proceedings of the summer schools, of which there have now been several hundred. In those early days many other ideas for international scientific co-operation were

10. None of the members of the committee had plenipotentiary powers so far as finance was concerned, and each of us was accompanied to our meetings by a small team which included a bureaucrat whose job it was to make his own assessment of the political implications of failing to back up with hard cash whatever brave promises about co-operation the committee suggested.

discussed, but only a few became implemented specifically because of the committee's efforts. Rabi continually urged the committee to realize that unless the European members of Nato pooled their scientific and technological resources, for example in the field of computers, they stood little chance of competing commercially either with the US or with Japan, whose emergence as a modern industrial power he could already foresee.

Off Duty

Both Rabi and I had many friends in Paris, both outside as well as inside the Nato community. When the committee was set up, Nato's Supreme Commander was the same Larry Norstad whose colleague I had been in the Mediterranean theatre in 1943. He was now a full US general, and in the year before the committee was formed I had delivered the opening address at a Nato conference on operational research at which, when introducing me, he had told a somewhat bemused audience that he and I still argued which of us had won the war. Different though Rabi's and my wartime military and political experiences had been, they provided an immediate interest additional to the affairs of the committee for the close relationship that developed between us. We often lunched or dined together, usually alone, but sometimes in the company of Bob Robertson and other US scientists in the Nato entourage. Rabi liked good food and wine. He soon reintroduced me to Derek Jackson, a scientist and wealthy post-war British tax exile, whose inherited fortune came from the popular Sunday paper *The News of the World*. Derek led a giddy social life, marrying and divorcing with unusual regularity, and paying out vast sums in alimony both to past wives and mistresses. I had met him in the thirties when he was a member of the Clarendon Laboratory in Oxford. He fascinated Rabi, possibly because, apart from their mutual scientific interests (Derek was a spectrographer and an FRS, and still worked somewhat spasmodically at one of the Sorbonne's laboratories), they were so totally dissimilar. Derek had distinguished himself during the war as a night fighter navigator, and, in his capacity as a physicist had experimented with the new airborne radar in whose development Rabi had played so big a part. There could hardly have been a meeting of the Science Committee when Rabi and I failed to meet him, and when he did not entertain us to dinner at some smart Parisian restaurant. For his part Derek was intrigued by what we were doing, and he became so interested in our critical talk about the nuclear arms race that Rabi encouraged him to publish in *The News of the World* a lengthy article on the subject, which must have surprised the bulk of its readers, by whom the paper was bought mainly because of the juicy scandals it reported. When Derek died in 1982 I sent Rabi a copy of an obituary that was published in *The Times*. In acknowledging it, Rabi wrote: 'I feel his loss deeply. In the drab uniformity of the upper class . . . he was a singular point. Brilliantly self-centered, an austere hedonist, a conventional aristocrat flouting convention, good company, sometimes good talk, always good wine, a good physicist immune to "grand" theory, an experimenter in the classic style. . . . He certainly found a wide selection of upper-class and varied bed-fellows and was willing to pay handsomely.' The letter was classic Rabi. He was always expert in seeing the interplay of positive and negative charges.

When I look back over the years that I was a member of the Nato committee, all I can really recall is Rabi. When we met in 1978 at the Nato headquarters in Brussels where the meeting to celebrate the twentieth anniversary of the committee's foundation took place, he was disappointed that because of official commitments in London I could not go with him to Paris to dine 'for old time's sake' with Derek Jackson. Several years before that an ancient European university had sounded me out about accepting an honorary degree at the same time as Rabi was to be honoured, but again, because the date of the ceremony clashed with an official commitment, I reluctantly had to decline the honour. 'You should have been there,' said Rabi when we met a few months later. 'They made us wear such funny hats, you would have enjoyed it.'

Encounters with PSAC

Happily my departure from the Nato Science Committee did not interrupt our exchanges. Rabi frequently stopped over in London when he attended meetings on the Continent, at the same time as official business often took me to the US. There was always a lot to talk about, and during the years when we both still led active lives scarcely one passed without our meeting in Washington, New York or London.

As the UK government's chief scientific adviser, one of my responsibilities covered the technical aspects of the negotiations between the US, the USSR and the UK for a comprehensive nuclear test ban which, at the end of the fifties and in the early sixties, were grinding on without making any obvious progress. I had also involved myself in operational matters, and had started to enquire into the military utility of so-called tactical nuclear weapons, taking as a basis for study actual war-plan scenarios. As a member of PSAC, Rabi was also involved in the test-ban debate, so that there was every reason why I should try to learn from him as much about his colleagues' views on the subject as I could. Equally, I knew that he had not seriously considered whether or how nuclear weapons could be used by correspondingly armed opposing forces in order to gain some military advantage. At the start he had had few misgivings about the wisdom of embarking on the development of the atomic bomb, and so far as I knew, in arguing later against the development of the hydrogen bomb, he had accepted Oppenheimer's view that there might be a rational military use for small fission weapons in field warfare. My experience as an operational planner during the war, coupled with what was emerging from my theoretical studies, had started to make me doubt whether, apart from their deterrent effect, nuclear weapons had any military utility at all.

I discussed all this with Rabi, who suggested that I should take the matter up with George Kistiakowsky, a distinguished Harvard chemist who had succeeded James Killian as Eisenhower's science adviser, and as such was the new chairman of PSAC. I should ask him, said Rabi, to bring to the UK a party of those members of PSAC who were knowledgeable about nuclear weaponry, to consider the argument with whatever group of British scientists I chose. I did what Rabi suggested, but Kistiakowsky, a tall, impressive man who, before coming to America, had as a young man fought in Wrangel's White Russian Army against the Bolsheviks, was at first nervous, believing that his responsibilities as the President's science adviser did not extend to commenting on military doctrine. Urged on by Rabi, however, he sought the necessary authority, and arrived in London with a small party of his colleagues for a two-day discussion. That was the first of a number of similar meetings with PSAC – at first biennial and alternately in London and Washington – that continued until the end of the sixties, and through a succession of four presidential science advisers, all of whom I outlasted, despite a joking remark by Rabi at the time I accepted my Whitehall post that he was certain I would not be able to stand the job for more than a year. Unlike my position in the UK, that of presidential science adviser changed as administrations changed. But, until PSAC died, Rabi, a Republican, remained a member or consultant from one administration to the next, Republican or Democrat.

The agenda for these small meetings was selected according to our current interests, as was the membership of our respective panels. But Rabi was always there, inspiring discussion, often impatiently blunt, but always creatively thrusting, even when we argued the merits of matters such as aircraft-carrier policy or the management of long-term environmental problems, in which he had only a marginal interest and which he regarded as irrelevant when viewed against the immediate dangers of the nuclear arms race and East/West confrontation.

His obvious confidence in me meant that I always had a welcome in PSAC circles. Occasionally, when a meeting of PSAC coincided with one of my visits to Washington, I was invited to join in discussions in which no special American secrets were involved, and in which the UK had an interest. Rabi often said that the US was only a few years behind the UK in committing some political or military blunder, and therefore always had something to learn from what was happening in England.

When John Kennedy succeeded Eisenhower as President in 1961, Kistiakowsky ceased to be chairman of PSAC, and I then found myself working with Kennedy's appointee, Jerome B. Wiesner of MIT, with whom I soon established close relations. Both of us were convinced that, despite the opposition from France and China, an internationally agreed comprehensive ban on nuclear testing would not only enhance the security of the West and East but would help prevent further nuclear proliferation. This view was strongly opposed in those quarters in the US where it was held that the US needed to add to the size and variety of its nuclear stockpile, and therefore had to go on testing. The opposition also constantly argued that whatever safeguards and measures of verification were specified in a treaty, the Russians would always cheat and find clandestine ways of testing. Maybe the Russians held the same view about the Americans. But Rabi was appalled by the arguments. I can still hear him expostulating: 'The Russians may be stupid but they are not mad! How can people believe that they will start cheating the day after signing a solemn treaty, especially when they must realize as well as we do that they would be bound to be found out if they did?'

The first of the talks that I had with PSAC, when Kistiakowsky was still in charge, had endorsed the conclusions that had emerged from my studies of actual nuclear-war plans – namely, that their use on a European battlefield could lead only to mutual disaster. Like me, Jerry Wiesner and his colleagues also saw no point in continuing testing in order to devise better nuclear artillery shells, or small warheads for ballistic missiles that were designed to hit enemy nuclear warheads in flight. Rabi, like Jerry and many other American scientists who were in full possession of the technical facts, was convinced that an operationally and strategically effective anti-ballistic missile (ABM) defence could never be devised, however many billions of dollars or roubles were spent in the effort. The argument that even a partially effective defence would be worth having because it might save a few tens of millions of American lives, while tens of other millions died, he regarded as Dr Strangelove madness. Once, when we happened to be in California at the same time, he arranged that I should debate the subject at a small luncheon meeting with Herman Kahn, that mountainous, bespectacled, twisted think-tank 'genius' who was the model for Dr Strangelove, and who was urging us all to 'think the unthinkable' and accept as a reality the prospect of all-out nuclear war, Rabi chipped in here and there, but his real purpose in arranging the meeting had been to reveal to me the kind of frightening nonsense that was encouraged in certain influential and hawkish quarters.

After PSAC

In 1979, I was invited to deliver a paper to the American Philosophical Society, to which I had many years before been elected as a foreign member. Although few attend the society's meetings in Philadelphia, Rabi encouraged me to choose a serious subject, and I therefore selected as my theme that of 'Science Advisers and Scientific Advisers', the idea being to highlight the difference between those official advisers of government who use their scientific talents and experience to satisfy their clients – with the military mainly in my mind – and those who try to exercise the same qualities of critical judgement in considering matters of national importance as they are expected to do in their academic research.

I began by reviewing the long history of scientific advice to government in the UK, and went on to consider – somewhat critically – C.P. Snow's celebrated story of the Cherwell/Tizard dispute at the start of the Second World War about the use of air power, and about the influence that Cherwell exerted on Churchill. I spoke about the contributions that scientists had made to the technological wonders of the war, and about the widespread hope that they would be able to achieve great things in the peace that was to follow. The core of my paper then became almost a synthesis of the many exchanges I had had with Rabi.

'In stimulating change,' I said, 'in promoting the birth of new industries, in devising new agricultural techniques, and in encouraging the launching of vast new technological projects, scientists and engineers have not been acting simply as servants of politicians and military chiefs who could not themselves have known whether what was being considered was either technically possible, or socially, economically, and politically desirable or necessary. . . . The scientists and technologists were themselves the ones who initiated the new developments, who created the new demands. . . . They were the ones who, at base, were determining the social, economic, and political future of the world. . . . Without any coherent concern for political values or goals, scientists and engineers had become the begetters of new social demand and the architects of new economic and social situations, over which those who exercised political power then had to rule. The nuclear world, with all its hazards, is the scientists' creation; it is certainly not a world that came about in response to any external demand. So, at root, is the whole of today's environment of ever-rising material expectation. So, because of biomedical advances, is the spectre of over-population. So, some protest, is environmental pollution. So is the world of instant communications. So is the world of missiles. So is the unending arms-race by which we are all now threatened.'

In winding up I quoted the words that President Eisenhower had used in his valedictory address to the American people when he warned them that they had to beware of the 'acquisition of unwarranted influence, whether sought or unsought, by the military industrial complex' and of the 'danger that public policy could itself become the captive of a scientific-technological elite'.[11]

I had not shown Rabi the text of my paper, but as I spoke I could see that he was becoming more and more worked up. As soon as I had ended, he moved to the rostrum, from where he made an impassioned speech saying that the time had come for psychiatrists to be brought in to stem the tide of technological madness by which we were being submerged. Why had we failed to get reason to prevail? he kept asking. When he had finished, I had a feeling that he had impressed the company of distinguished elder scholars – as I remember, few of them scientists – far more than my formal presentation had done.

He was still worked up that evening when he got Emanuel Piore, a mutual friend who was then the vice-president of the society, to join us. 'Manny', like Rabi, was a physicist, and I had met him on my first visit to Washington after the war, during which he had been connected with the Office of Naval Research, which he left to become a vice-president of IBM and the head of its vast research laboratories. Like Rabi, he was a continuing member of PSAC, remaining one of its members or consultants regardless of which administration was in power. Over beer and sandwiches that evening Rabi expanded on his worries about the way the nations of the world were driving themselves to destruction, and about the need to do something about it. He simply could not understand why scientists such as ourselves should have failed to get the literate world to realize that the arms race had set mankind on a course that could end only in disaster. I do not know about Manny, who spoke slowly and softly between puffs on his pipe, but I felt that I had disturbed a hornets' nest in Rabi's mind, and that he was trying to urge us to embark on some new kind of crusade.

11. D.D. Eisenhower, *Public Papers of the President, 1960–1961* (Washington, DC: United States Government Printing Office, 1961), p. 1038.

When, a few years later, I asked Rabi what he thought of President Reagan's idea of protecting the United States by way of a space-based anti-ballistic defensive 'astrodome', he lost all patience. It was technologically impossible and strategic madness, he said. The President's scientists were destroying American culture. He simply could not understand why the rational men of science had lost out. When I brought up the name of one of his brightest post-war pupils, he reacted by saying sharply that the man was throwing away his genius, and that however much he disagreed with their views, he was wasting his time by remaining associated with defence scientists who were leading their country astray. 'Sometimes I doubt my own sanity since I find my words find no echo,' he said to me in a letter.

He had expressed similar worries in 1967, on the occasion of a symposium that was organized in his honour to mark his retirement as head of Columbia's Department of Physics. 'My life', he said, 'has been separated essentially into two parts.

'The first was the prewar, where we devoted ourselves wholeheartedly and continually to scientific efforts. . . . Then came the war and I did as much as anybody to stop all scientific research in the United States and devote ourselves completely to the war effort because it was then that we were fighting a beast which was inimical to all nationalities, to all humanity. . . . From the end of 1945 on, whenever opportunity came to me, I hoped . . . to do whatever could be done by an individual who earned the right to have some small voice in affairs by being actively concerned with those who determined affairs, and therefore since 1945 to now, a period of twenty-two years, I have lived a dual existence. On the one side, I came back from war to build up again the Department of Physics, after the grievous losses suffered through the departure of Fermi, Urey and other great scientists. Well I am sorry to say that, while I feel quite confident that we have a great Department of Physics, I do not feel so confident that we have even begun to tame the atom so that it doesn't kill us ultimately. I far underestimated the problem; I far overestimated the rationality . . . of human beings. I far underestimated the capacity of people to put the obvious, the fearful, out of their minds, to refuse to look at the longer distance for the sake of immediate advantage, and the results have been in the last twenty years that we have had this mounting conflict fed by fears of itself.'[12]

12. *A Tribute to Professor I.I. Rabi* (New York: Columbia University Press, 1970).

In yet another address Rabi proclaimed that

'. . . the greatest difficulty which stands in the way of a meeting of the minds of the scientist and the nonscientist is the difficulty of communication. . . . The mature scientist, if he has any taste in these directions, can listen with pleasure to the philosopher, the historian, the literary man, or even the art critic. There is little difficulty from that side because the scientist has been educated in our general culture and is living in it on a day-to-day basis. He reads newspapers, magazines, books, listens to music, debates politics and participates in the general activities of an educated citizen. Unfortunately, this channel of communication is often a one way street. The nonscientist cannot listen to the scientist with pleasure and understanding. Despite its universal outlook and its unifying principle, its splendid tradition, science seems to be no longer communicable to the great majority of educated laymen'.[13]

Rabi epitomized the kind of scientist about whom he was talking. He had achieved that synthesis of knowledge and experience which leads to wisdom. Yet he was also, as he told his biographer, an intuitive person who could not explain why his hunches led him to do this or that. The knowledge that science provided was never enough for Rabi. It could never create a finite picture of all that he wanted to comprehend. Rigden quotes a speech that Rabi delivered in 1950, in which he said that 'to science the unknown is a problem full of interest and promise; in fact, science derives its sustenance from the unknown; all good things have come from that inexhaustible realm'. The unknown – which goes on expanding as science chips off from it a little that then becomes part of knowledge – created for Rabi 'an awareness that there is a reality both greater than and external to himself'. If we survive into the future, said Rabi, we can hope 'that men will realize deeply that their most noble goal is to understand themselves within the universe and that this goal will override all the petty and parochial aims that so disturb the peace and endanger mankind's future existence'.[14]

I saw Rabi for the last time about two months before he died. He was not long out of hospital, where he had undergone a serious operation, but he was as cheerful and vivacious as ever during the two hours that I was with him, piecing together bits of the past in which we had been colleagues,

13. I.I. Rabi, *Science and the Humanities: Morris Loeb Lecture*, 1955, quoted in John S. Rigden, *Rabi: Scientist and Citizen* (New York: Basic Books, 1987), p. 257.
14. Ibid., p. 261.

and speculating about what the future held now that Mr Gorbachev had taken a major step towards ending the Cold War and the nuclear arms race. When I left him I promised to return in three months to carry on with our talk. But it was not to be. I was later told that on his deathbed he was visited by a rabbi who suggested that they should pray together. No, said Rabi. Sing to me instead.

Shortly after his death, a Celebration of Thanksgiving took place in Columbia's St Paul's Chapel in February of 1988. I was unable to attend, but sent a tribute,[15] in which I said that 'the full extent of Rabi's enormous contribution to science and society will be appreciated only by those who followed him into the new horizons of understanding that his genius opened up. . . . My own debt to him is immeasurable, not only for the warmth and joy of a friendship in which I basked for some thirty years, but for the wisdom that I was able to imbibe'.

---

15. Included in the volume that records the speeches of those who spoke at the ceremony.

TWO AIR CHIEFS

*   *   *

Marshal of the RAF
Lord Tedder

General Carl A. Spaatz

Marshal of the RAF, Lord Tedder

1890–1967

The Politically Sensitive Airman

* * *

Arthur Tedder was an airman who rose from an obscure posting at the start of the Second World War to become the Deputy Supreme Commander of all British and American forces which were ranged against Hitler. He avoided the limelight, and his superior, the Supreme Commander, General Dwight D. Eisenhower, had infinite faith in the judgement that he quietly exercised in the background. Theirs was a superb partnership. In matters that specifically concerned the air, Tedder's American opposite number was General Carl Spaatz, the Commander-in-Chief of the US Army Air Forces in the European theatre of operations, and which technically were part of Eisenhower's command.

In background, Tedder and Spaatz could hardly have been less alike. Like most American commanders, Spaatz was a product of a military academy. Tedder, like several other top RAF commanders – with Air Chief Marshal Sir Arthur Harris, the head of RAF Bomber Command, a notable exception – was one of a group of Oxford and Cambridge graduates who, instead of pursuing the professions for which their university education had prepared them, were swept into a military career by the First World War.

The two men could also hardly have been less alike in character. Where Spaatz was outgoingly friendly and gregarious, Tedder was friendly but quiet and reserved. Spaatz was an addictive poker-player who enjoyed his whisky, and who in his last years became an ardent bird-watcher. Tedder's hobby was sketching. When he was in the mood, he would make small, delicate pencil sketches, of the kind with which he illustrated the autobiography that he wrote to cover the years 1940 to 1945.[1] He drank only sparingly and did not play cards.

Tedder was quick to notice when people were either humourless or pompous, but where Spaatz was always ready with a wisecrack, Tedder's wit was ironical, even sardonic, and at times wounding. Tedder's second wife affectionately and teasingly called him BOM, which at first I mis-

---

1. Lord Tedder, *With Prejudice* (London: Cassell, 1966).

65

takenly took to be Bomb, but which turned out to be short for 'bloody old man'. His personal staff referred to him as 'the Chief', but in the world in which I met him he had no nickname. He was always referred to as Tedder. Spaatz on the other hand was Tooey to his friends and staff. Eisenhower was the only person whom I ever heard addressing Tedder by his Christian name, Arthur. For more than two years of the Second World War I worked more closely with him than with anyone else. But in those days I never knew how to address him, and he, like Tooey, called me 'Zuck'. Only after the war did we start to address each other by our first names.

Like Tooey, Tedder bothered little about dress, but his presence, if not imposing, was always impressive. His entry in the *Dictionary of National Biography* describes his facial expression as 'sometimes vague'. I never saw him like that. He always looked purposeful, either when he listened or when he questioned, even when an ironical or quizzical remark preceded the statement of an opinion or of a decision. Above all, where Tooey viewed the war in which they were colleagues in a single-minded way, as an opportunity to show what 'the Air' could do, Tedder saw it in its historical perspective, without being obsessed about the place of 'the Air' in Britain's military establishment. Right to the end he remained intellectually concerned by the far-reaching political and technological events that were transforming the world scene.

The Early Years

Tedder was born in 1890, the youngest by eleven years of three children. His father was a civil servant in the not very exciting Excise department of the governmental bureaucratic machine, in which he rose steadily, being knighted before he reached the age of retirement. Tedder's mother, whom he later described to his biographer, Roderic Owen,[2] as a martinet, was a distant cousin of his father. Husband and wife shared wide, if somewhat conventional, cultural interests.

Tedder spent his early years in Scotland, where his father was then stationed. When the family moved to London, he was enrolled as a day-boy in an excellent grammar school, from which he moved at the age of nineteen to Magdalene College, Cambridge.[3] His subject was history, and his academic and athletic record both at school and at university, while not outstanding, was well above average. He won a few prizes, and

2. Roderic Owen, *Tedder* (London: Collins, 1952).
3. The same college as Patrick Blackett's.

after taking his degree at the end of his third year, he stayed on at the university for a fourth, during which he carried out a piece of somewhat narrow historical research which was later published under the title *The Navy of the Restoration*. During his post-graduate year he also tutored a few history undergraduates, so adding a little to the sparse allowance he had from his father, and which had paid for his university education.

It has often been said that, had there been no First World War, Tedder would have pursued an academic career. This I doubt. At the end of his fourth year in the summer of 1913, his efforts to obtain a university post were motivated not by an urge to continue in academic life but by the need to find a job, and he was not unhappy when he proved unsuccessful. He then obtained a probationary appointment in the Government's Colonial Service, and was sent to Fiji, which he reached in mid-March of 1914, that is to say five months before 'the war to end all wars' started.

Both at school and at university he had been a keen member of the Officers' Training Corps (OTC), and on hearing that the UK was at war, he immediately applied for permission to join up. When this was refused, he had no hesitation in sending in his resignation from the Colonial Service and, having borrowed money for the fare, set out for England by way of Australia. While waiting for a passage, he tried unsuccessfully to join the Expeditionary Force that the Australian Government was sending to the UK. He was more successful in renewing contact with Rosalinde Maclardy, an Australian whom he had met at an academy in Berlin to which he had gone during a Cambridge Long Vacation in order to learn German, and with whom he had since corresponded. Before he resumed his journey to the UK, he and Rosalinde had become secretly engaged.

Tedder reached England in early October, two months after the war had begun, and was straight away given a definitive commission as second lieutenant in the infantry regiment in which his performance in the OTC had gained him a reserve commission. Accident then struck. In a field exercise in February 1915 he damaged a knee so badly that he was laid up for two months and then declared unfit for active service in the field. He cabled his fiancée in Australia and asked her to come to England to marry him, which she did. He had already decided to seek a transfer to the Royal Flying Corps, but before this was granted, he was sent to France to help run his regimental base camp. Only after some months of persistent badgering of the authorities was the transfer allowed.

Following a period of intensive training, Tedder, now a captain, was posted in June 1916 to a front-line squadron that was engaged in bombing patrols and in reconnaissance of enemy positions. Within a short time he saw action in an air battle in which his aircraft was hit, and from which he escaped death almost by a miracle. He was somewhat older than most of his colleagues, and had been noted by his superiors as a responsible officer, quiet, assured and methodical, with none of the flamboyance that characterized so many of the young pilots of those dangerous days. He was soon promoted to the rank of Major and given command of his own fighter squadron, in which he revealed a highly flexible mind, devising new tactics, as necessary, to deal with the aerial opposition that was costing so many lives.

After a full year in France without leave, he was posted to England to take command of a training squadron, a move that allowed him for the first time to enjoy a home life with his wife and a baby son. This phase of domesticity did not last long. In May 1918 he was sent to Cairo as navigation instructor to a training school for airmen. Once again events did not run smoothly. One night on the journey out his ship was torpedoed and sunk. Tedder succeeded in dressing and packing his papers in a haversack before sliding down a rope into a lifeboat, from which he was rescued by an accompanying destroyer.

On his return to the UK at the end of the war, he declined an invitation to return to the Colonial Service. Major-General Sir Hugh Trenchard, as he then was,[4] had marked him out as an officer who would be needed in the new and independent Royal Air Force, which superseded the Royal Flying Corps, which he had commanded. He had noted that Tedder had the ability to recognize the 'essentials' of a problem, and that he had 'a great gift for getting his priorities right'.[5] Tedder's career in the inter-war years, as in those that followed, more than fulfilled this judgement.

Unlike Tooey Spaatz, Tedder was not a charismatic airman, and at first he seems to have behaved as somewhat of a disciplinarian in his command of a peacetime squadron. He was then posted to take charge of training schools, and in 1929 and 1930 became assistant commandant of the RAF Staff College, which he left in the rank of Group Captain.

After two years as head of the RAF's air armament school, he was posted in 1934 as Director of Training in the Air Ministry. Two years later, with the rank of Air Vice Marshal, he was given his first major operational post, as Air Officer Commanding the RAF forces that were deployed in the Far East. His final pre-war appointment came in 1938, when he was made the Air Ministry's director-general of research and development. He had improved operational efficiency in the Far East by restructuring his command organization. He had also tried, less successfully, to encourage inter-service co-operation. As head of research and development he

---

4. Later Marshal of the Royal Air Force, Viscount Trenchard.
5. From Air Chief Marshal Sir Christopher Foxley Norris, in *The War Lords*, ed. Field-Marshal Sir Michael Carver (London: Weidenfeld & Nicolson, 1976).

played a crucial role in the rearmament programme that was gathering force as war approached. It was a job in which he had to be firm in deciding his priorities. He encouraged projects that were clearly operationally desirable, and which had a chance of being realized, given the limitations imposed by time, the availability of professional manpower, and of industrial and other resources. For example, he furthered Whittle's jet engine, and such radar developments as improved early-warning as well as navigational accuracy. He rejected others that he found fanciful – for example, aerial mines, one of Lord Cherwell's pet schemes that brought him into direct conflict with Lord Beaverbrook, the minister who had become responsible for aircraft production, and with Winston Churchill, who had now become Prime Minister. It was in this post that he first met Sir Henry Tizard, who by then was chief scientific adviser to the Chief of the Air Staff, and who was the doyen of the scientists who were involved in work for the armed services.

The Middle East Air Forces

The war had been in progress for little more than a year when Air Marshal Longmore, the Commander-in-Chief of the RAF forces in the Middle East, asked Air Chief Marshal Portal who, immediately after the Battle of Britain, had become Chief of the Air Staff in succession to Air Chief Marshal Sir Cyril Newall, to send Tedder out as his deputy. Churchill vetoed the appointment. But, once again, luck played into Tedder's hands. The aircraft carrying the officer who was appointed in his stead was forced down in Sicily. Tedder duly took his place in November 1940.

The Prime Minister could well have had several reasons for vetoing Tedder's appointment, of which one would certainly have been the firm way in which Tedder had stood up to him and Beaverbrook, and indirectly Cherwell, when they challenged his professional judgement. Some six months later, when Longmore was recalled to London, Tedder's appointment to succeed him, with the rank of Air Marshal, was not opposed. Then, after little more than a year, at a meeting in Cairo in August 1942, Churchill found himself congratulating Tedder, now an Air Chief Marshal, for all that he had achieved in the Middle East, and apologizing for having failed to recognize that Tedder's ability to get to the essentials of a problem, to get his priorities right, applied to him not only as a 'nuts and bolts' man concerned with military hardware, but to his vision over the whole spectrum of military organization, tactics and strategy.

Tedder was fifty years old and unknown to the British public when he left London for Cairo at the end of November 1940. The responsibilities of the Middle East Air Forces were then enormous, and covered a vast geographical area which included the whole of the Mediterranean, through the Balkans into Yugoslavia to the north, eastward to the Persian Gulf, and south into East Africa. A few months before Tedder arrived, Mussolini had proclaimed that Italy was going to blockade the Mediterranean and put an end to British control of the Suez Canal and Red Sea, so depriving the British Middle East Forces of their supplies of oil. Italian troops invaded Greece in order to enforce the dictator's control of the eastern Mediterranean, and also moved into Egypt from Libya, then an Italian colony known as Cyrenaica, in order to drive out the British.

Tedder could not have chosen a more invigorating moment to arrive. Longmore immediately assigned Libya and Egypt to him as his main area of responsibility, and Tedder began by taking operational command in the field of the Desert Air Force, standing in for its commander during a period of ten days when he was away sick. The Western Desert Force (later to be known as the Eighth Army) had just begun a 'push' to drive the Italians back into Libya, and during the year that followed, as British troops advanced – capturing tens of thousands of Italians on the way – other Middle East ground and air forces had had to be in action both in Iraq and in Somaliland. In addition, and almost at the same time as the start of the December 1940 push in the desert, yet other Middle East forces had had to be sent to help the Greeks in their fight against the Italians and the Germans, but only to be withdrawn under fire barely six months later. Not long after came the fall of Crete – the operation in which Lord Louis Mountbatten's destroyer *Kelly* was sunk.

Towards the end of 1941, and some six months after Tedder had succeeded Longmore as Middle East Air Commander-in-Chief, Hitler's brilliant general Erwin Rommel entered the scene, and in February 1942, by when the Western Desert Force had reached well beyond Benghazi, a German Afrika Korps arrived in Tripoli from Naples, and with practically no delay at all began a counter-attack which, by late April, two months later, had driven the Western Desert Army back into Egypt, but leaving Australian troops to hold out in Tobruk. Some two months later, a counter-attack against Rommel failed almost as soon as it began.

Tedder's command in the Middle East turned out to be a story of two years of attack and counter-attack. He decentralized the control of the Desert Air Force, and improved the communications between groups and squadrons so as to enhance the flexibility with which his fighters, fighter bombers and medium bombers could be used. The appointment of Air Vice Marshal 'Mary'[6] Coningham to command the Desert Air Force was a

6. 'Mary' was a corruption of 'Maori', which denoted Coningham's New Zealand origins.

brilliant move. Coningham, a tall, imposing, flamboyant and outgoing man, who managed to live well even in the desert, and Tedder, modest, quiet and reserved, and undemanding so far as physical comforts were concerned, complemented each other perfectly. Communications with the Army were improved – they had been all but chaotic when Tedder took over. In the interests of flexibility he was firm in his opposition to the use of his forces in what he called 'penny packets', and he was adamant in refusing to assign squadrons specifically either to naval or army commanders, to be used when and how they wanted. After the loss of the *Kelly*, Mountbatten was taken to Alexandria and managed to see Tedder, to be told politely but firmly that all the aircraft in the Middle East that could then be spared had been covering the withdrawal of British and Australian forces from Crete. Range of operation limited what could be done, and regretfully there were higher priorities at the time than giving special protection to Mountbatten's squadron of destroyers.

Until Rommel's dominance in the desert came to an end at El Alamein, command of the air fluctuated as attack and counter-attack moved the battle back and forth over the five hundred and more miles that the desert war covered. The further west the Eighth Army pushed, the easier it was for Rommel, with a plentiful supply of transport aircraft, to obtain reinforcements from Sicily. At times the Luftwaffe's command of the air was so overwhelming that British naval and supply ships did not dare to move without air cover from close to the African shore, or from Malta, which was itself under constant air attack. Tedder's chief staff officer, Air Vice Marshal Peter Drummond, had created a superb repair and maintenance organization, as Coningham had of airfields and airstrips. Lose these, said Tedder, and you retreat; hold them, and you advance.[7] But his forces were rarely up to strength, and priorities often had to be changed. Reinforcements that had been promised were diverted to other theatres. He had to agree to send aircraft to India when Japan entered the war. At times he had to reinforce his RAF squadrons in Iraq to guard against a possible thrust of German forces southwards, which would have threatened the Iraqi and Iranian oilfields.

Tedder's vision had to be not only tactical and strategic but political. The desert war had to be viewed in the context of the whole war. If the Germans succeeded in overcoming the Russians in the Caucasus, the Persian Gulf would be in danger. Churchill included Tedder in the party he took to Moscow in August 1942 in order to discover, unsuccessfully as it turned out, how confident the Russians were of holding the German forces on their southern front. Because they knew him well, Tedder

7. H.H. Arnold, *Global Mission* (New York: Arno Press, 1949), p. 324.

enjoyed the full confidence of Portal and of Wilfrid Freeman, the Vice-Chief of the Air Staff, both of whom relied upon him to let them know – needless to say, in the most secret way and in the deepest confidence – what he felt about his fellow-commanders in the other two services, both British and then American. He wrote easily and well, and his handwritten letters were as blunt as his appearance was deceptively mild. 'The land battle', he wrote on one occasion, 'had been a series of lost opportunities and lack of inspired leadership', with one army general described as being an 'utter failure', and another as, 'no commander to put up against a quick-witted and thrusting opponent' – meaning Rommel.[8] In turn, he also had no hesitation in letting Portal know when he disagreed with him or with the directives that were sent him on behalf of the Chiefs of Staff, or even the Prime Minister. The Air Ministry may be omnipotent, he once signalled, but it was not necessarily omniscient.

The remarkable thing is that neither Tedder nor Coningham cracked under the strain in which they were living, as did a few other Middle East commanders. The two were always in the thick of things, resilient and unflappable, angry only when the press and radio criticized the RAF because it had not done enough to help the Navy or Army. Unfortunately, however, 'Mary' Coningham managed to get himself disliked in Eighth Army circles, where it was not long before he was regarded as too much of a prima donna.[9] His grandiloquent style and his penchant for good living, even in the desert – not only for himself but also for his squadrons – did not endear him to his fellow Army commanders. After the end of the war, when Tedder succeeded Portal as head of the RAF, Coningham's behaviour even lost him the support that he had enjoyed from the man who had been his chief in the desert.[10]

Longmore, whom Tedder had succeeded, had been withdrawn from his position as Air Commander-in-Chief because it was felt that he lacked the drive and determination that was needed. Soon afterwards, General Wavell, the Commander-in-Chief of the armies in the Middle East, was moved to the quieter theatre of India. General Auchinleck, who succeeded Wavell, and with whom Tedder got on well, was replaced by General Alexander only a few months before the final push that was to defeat Rommel.

For a variety of reasons, too, command of the Eighth Army had frequently changed. When Tedder arrived in the Middle East, its com-

8. Vincent Orange, *Coningham* (London: Methuen, 1990), p. 100.
9. General Sir Charles Richardson, *Send for Freddie* (London: Kimber, 1987), pp. 122 and 124.
10. Orange, op. cit.

manders were Generals Neame and O'Connor. Both were captured by Rommel's forces in their first major counter-attack. For a short spell General Evett took O'Connor's place, to be followed by General Cunningham. At the end of June 1942, he in turn was replaced by General Ritchie, whose place at a critical moment in the field was taken by Auchinleck himself. Less than two months later, at his meeting in Cairo in August, Churchill decided that Ritchie had to go, and to succeed him he nominated General Gott, one of the Eighth Army corps commanders. But Gott was shot down and killed on his way from the front to meet the Prime Minister in Cairo. Montgomery was appointed in his place, and arrived in time, first to hold Rommel when he attacked at Alam Halfa in the final attempt that he was to make to capture Cairo, and then, having defeated him at El Alamein, to drive the Afrika Korps from Egypt, and finally out of Africa. Over the period of the war in the desert there were also a number of changes at army corps commander level. Montgomery's failure to turn Rommel's withdrawal after El Alamein into a rout was the beginning of Tedder's well-known antipathetic attitude to him over the remaining years. In a letter to Portal he wrote that while Monty's 'supreme self-confidence and personal drive' had been invaluable at the start, 'from that time on, there has been no spark of genius, no glimmer of an attempt to exploit the initial smash'.[11]

The Overall Mediterranean Command

Rosalinde had come out to join Tedder in Cairo in early 1942, spending her time visiting hospitals and rest-camps. She was on her way back to Cairo from a visit to a hospital in Benghazi when her plane crashed as it circled before touching down. Tedder had gone to Heliopolis to meet her, and saw her aircraft as it hit one of the hills near the airfield. I was told that when he saw the crash he waited absolutely silently, his pipe in his mouth, until he was told that there was a dead woman in the wreckage, whereupon he turned to his companion, saying: 'Come on, let's go, there's no point in waiting any longer.' He had realized at once that there could be no survivors. He had already lost the elder of his two sons, a young RAF officer, in a raid over Germany.

Deeply affected though he was by Rosalinde's death, Tedder could not allow it to affect the routine of his life. Not only could he not afford to relax his hold on his command, he had to consider the likely implications on his operations of the projected invasion of North West Africa, code-named

11. Ibid., p. 122.

Torch, into the planning of which Cairo does not appear to have been drawn.

In July 1942, General Eisenhower had been appointed Commander-in-Chief of all US Army Forces – air as well as ground – in the European theatre of operations. The projected landings of the British and American forces in North Africa in November 1942 were under his supreme command, and in view of the poor state of the relations between the UK and France at the time, the hope was that the Vichy French forces, which then controlled North Africa, would view the operation as primarily an American affair. It was a vain hope. Soon after he had made his base in Algiers, Eisenhower discovered that the political task of bringing the French forces in North Africa over to the Allied side was anything but easy. So too was the job of co-ordinating the advances of the British First Army and the less experienced American troops which, as they pushed eastwards, were being supported by RAF units under the command of Air Marshal Welsh, and by the 12th US Army Air Force under General 'Jimmy' Doolittle – a force that had been created mainly by detachment from Spaatz's 8th US Army Air Force in the UK. These two North African air commands were operating independently of each other, and also under great difficulties. Co-ordinating their activities with those of Tedder's Middle East Command – with his HQ in Cairo about a thousand miles to the East – had not been considered when *Torch* was planned.

Tedder had already been the Middle East overall air commander for some two years, and had under his general command 'Mary' Coningham's Desert Air Force, whose job it was to provide direct support for the Eighth Army as it fought the Italian and German forces under Rommel, and a Mediterranean Coastal Command, which was there to help protect the movement of naval and merchant vessels. He also had under his command an RAF force based in Malta, which was operating in concert with the Royal Navy to prevent supplies reaching Rommel. In addition, he had under his strategic control, but not direct command, a small force of US aircraft, under General Lewis Brereton, which had been sent to the Western Desert in mid-1942. Despite the lack of any formal link between the Middle East Air Forces and those which Eisenhower commanded, Tedder had seen to it that in order to help the *Torch* operation at the time the Allied landings took place, his bombers attacked a number of targets on the North African coast, among them Tunis and Bizerta. He had also continued to help by adjusting some of his own operations in order to meet urgent requests for assistance from Eisenhower's air forces.

Soon after the landings Tedder had paid a flying visit to Malta, and before returning to Cairo stopped in Algiers to call on Eisenhower. He was much disturbed by what he learnt about the Supreme Commander's loose command set-up, and was convinced that despite personality problems – American and British staff officers were finding it difficult to work in harmony – what was needed was an overall air commander for the whole Mediterranean Theatre. Eisenhower, however, was at the time far more concerned with what was happening on the ground than with what he then regarded as a long-term problem, but as a first step to improve matters, he detached Tooey Spaatz from the 8th US Army Air Force in the UK to serve as 'Acting Commander-in-Chief for Air' – in effect co-ordinator – of his two North African air forces. At Eisenhower's request, Tedder soon returned to Algiers to discuss what needed to be done in the longer term. Once again, however, the Supreme Commander was not prepared to go further than appoint Tooey executive commander, not merely co-ordinator, of his two air forces. He was worried lest any more fundamental move would jeopardize the call he had on the remaining US air forces based in the UK. In his view, too, the question of uniting all the Allied air forces in the Mediterranean Theatre was something that would have to be decided by Roosevelt and Churchill when they met at Casablanca in mid-January of 1943.

The outcome was what Tedder had proposed. At the end of the summit meeting between the two political leaders, it was decided, with Eisenhower in full agreement, that Tedder was to be Air Commander-in-Chief for the whole Mediterranean Theatre. He was to set up his headquarters side by side with that of the Supreme Commander, to whom he was to become deputy for air operations. Tooey Spaatz was made C-in-C, under Tedder, of both air forces in North West Africa, at the same time taking under his wing Coningham's Tactical Air Force. Tooey had not liked being moved from the 8th Air Force. Becoming C-in-C of the North West African Air Forces was at least some slight consolation.

Before it was decided that there was no one better than Tedder to take command of all the Mediterranean air forces, Portal had intended to move him to London as Vice-Chief of the Air Staff, and had nominated Air Chief Marshal Sholto Douglas, an ex-Chief of RAF Fighter Command, as his replacement. Sholto Douglas was an Oxford man who had joined the RFC in the First World War, and whose career during the inter-war years had followed much the same path as had that of Tedder, for whom it was now a slight embarrassment to find himself superior in the new Mediterranean command structure to his distinguished friend. Fortunately, as it turned out, no difficulties arose between the two, which was not at first the case between Tedder and Spaatz. Tedder had hoped that his own staff, as well as the staffs of all the subordinate air commands that now came under him, would be fully integrated, with British and American officers working side by side. Neither he nor Eisenhower was prepared to tolerate any international bickering or, as they put it, any 'them and us', in the Allied command. Arguments did, however, soon arise about relative ranks and seniority, and national prejudices were not slow to surface. When Tooey Spaatz protested about the way the exercise of integration was proceeding, Tedder promptly reacted by telling Tooey 'if you want a divorce, you can have one here and now, repeat now'.[12] Fortunately the tiff between the two soon blew over, and Tedder decided not to try to formalize the working arrangements of his subordinate commands. He would operate simply as Eisenhower's strategic *alter ego* in charge of air policy, responsible for making sure that his various commanders had both the resources and the ability to carry out the orders they were given. He ran his new organization as he had his Middle East command, following and overseeing, but not interfering with the way his subordinate commanders discharged their responsibilities.

Working with Tedder

The process of organizing the new Mediterranean air command was still in full swing when in mid-March of 1943 I became attached by accident both to Tedder and Spaatz. At the time I was a member of Admiral Lord Louis Mountbatten's staff in Combined Operations headquarters in London, and had been sent to the Middle East to make a study of the operations of the Desert Air Force. In the two and a half months that I was in the field I managed to carry out a number of studies, in particular one of Tripoli, where for the first time in the war it became possible to compare the daily intelligence information that we received about what our bombing attacks on shipping had achieved when the town was in Italian and German hands, with what had actually happened. I had been flown from Tripoli to Algiers by Air Vice Marshal Sir Hugh Pughe Lloyd, who then headed the Mediterranean Coastal Air Command, which had also now become part of Tooey's new empire.

My first meeting with Spaatz was in the company of a number of his staff officers; that with Tedder, on the second day I spent in Algiers, lasted

---

12. Tedder, *With Prejudice*, p. 399. In a debate in the House of Lords in November 1953, Lord Tedder refers to a similar incident which occurred in the early stages of the development of the Normandy command organization. (Hansard, Col. 418) Some months after the first difference between the two, and after Allied forces had landed in southern Italy, Tedder in a letter to Portal described Tooey as suffering from a 'violent inferiority complex'. One spends much of one's time and energy, he wrote, 'jollying him along – very wearing' (Orange, op. cit. p. 165).

the entire afternoon, during which we were alone for all but the first hour. He wanted to know everything that I had learnt about the results of the operations for which he, as C-in-C of the Middle East Air Forces, had been responsible during the preceding two years. He had been sent a copy of a preliminary report that I had prepared for Sholto Douglas, on whom I had called in Cairo before leaving the Middle East, and Tedder cross-examined me closely, particularly about what I had discovered in my detailed study of the damage that air attacks had caused in Tripoli. He had obviously instructed his private office that he was not to be disturbed, and in the hours that we were together our discussion ranged over all manner of things that had happened in the war, not just in the desert. I had to tell him how it had come about that I, an academic biologist who previously had been engaged only in fundamental research on totally different problems had, when war came, opened up the subject of 'wound ballistics', and had then moved, without formally joining any of the services, to Mountbatten's staff in Combined Operations. Tedder was obviously hungry for conversation with someone who was not directly concerned with his day-to-day preoccupations.

On the following evening we continued to talk over dinner, and carried on until well after midnight, for he had had my bags moved to his house from the officers' mess where I had been billeted. Next morning he had me driven to the plane for London. While I had enjoyed the party spirit of the start of my friendly relations with Tooey Spaatz, the beginning of the long relationship I was to have with Tedder was much more to my style and intellectual taste. His wide interests and inquiring mind inspired an immediate respect.

When I returned to Algiers two months later for the Pantelleria operation, I was taken straight from the airfield to his office. He looked up as I entered, and said with a smile: 'You're late.' He then sat me down at a table on which were laid out all the daily operational reports he had received since I was last with him, saying in a joking way, but at the same time seriously: 'Read those and tell me where we have gone wrong.'

I again spent the night under his roof, but he did not tell me why I had been summoned back. 'You'll know tomorrow,' he said, 'when I fly you to Constantine to meet Tooey Spaatz. He'll explain it all to you, and if you judge that what he wants can be done, telephone me at midnight, and with as few words as possible, tell me whether it's on.' 'It' was the Pantelleria operation.

When Eisenhower's forward headquarters were moved to La Marsa near Tunis, Tedder provided himself with a modest house about a mile from the grander d'Erlanger villa which Tooey had made his home. As often as not, when I had to fly back to Tunis after Palermo had become my working base, I stayed with him even though there was always a bed available for me in Tooey's villa. Tedder wanted to know, with as little delay as possible, what I was finding out about the effects that air attacks in Sicily and southern Italy were having on military operations, and particularly what I was discovering about the results of the bombing of the Sicilian and southern Italian rail system. He sent a signal saying that he and Portal would be visiting me in Palermo on the latter's way back from the Teheran Conference to see for themselves how the work was proceeding. He arrived in the middle of December, without Portal, but accompanied by his new wife, 'Toppy', the head of the Malcolm Clubs which she had set up for airmen on leave. As he indicated in his autobiography, he wanted to satisfy himself that my recommendations about targets were as soundly based as they could be, for, unlike most of the other commanders with whom I was dealing, Tedder, given there was a chance that he himself could get closer to the facts, never committed his own judgement on the basis of what he was told by intelligence officers and by planners. He spent two days in Palermo, and shortly after he left, he sent an aircraft to fly me to La Marsa where, at dinner, he got me to go over the ground fully with Portal, who had stopped for the night on his journey back to London from Teheran.

When I first set up my Bombing Survey Unit in Palermo, Tooey Spaatz had assigned to me as administrative officer a Colonel Willis, who in peacetime was a Harvard historian. Willis was a man of style, and instead of finding quarters in war-torn Palermo, had requisitioned for the nucleus of my staff three empty houses in the nearby seaside resort of Mondello. My unit soon outgrew these quarters – it eventually comprised some twenty specialist officers and about fifty supporting staff – and we were moved to a large and somewhat dilapidated *palazzo* in Palermo itself.

In the meantime I had got to know Signor de Cruz, the owner of the larger of the Mondello houses, and to which he and his wife, an American, had returned from their country estate after we had moved out. They readily agreed to a suggestion of mine that they should lay on a dinner for the Tedders on one of the two nights that they were to spend in Palermo, in order to give them the opportunity of telling Tedder about conditions in Italy and Sicily during the early years of the war. Unknown to me, our hosts had asked the deputy head of the Allied Military Government (AMGOT) that had been set up in Sicily to join us after dinner. He was a Colonel Poletti, an American politician of Italian descent, who had formerly been Lieutenant Governor of New York State. I had told Tedder that there were rumours that food and other necessary supplies that were being sent from the US to Palermo for the troops were disappearing into a black market, and that AMGOT was proving ineffective in stopping what was going on.

When Poletti came into the de Cruzes' sitting-room he was a little merry with drink, and had on each arm a pretty Sicilian girl. 'Meet my Botticellis,' he said as he entered. We all rose, and Tedder greeted him by saying: 'I have long been wanting to meet one of the men who have taken so little time to undo what it took us so long, and cost so much, to achieve.' Poletti did not know what to say in reply. That was one side of Tedder – blunt and sarcastic.

Overlord

The other Tedder had all the patience, tact, cunning and political sense that was needed when he returned to England at the beginning of January. As Eisenhower's deputy he was concerned with every aspect of the *Overlord* operation – not just the air – and he was not helped by the fact that Montgomery, who had been put in charge of the initial assault phase, was behaving like a Napoleon. As I have said, the two had taken a dislike to each other after El Alamein, and Tedder regarded the Eighth Army commander as overwhelmingly conceited and insensitive. But if working with Montgomery caused him trouble, it was not a patch on his difficulties with the 'air barons'.

Several months before Eisenhower, in December 1944, was appointed C-in-C for *Overlord*, with Tedder as his deputy, Air Chief Marshal Sir Trafford Leigh-Mallory, a distinguished airman who had played a significant part in the Battle of Britain, and who was now C-in-C of RAF Fighter Command, had been designated C-in-C of the Allied Expeditionary Air Force (AEAF) that was to be allocated for the *Overlord* operation. Serious planning of what the air should do to prepare the ground for the landings began in January 1944, and it soon became apparent that, in addition to the AEAF fighter and medium bomber 'tactical' forces which were to come under his command, Leigh-Mallory would need to call on the heavy bomber forces of USSTAF as well as of the RAF, given that the plans he was laying were to be accepted by Eisenhower. Montgomery was relying on the air forces to clear the skies over the landing beaches, and also to make it impossible for the Germans to prevent the consolidation of an Allied beach-head by bringing up reinforcements by rail. To this end, all that the Army planners had requested was that seventeen rail links – lines and bridges – should be 'cut' in an arc some hundred miles from the beaches on which the Allied troops would be landing, the air attacks to begin about the time of the assault. Another requirement of the *Overlord* air plan was the neutralization of the coastal defences that covered the approaches to the beaches.

On my return to the UK at the end of December 1944 I had been appointed chief scientific adviser on strategic air planning both to Leigh-Mallory and to Tedder. In place of the limited 'tactical' plan which was under discussion when I arrived, and whose execution depended, among other important considerations, on an assurance of good weather at the time of the landings, I encouraged Leigh-Mallory to put forward a plan that was based on what had been learnt from the attacks on the Sicilian and Italian railway systems, and which made no distinction between operations that were conventionally regarded in bomber circles as strategic as opposed to tactical – that is to say, operations in direct support of ground forces. The plan proposed that the whole rail network of France and the Low Countries, and extending into Germany, should be disrupted by striking at the nodal points of the system – at the main rail centres that regulated traffic. Bridges were also to be attacked, but, for security reasons, not until close to the time of the land assault. In so far as the plan was designed not only to impede military movement but to disrupt the German railway system, it was therefore as much strategic as tactical. The deeper that attacks on the railway system were pressed into Germany, so the plan claimed, the sooner would *all* German industry be brought to a standstill. Instead, therefore, of being called upon to help the *Overlord* operation just before and during the assault phase, as Tooey Spaatz and Harris hoped, the AEAF plan was presuming to play a part in stating what their long-term strategic objectives should be.

Harris knew that Tedder was behind the AEAF 'transportation plan' which Leigh-Mallory had put forward. He was, however, adamantly against the idea that RAF heavy bomber forces should be used in the preparatory phase, or indeed in any phase, of the invasion. By mid-February Spaatz also put forward – as an alternative to the transportation plan – an 'oil plan', in whose preparation his people had co-operated with the American economists who, as an Economic Objectives Unit, worked in parallel with a corresponding unit of the British Ministry of Economic Warfare.[13]

As we moved into February, Leigh-Mallory had become increasingly worried about the way opposition was mounting to the plan to which he

13. The American unit, to quote Dr Mierzejewski (Alfred C. Mierzejewski, *The Collapse of the German War Economy, 1944–1945*, Chapel Hill Calif. and London: University of North Carolina Press, 1988), struggled 'with every intelligence organization that it encountered. Its unique degree of egotism made it a bitter opponent of all who disagreed with it and prompted it to subvert even those whose views coincided with its own'. I myself do not recall that it had any arguments with other planning and intelligence bodies in so far as they were opposed to the transportation plan.

had committed himself. He was also being regarded as an unnecessary link in the chain of command – even by his forward commander, 'Mary' Coningham – and the opposition was also becoming more personal. 'If only Tedder would speak out,' he said to me one day, 'all could be settled.' But even though those who opposed the plan had little doubt that it had his backing, Tedder at first held his counsel. He did not argue when Tooey Spaatz told him that he had been assured by his intelligence officers and planners that it would take every bit of a year before the bombing of the rail network of France, Belgium and western Germany could have any significant effect either on military or economic traffic. Nor did he controvert Tooey when he first asserted that an offensive against Germany's synthetic oil plants would quickly make it impossible for its armies to move and the Luftwaffe to fly. He remained silent as Harris continued to reaffirm his faith in the strategic value of area attacks on German cities. Nor, indeed, did he clearly indicate his belief in the transportation plan at a mid-February meeting of the air barons, when he dismissed as pure speculation Tooey's statement that the Luftwaffe would fight to defend oil installations but not railway centres.

The argument about the AEAF plan – essentially the transportation plan – was formally, if not finally, settled at a meeting between Eisenhower and the air chiefs that Portal arranged towards the end of March. They were at one that the maintenance of air superiority had to have first priority. This proposition was of course axiomatic to all airmen, whatever their nationality, for however employed, there is little purpose to an air force if its operations can be successfully countered by the enemy. With Eisenhower in full agreement, Portal then summed up the argument that had developed around Leigh-Mallory by declaring that there was no suitable alternative to the transportation plan. This conclusion was endorsed a couple of days later by the Joint UK/US Chiefs of Staff, who at the same time directed that control of the strategic bomber forces should now be handed over to Eisenhower, with Tedder, his deputy, co-ordinating their operations. Acting behind the scenes, Tedder had in fact been more responsible than Leigh-Mallory for the promotion of the AEAF plan; and even if only secretly, Eisenhower had made it clear before the meeting that he intended to ask to be relieved of the command of *Overlord* if the strategic bomber forces were not placed under his command.[14]

The decision at the end of the meeting that overall command of the heavy bomber forces should pass to the Supreme Commander, with Tedder acting on his behalf, was clearly a blow to Leigh-Mallory's status as Commander-in-Chief of the air forces that were to be engaged in the

14. Alfred D. Chandler (ed), *The Papers of Dwight D. Eisenhower* (Baltimore, Md, and London: Johns Hopkins Press, 1970), Vol. 3, *The War Years*, p. 1785.

Overlord operation. But he accepted the situation with quiet dignity as a price that would need to be paid if the central part of the whole air plan over whose preparation he had nominally presided was to be implemented. But I could sense how deeply he had been bruised, and knew that he would not allow himself to be further demeaned. At a meeting less than a week before D-Day, when both Spaatz and Tedder argued strongly against his plan for the use of the heavy bombers in the opening stages of the Normandy assault, he insisted just as bluntly that the responsibility for the plan according to which they were going to be used was not theirs but his. Later that same day Montgomery telephoned to ask if any changes had been made in what the two had already agreed. Leigh-Mallory told him 'No' and that, had there been, he would have resigned there and then.

Leigh-Mallory and Tedder had co-operated in their different ways, even if distantly, to get the transportation plan adopted. Leigh-Mallory undoubtedly felt that Tedder, whose behaviour he could not understand, had let him down. Tedder, however, was not one to allow personal relations to influence his judgement about major decisions. He liked Leigh-Mallory but had to keep the peace with the bomber barons, and in particular with Spaatz, and he could not have behaved differently from the way that he had, even if it meant, what he deeply regretted, sacrificing an old friendship. He and Leigh-Mallory had not worked together in the earlier years of the war, and I do not know what their relations had been during the inter-war years. But much later I learnt that they had been contemporaries at Cambridge and, what was even more interesting, both members of the same small college.

As I have said, Eisenhower had secretly made the control of the heavy bomber forces a resignation matter, and if the question of command had not been settled the way it was, Tedder would almost certainly have had to resign. The possibility of resignation faced him again when Churchill decided to challenge the political acceptability of the transportation plan. This he did at a series of meetings of the Cabinet Defence Committee, gatherings that used to begin at about ten in the evening and end in the early hours of the morning whenever the Prime Minister tired. They were known as Winston's 'midnight follies'. I accompanied Tedder and Portal to the first of the series, which the Prime Minister opened by asking whether both of them backed the plan. When each replied that he did, Churchill asked Tedder whether he could not think of a better plan. 'There is no better plan,' replied Tedder. 'I'll show you a better plan,' replied the Prime Minister. I was sitting beside Tedder, and could see how tense he was. His knuckles were white as he gripped the edge of the table. When at about four in the morning he drove me back to my flat, he said, only half jokingly: 'I wonder how much it will cost to set up as a tomato-grower?'

After five such meetings (of which I attended three), Tedder refused to yield other than by agreeing to delete from the list of rail centres that the plan had specified for attack a few where the risk of French civilian casualties was highest. Doing so, however, did not lessen Churchill's opposition. He decided to refer the matter to President Roosevelt, which is where the debate ended – at the highest level. The President replied that he was unprepared to impose 'any restriction on military action by the responsible Commanders that in their opinion might militate against the success of Overlord'.

The decision was a victory for Tedder. But the strain under which he was living did not lessen. Churchill kept pressing him, still determined to break his will. On mornings after a French railway centre had been attacked, a note would appear on Tedder's desk which in effect read 'Pray, how many French civilians did you kill last night?' and initialled W.S.C. Equally, the Director of Plans in the Air Ministry never stopped deprecating the value of whatever results intelligence sources indicated the attacks on railway centres were having, at the same time declaring that the plan was diverting effort which, if applied to 'strategic' targets in Germany, would soon bring the war to an end. Harris's own intelligence staff and the members of the US and UK Economic Objectives Units followed suit. As Tedder relates in his autobiography, he had constantly to deal with the 'red herrings' that kept being introduced into the argument. All the intelligence organizations seemed to be echoing the parrot cry that the bombing of railway centres was having no effect. Even the intelligence section in Eisenhower's own headquarters joined the chorus. Less than two weeks before D-Day, and again soon after the landings, they reported that the transportation plan had not seriously impaired the movement of German military traffic. Claims began to be made that attacks on bridges alone would have had a greater effect on rail traffic than would the combined assault on rail centres and bridges, for which the plan had called. Within the command organization that they headed, Tedder and Eisenhower – and Leigh-Mallory – were all but alone in their faith in the plan.

The fact that Tedder had backed his own judgement in rejecting the advice that emanated from air-staff planners and intelligence officers in favour of what he was being told by an adviser who was not officially part of their world – to wit, myself – certainly did not help.[15] Neither did the

15. David R. Mets in his biography of Spaatz (*A Master of Air Power: General Carl A. Spaatz*, Novato, Calif.: Presidio Press, 1988, p. 207) writes that 'Eisenhower, they felt, was about to make a decision based on the findings of "*one* investigator"' – meaning me – who had not taken the trouble to consult 'the War Office's military transportation experts'. The italics are his.

fact, clearly stated in the paper he tabled at Portal's March meeting, that while the plan was directed in the first instance at the 'tactical' requirement of impeding German military traffic, it also had a longer term objective that was in conflict with what the commanders of the heavy bomber forces saw as the unique 'strategic' mission that they had been set by the Allied political leaders. What was not understood was that the confidence that Tedder had in me, about which he writes in his autobiography, was not based on blind faith or on any powers of persuasion on my part. He used his own judgement to assess the data I continued to lay before him. They were the best facts that were available at the time, in contrast to the assumptions based on wishful thinking of those who opposed the plan. What we simply could not understand was the inability of our opponents to appreciate that an integrated system such as a vast railway network constitutes far more than the sum of its separate parts; that it is more akin to a biological organism in which each system interacts with the others, and that the whole would inevitably break down if the co-ordinating mechanisms that united the parts were disrupted.

There was, of course, another reason why the stand taken by Tedder caused so much controversy in air force circles. Tooey Spaatz was concerned not only to uphold national honour but to maintain the independence of the US air forces, as well as his commitment to the doctrine that bombing alone could defeat an enemy. His people kept arguing that the AEAF plan was not strategic as demanded by the doctrine, but purely tactical.

As Deputy Supreme Commander, Tedder was, however, not concerned to play a national card. If anything, it was usually believed that he was more favourably disposed to American than to British commanders. After the landings had taken place, he became even more outspoken than Eisenhower in his criticism of Montgomery's delays and cautionary tactics in breaking through the German defences on the Caen sector of the front, and later of his demand that he should be given the star role in the Allied drive into Germany. Unlike Harris, too, Tedder had no emotional commitment to any one of the major British air forces. He regarded the part the air had to play in the defeat of Germany as vital, but he did not believe that the power of the bomber meant that navies and armies were unnecessary or redundant. Above all, he did not believe that there was a fundamental divide in the air war between what was regarded as tactical and what strategic.[16] But what he certainly never anticipated was that the antagon-

---

16. Sixteen years after the war ended, I received a letter from him expressing his disquiet over the issue. He found it difficult to understand, so he wrote, what was being said about 'defence', and did 'not like the way the words "tactical"

ism to the transportation plan of the planning and intelligence staffs – even those in Eisenhower's headquarters – could lead, as it did, to a deliberate misrepresentation of what Ultra intercepts and other intelligence information showed was in fact happening.

The Results Analysed

Soon after the lodgement area in Normandy was secure, Tedder arranged for me to set up a Bombing Analysis Unit to conduct field studies in the battle zone similar to the one I had established a year before in Sicily and southern Italy. When Paris was liberated at the end of August, I detached a few members of the unit to co-operate with a group of French scientists and railway officials to analyse the records of rail traffic during the course of the pre-D-Day bombings. This work was carried out in the offices of Paris's two main railway stations, and Tedder was kept posted about the results as they emerged. The analysis showed that the offensive had had a far more devastating and immediate effect on rail movement in France than even we had anticipated. In the more heavily bombed French north-eastern railway region the decline in the volume of originating traffic, expressed in numbers of wagon loadings, had fallen by the end of May, that is to say, before the landings, to 20 per cent of its previous peak level. The decline and the dislocation of traffic had become almost complete before the Seine bridges were destroyed in the last week of May. In addition to disrupting traffic between the separate French railway regions – the *total* volume of rail traffic in the whole of France by the end of July had fallen to about 20 per cent of its January level – the attacks had had a disastrous effect both on the military and the non-military traffic that was circulating between France, Belgium and Germany.[17]

Needless to say, Tedder was relieved that the French records had so fully justified his confidence in the plan. He was even more so after he had studied charts of rail movement that were found in Brussels some weeks after the city was captured in early September. There were three of them, in rolls about a yard wide and seven yards long, on which German railway officials had plotted the daily figures for different categories of rail traffic in Belgium and north-east and eastern France in the railway region which

and "strategic" are bandied about' (Letter to SZ, 16 June 1961). He elaborated the same theme in a speech he delivered in the House of Lords after his retirement.

17. The analysis of the French records was published early in November under the general title *The Effects of the Overlord Air Plan to Disrupt Enemy Rail Communications* (BAU Report No. 1, November 1944).

they had styled 'HVD Brussels'. In addition to military trains, one chart included a plot of the amount of iron ore that was mined in eastern France and Luxemburg, and moved every day to the steel mills of the Saar. Another dealt with the transport of coal from the Ruhr into France, whose industries were then working mainly in the German interest. The plots had been started when the Germans entered Brussels in January 1940, and had come to an end on 27 May 1944, a week before the Normandy landings, by when the HVD railway officials presumably found it impossible to discover what trains, military or civil, were running, and where.

Tedder was out when I brought the charts to his office, and Wing Commander Leslie Scarman,[18] his chief personal staff officer, and Air Marshal Robb and I had unrolled them on the floor of the ante-room to his office. When Tedder returned, he got down on his knees and crawled along the charts to see what they showed. They revealed that by the end of May 1944 the daily number of all trains moving in the region had fallen to about a third of their normal level. Coal and ore traffic, general goods and troop trains had declined catastrophically, with the overall result that industry in the whole region had for all practical purposes come to a standstill before the Allied troops landed in Normandy. The cessation of the Minette-ore traffic was the first major shock suffered during the war by the German steel and armaments industry. What traffic continued to flow in the region was devoted almost entirely to military supply trains.

On 26 October, a day or two after Tedder had examined the German HVD records, he summoned a meeting at the headquarters of the Supreme Command, now in Versailles, where, as he notes in his memoirs, he told the bomber chiefs 'not for the first time, that they had been wrong about the communications offensive'.[19] He had asked me to stand by, ready to be called in with the German charts. This did not prove necessary. No one was prepared to question his recital of the facts, which he did, so I was told as the meeting broke up, with a fair measure of his sardonic humour.

When Eisenhower surrendered control of the heavy bomber forces in September, the Combined Chiefs of Staff had immediately endorsed a recommendation of the Combined Strategic Targets Committee (CSTC) that synthetic oil plants should from then on be first priority targets for heavy bomber attacks, with 'transportation' bracketed in second priority with tank, ordnance and motor transport plants and depots. The upshot of Tedder's September meeting was that transportation targets were officially assigned to a category of their own, second in priority only to oil.

18. Later Lord Scarman, the High Court Judge and Lord of Appeal.
19. Tedder, *With Prejudice*, p. 610.

But, as Tedder also records, the CSTC continued to regard attacks against the German communications network as a 'diversion' of the strategic offensive from more worthwhile objectives. It also continued to insist that the network still had considerable spare capacity, capacity vastly in excess of what the German military could ever require. Nor, it was contended, could attacks on the railway network have any appreciable effect on the German economy in the period of ninety days within which the Joint Chiefs of Staff then hoped that the war in Europe could be won.[20] Tedder's constant reminder that the transportation system was the 'common denominator' on which all German economic activity, as well as military traffic, depended, was turned on its head. Because it was the 'common denominator', so the opposition argued, because of its 'fragmentation and dispersal', the railway network was the least vulnerable target within the whole German economic system. It was not at all surprising, therefore, that the bomber chiefs continued to treat railway centres as targets to be bombed only when conditions precluded attacks on what they were advised were more worthwhile targets. Tedder simply had to go on battling against a tide of opposition. One day when I expressed astonishment that he had arranged with Portal to have transferred to his staff at Supreme Headquarters the deputy head of the Air Ministry's Directorate of Bomber Operations, from where the main opposition to his policies emanated, he looked at me with a smile and asked whether I had forgotten the adage 'Embrace thine enemy'.

In mid-December of 1944 the Germans launched their unexpected counter-offensive in the Ardennes. It then transpired that in the preceding three months, that is to say in the period after Tedder and Eisenhower had ceased to have control of the heavy bomber forces and after transportation had been placed in second priority to oil, only sixteen out of 120 heavy bomber attacks on transportation targets had been carried out under visual conditions.[21] Desultory, however, as they were, they had, as is now known, caused far-reaching damage to the German industrial system, as indeed had those by which they had been preceded. On the other hand, they had not caused sufficient damage to prevent the rail network behind the German lines from being used to prepare for the counter-attack in the

---

20. Ibid., p. 612.
21. After the Combined Strategic Targets Committee had been instructed to place attacks on the railways in second priority to oil, they prepared a priority list of targets to be hit. But 'the air forces as often as not ignored the CSTC priority lists. From the beginning of November to the end of January only 53 percent of the total bomb tonnage dropped on transportation targets was directed against those recommended by the CSTC. Moreover, 96 percent was dropped using radar'. (Mierzejewski, *The Collapse of the German War Economy*, p. 131).

Ardennes. For a couple of weeks Tedder was able to enforce his authority to the extent that the heavy bombers were directed in a concerted way against the German rail centres that might be involved in the movement of supplies and reinforcements to the forces that were engaged in the German counter-attack.

It was not until the beginning of March 1945 that the intelligence organizations started to acknowledge that the German industrial complex had been seriously affected even by such attacks on railway installations as had been carried out. Partly because Upper Silesia had then been overrun by the Russians, and partly because of a critical fall in the transport of coal from the Ruhr, German industry, it was now admitted, was in serious trouble. 'Even the most important war factories', the Joint Intelligence Committee was now ready to report 'are affected.' It was not long before all were. Two months later, on 8 May, the European war ended.

The Judgement

In 1966, when Tedder's autobiography appeared, the policy he had so consistently promoted was still being attacked both in books and in articles, and the title he gave his own book – *With Prejudice* – was at least in part his ironical way of indicating that he had not changed the views that had led to so much controversy. To this very day, criticisms continue to appear. This is partly because apologists for those by whom his policy was opposed have rarely taken the trouble to read either the original texts of the plan or Tedder's contemporary minutes on the subject – or, for that matter, the reports of the official bombing surveys that were set up at the end of the war by the British and American governments. The spurious notion – sometimes deliberately contrived – that the dispute was about the relative merits of bombing railway centres instead of railway bridges still continues to engage the attention of a category of would-be historians, despite the fact that the destruction of bridges was an integral part of the plan.[22] Nor, as some writers have contended,[23] was Tedder's a 'tactical'

22. See, for example, Charles P. Kindleberger, 'World War II Strategy', *Encounter*, 51, No. 5 (1978), and Henry D. Lytton, 'Bombing Policy in the Rome and pre-Normandy Invasion Aerial Campaigns of World War II', *Military Affairs*, 47 (1983), 53–8.
23. Even the official British *History of the Strategic Air War* incorrectly states that the pre-D-Day attacks on rail centres had been made only for 'tactical purposes' (Vol. III, p. 245). There is no mention there of the studies that were made in Paris or of the German records found in Brussels which showed how rapidly the attacks on rail centres had affected the movement of coal and iron ore. The

plan merely concerned with the dislocation of enemy movement into the area of the Normandy landings. From the very start, as he put it in the paper he submitted to Portal's meeting of 25 March 1944, it was an overall plan designed at one and the same time to dislocate and paralyse economic as well as military traffic. The policy of concentrating on communications was a coherent way of engaging all the air forces to achieve an objective that at one and the same time helped our armies and destroyed the German economy.

The official British and American histories of the air war were based on contemporary American and British records, and on the results of surveys carried out in Germany during the two years after the end of the war[24] by organizations appointed for the purpose. They have now been superseded by a new and far more exhaustive analysis of what happened to the German war economy in 1944 and 1945. It is the work of Alfred C. Mierzejewski, an historian who, conscious of the controversial nature of the subject, describes himself as someone 'who has no institutional ties past or present to any of the actors'. What he has written is largely based on German records that were either not available or not fully assessed by the official American or British post-war bombing survey teams. Mierzejewski has also studied British and American archival material, as well as German historical studies of what happened to the Reich's economy in the final two years of the war.

His book begins by providing a detailed picture of the layout of the German rail system as it was during the war years, and of its crucial importance to the maintenance of the German economy, in particular to the transport of the coal on which more than 90 per cent of the Reich's energy supplies depended. Slightly less than half of Germany's hard coal came from the Ruhr, with Silesia next in importance. The Saar produced 10 per cent, and was a significant source of supply because it was the only coal-producing area which, in addition to producing its own iron ore, was adjacent to the Minette mines of Lorraine. 'The smelting of every kilogram of iron', Mierzejewski writes, 'required the consumption of almost twice its weight in coal. Six tons of coal stood behind every ton of synthetic gasoline. A heavy tank could rumble from the factory only after 115 tons of coal had been burned by a myriad of companies to produce it. Coal was at

---

authors do, however, admit that the post-war records indicated that Tedder's optimism was 'nearer the truth than the more sceptical attitude' of the planning and intelligence agencies in London, and that even before the rail links with the Ruhr had been cut, 'the attack on communications had had devastating effect on the whole of the German economy' (Vol. III, p. 255).

24. The US survey was concluded in one year, the British in two.

once the indispensable basis of the German economy and the life blood of its everyday activity.'[25]

When the transportation plan was being prepared, neither Tedder nor I was concerned with any detailed statistics. What we knew was that almost everything in an industrial economy is dependent on everything else, and that no industrial plant is self-contained. Raw materials have to be moved, components have to be moved, and finished products have to be moved. Even coal had to be moved to synthetic oil plants, and its finished product, fuel, then moved – and we knew that most movement had to be by rail. Mierzejewski has now shown conclusively that by October 1944 the bombing of German railway centres was already destroying the German economy, and that Speer, Hitler's armaments minister, as well as the German railway authorities, fully understood what was happening and what would be the inevitable consequences if the offensive against the nodal points of the railway network were to be conducted in accordance with a coherent plan, instead of in a haphazard way. As it was, all the repair facilities that could be mustered in Germany could not cope with the damage that the desultory bombing of railway centres and other railway installations was inflicting. Four months after the September attacks began, writes Mierzejewski, 'the exchange of vital commodities in the Reich economy, especially coal, had broken down and every form of industrial production was in decline or had ground to a halt'.[26] Mierzejewski pinpoints the marshalling system as the major factor in the breakdown of the transportation network. Neither empty nor loaded cars that piled up in one railway centre could be moved to where they were wanted, as had also been noted by both the British and US post-war bombing survey teams. The railway network had in truth behaved like the integrated series of systems that make up a living organism.

In putting forward his plan, Tedder relied on commonsense to appreciate this point; commonsense backed not just by logical argument but by the facts that had been first revealed by the analysis of the 1943 records of Italian rail movements. If he had not judged the issue for himself, his confidence that he was in the right could hardly have persisted in the face of the orchestrated dissent of the Allied intelligence and planning staffs, backed as it was by the opposition of the bomber chiefs and of Winston Churchill.

Fortunately both Eisenhower and Portal knew that the intensely unpopular stand that Tedder was prepared to take was based on the hard facts that were available at the time. They knew that he was talking sense

25. Mierzejewski, op. cit., p. 22.
26. Ibid., p. xi.

when he continued to argue that transportation was the common denominator that held the German economic system together, and that its dislocation and destruction would at the same time bring down the home front as well as affect military movements. Obviously he appreciated that such damage as was inflicted by the bombing of Germany's dispersed synthetic oil plants also seriously affected the German armies and air forces. But what he did not believe was that this could become as critical to the future conduct of the war as would the disrupting and blocking not only of the flow of the coal on which the plants depended but of the despatch of their product to the points where it was wanted. But in any event, so Mierzejewski writes, 'Oil was not crucial to Germany industry. Even if EOU's [the Economic Objectives Unit] prescription had been fulfilled in its entirety, the assault on Germany's petroleum resources could not have harmed the Reich's basic industrial economy and, given the fanaticism of Nazi resistance, could not have ended the war alone.'[27]

None the less, and for all the cynicism he often displayed, I doubt whether Tedder could ever have believed that the antipathy to the bombing of transportation targets had become so deep-rooted that it could have led intelligence agencies to suppress, as they did, masses of the Ultra intercepts they received which indicated what was really happening as a result of the breakdown of the railway network.[28] One, dated 20 October 1944, stated that the 'Reich Minister for Equipment and War Production reported that, on account of destruction of traffic installations and lack of power, from 30 to 50 per cent of all works in west Germany were at a standstill.' If this intercept had been in Tedder's hands at his Versailles meeting with the air barons in October 1944, to complement the three German charts of railway movement 'captured' in Brussels which he already had, and if what was happening to the German rail network had been drawn to the attention of the Joint Chiefs of Staff by those who were simply sitting on the information, it is inconceivable that a concerted and coherent continuation of the transportation plan would not have been accorded the highest priority of the strategic bomber campaign. Had it been, it is clear from what Mierzejewski has discovered about the speed

27. As Mierzejewski also writes (p. 181), and as both official surveys discovered, the failure to follow up attacks on oil plants also allowed repair teams to bring those that had not been fully destroyed back into operation.
28. Mierzejewski (p. 167) writes that in February 1945, 'Sir Norman Bottomley, Deputy Chief of Air Staff of the RAF, ordered a complete review of Ultra, relating to the transportation offensive. The study demonstrated that for months the CSTC has been suppressing Enigma information on the Reichsbahn and the economy. Oliver L. Lawrence said that 20,000 commercial intercepts were made weekly but they were not analysed because they were not "likely to be particularly instructive".'

with which the system was breaking down, even as a result of uncoordin-
ated blind bombing attacks, that the end might well have come far sooner
than it did.

But it did not go that way. Instead, there was a powerful move towards
the end of 1944 to have Tedder removed from his post, a move which
fortunately came to nothing. One reason why this happened was almost
certainly the environment of controversy that marked his relations with
the air chiefs. Tedder never disguised his misgivings about the way the
Strategic Air Forces were controlled after their command had been transferred from Eisenhower to the Joint Chiefs of Staff. 'Running the war by
committee', as he put it, was not the way to inspire confidence. Another
reason for the plot to get rid of him was his outspoken support of
Eisenhower's plan for a broad Allied advance into Germany after the
failure of the German counter-offensive in the Ardennes, and his opposition to what Montgomery was urging – a concentrated push in the north
with him in command. Montgomery had told Alanbrooke, the British
Army Chief of Staff, that getting Tedder out 'might go some way towards
putting matters straight'.[29] Tedder no doubt felt the same way about
Montgomery.

The Post-war Years

Tedder succeeded Portal as Chief of the Air Staff in January 1946. Despite
the controversies in which he had been involved, he was unquestionably
the most suitable candidate for the post. But none the less I doubted, as
indeed he did, whether the succession to the office would have been his
had Winston Churchill still been in power, and if Clement Attlee, the
leader of the Labour Party, had not become Prime Minister. Tedder was
not Churchill's favourite air marshal.

Soon after Tedder knew he had been selected, he asked me to join him
as chief scientific adviser to the Air Staff, an invitation which, for a number
of reasons, but mainly because I was unprepared to abandon academic
life, I regretfully declined. 'I don't know', he said to me, 'whether my job
means burying the RAF or keeping it alive.'

Neither he nor anyone else could see how even the immediate future
was going to unfold. The lights may have come on again in England, but
German bombs had caused widespread destruction and the country was
all but bankrupt. Rebuilding and restoring the UK's fortunes were going
to prove a formidable task. The public's expectation of a better life than the

29. A. Bryant, *Triumph in the West* (London: Collins, 1959), p. 376.

one they had known before the war was high, yet the lack of resources made it impossible even to end the wartime rationing of food and clothes. The UK, as head of an empire, still had extensive overseas military commitments. Demobilization had had to start, but national service – conscription – continued. There was also 'the bomb'.

Tedder's job as CAS became ever more difficult when the Cold War started to set in. The airlift to beat the Russian blockade of West Berlin in 1948 had to be organized. He had to participate in the negotiations that led to the formation of Nato. With the threat of renewed conflict never out of sight, the services, as always, struggled against each other for the limited resources that the Government could make available for defence. Despite financial constraints, many costly military projects that had not been completed when the war ended could not be summarily stopped. Nor could new ones that looked promising be nipped in the bud. When the US decided to terminate its wartime nuclear collaboration with the UK, Attlee's government almost unhesitatingly committed itself to developing an 'independent' British bomb. This meant that the RAF had to be provided with new bombers to carry the weapon, as well as new jet fighters as escorts and for home defence.

Scores of Flying Fortresses, Liberators and other US aircraft were then being sent back to the USA from their airfields in Europe and the Pacific. But Tooey Spaatz's staff was at the same time working on plans to establish permanent air bases around the world, and in particular, bases to accommodate the B.29 Super-Fortresses. None of the fields that the US forces had occupied in Europe had runways long enough to allow for the new aircraft. After some discussion at staff level, Tooey decided to fly over to the UK in June 1946 to seek Tedder's agreement as Chief of Staff of the RAF for adapting a few of the airfields which the US forces were still occupying in the UK for the reception of their bigger bombers, and for handling new armament, presumably atomic bombs. Since American heavy bomber squadrons were still being moved around between airfields before their return to the US, Tedder did not object to what Tooey asked, provided that in return he agreed that a squadron of the B.29s would take part in a major fly-past that was being arranged for the following year to commemorate the Battle of Britain. The two air chiefs also agreed to treat the matter as a purely routine affair between their respective air staffs, just as similar arrangements had been made over the previous five years. Tooey was not asking for any permanent arrangement, nor did he know when the new armament would become available. Both air chiefs, however, agreed that were his request referred to higher authority, bureaucratic and then political delays were bound to follow. The two therefore agreed to go ahead on a personal and 'just-in-case' basis.

Two years later, when the Berlin airlift had started, more accommodation was needed for US aircraft, and questions started to be asked. A Member of Parliament wanted to know whether the presence of two groups of B.29s already in the UK was covered under treaty arrangement. The Government's reply was that the aircraft were there under 'informal and long-standing arrangements between the United States Air Force and the RAF for visits of goodwill and training'.[30] Questions continued to be asked. Who was going to pay for adapting British airfields for the accommodation of US aircraft? How long would the arrangement last? The Chiefs of Staff – and here I have no doubt, this in the main meant Tedder, the member with the greatest political sense and experience – became concerned about the possibility that, under the existing unofficial arrangements, the US might in certain circumstances decide to use the atom bombs that it had on UK airfields without first consulting the British Government. It was not until 1949 that Washington formally requested that stationing US aircraft in the UK should become a permanent arrangement.

By then Tedder had made his own views clear. The UK, he said, should not rely on the US for nuclear protection. Doing so 'would involve a close military alliance with the United States in which Britain would be merely a temporary advance base, would involve complete subservience to United States policy, and would render Britain completely impotent in negotiations with Russia or any other nation'.[31] It was only at the end of 1951, after he had ceased to be CAS, that the Government formally agreed to the permanent arrangement that the Americans wanted, but subject to the condition that the new weapons could not be used without prior consultation, and with the UK retaining the right to terminate the agreement when and if it so decided. The US also had to be responsible for whatever costs were entailed in adapting the airfields they were using.

For most of the four years that Tedder was head of the RAF, his colleagues on the Chiefs of Staff Committee, of which he soon became chairman, were Montgomery and Admiral Fraser. I saw him frequently during this period, and doubt whether he found it a congenial one. Montgomery constantly tried to override his two colleagues, and was always ready to make them feel that only he knew how a war should be conducted. He produced papers on the organization of defence with which his two colleagues rarely agreed, owing, according to their author, to 'incompatibility of temperament'[32] and to their lack of vision and cour-

30. Hansard, House of Commons (28 July 1948).
31. Margaret Gowing and Laura Arnold, *Independence and Deterrence: Britain and Atomic Energy, 1945–52*, Vol. 1, *Policy Making* (London: Macmillan, 1974), p. 185.
32. Field-Marshal Montgomery, *Memoirs* (London: Collins, 1958), p. 489.

age. On one occasion he intrigued unsuccessfully and clumsily to get rid of the then Minister of Defence. On another he took it upon himself to discuss with Harry Truman, the US President, matters that should have been left to the British political authority. He regarded the committee as a useless body, and wrote to his ex-Chief of Staff, General de Guingand, that Tedder was 'utterly useless as a Chairman; he sits on the fence and never gives a definite opinion on any matter'.[33] Montgomery's pretensions both amused and irritated Tedder, to whom the Chiefs of Staff organization was a military institution through which the three services had to work harmoniously, compromising with each other when necessary, but always recognizing that the services were subject to political authority, and not the other way round. To Montgomery the committee was a nuisance.

At the end of Tedder's first year as CAS, Air Vice Marshal Claude Pelly, the executive head of the British Bombing Survey Unit (BBSU), and I, its scientific director, presented Tedder with the organization's final reports. The Air Staff, however, and that must have included Tedder himself, decided both to delay and to limit their circulation. Like others who had worked for two years in the unit, I felt somewhat let down by the decision, but I can see now that it was a wise thing to do. RAF Bomber Command's policies had been a highly contentious issue in parliamentary and influential public circles, and had proved costly both in lives and resources. The American bombing survey organization, whose reports had already been made public, had concluded that area bombing by the RAF had failed as a war-winning strategy. There would, therefore, have been little good in the Air Staff publishing British reports to the same effect, for, with the publicity that they might have received, doing so could only have added to the grief of thousands of families which had lost fathers and sons in a bombing campaign that was based on a policy which was now branded as ineffectual. On the other hand, today I greatly regret that histories of the air war of the Second World War almost never refer to the BBSU reports, only the American.

The Final Years

When Tedder's four-year term as CAS came to an end, he agreed to spend two more in Washington as head of the British Military Mission, simultaneously serving as the UK representative on the newly formed Nato

33. General Sir Charles Richardson, *From Churchill's Secret Circle to the BBC* [The biography of Lt-General Sir Ian Jacob] (London: Brassey's, [UK], 1991), p. 267.

Military Committee. In accepting this appointment, he knew of course that he had something to look forward to at its conclusion – the freedom to speak as a peer in the House of Lords, and the pleasures associated with the office of Chancellor of Cambridge University, a position to which he was elected in 1950 in succession to the distinguished South African, General Smuts, whom he had known well and had greatly admired. The year before he was elected to this lofty academic position, he had delivered the university's Lees Knowles Lectures, in which he reviewed the place of the air in modern warfare, as well as the controversies about strategic bombing in which he had been involved. Being chancellor was a happy experience for him. The office is a highly prestigious one and normally demands little more than appearances at major university functions. But there he was, the notional head of one of Britain's two most ancient universities and, ironically, the one where he, some forty years before, had failed to find a footing on the lowest rung of the academic ladder.[34]

Tedder was a witty and cultivated conversationalist, and never a bore. He admired good scholarship, and had that rare gift of being able to listen and to make people talk about their subjects. He was also a good public speaker and enjoyed the functions at which before long he found himself being increasingly asked to appear. I recall how impressed I was by his demeanour in front of a large company of civic leaders and industrialists at Birmingham City's big annual event, the Jewellers' Dinner. This was one of several occasions when he and Toppy stayed with my wife and me after I had moved from Oxford to the University of Birmingham, which, at my suggestion, his second son, John, entered as a post-graduate student in chemistry. The Tedders had another connection with us in Birmingham. When they left to take up their two-year stint of duty in Washington, they parked their big black retriever with us.

By the end of the war, the fact that Tedder was clearly a man whose good judgement was not limited to military affairs was widely recognized. Shortly after his return from his posting in Washington, he was asked by the Government to chair a Royal Commission that was set up to recommend how to resolve a dispute between the University of St Andrews in Scotland and the claim to independence of its associated college in Dundee. The commission sat for almost a year, taking evidence from all relevant quarters, with most of its recommendations then becoming in-

34. Lord Mountbatten's name had also been canvassed for the honorific post of chancellor. Many years later he told me that when he learnt that Jawaharlal Nehru's name was also on the list of possible candidates, he asked that his name be removed, out of respect for the man who had helped him so much when he was the last Viceroy of India. I think he always envied Tedder the appointment, to which his nephew, Prince Philip, was later to succeed.

corporated in a Government bill that was laid before Parliament in January 1953. This was the occasion for Tedder's maiden speech in the House of Lords. He spoke for twenty minutes, almost twice as long as is customery for maiden speeches, and the Hansard record reads as if on this occasion he was following a written text, from which he occasionally departed to make an extemporaneous remark.

He sat as an independent, and his speeches – he spoke about a dozen times between his first in 1953 and the last in 1962 – were usually contributions to debate, not readings from a fixed text, although, like most peers who participate in debates, he would have had notes in his hand when he rose to speak. He did not mind being interrupted; he commented easily on points made by previous speakers; he was lucid, erudite and on occasion witty. He never minced his words. In a debate at the end of 1956 on the Suez fiasco, he had no hesitation in declaring that Suez was 'A tragic mistake and a folly because it was the wrong action at the wrong time and in the wrong way.'[35]

Most of the debates in which he participated related to defence, and on a few occasions he spoke for as long as forty minutes. He was forthright in stating his views about the atom bomb. In one debate he rhetorically asked: 'Would anybody with the prospect of being atomised, think it worth while going to war?' Another he ended equally bluntly:

'I ask your Lordships to believe me when I say that I have not spoken as I have, of airmen, bombers and bombs, because I was once an airman. I have spoken as I have because I believe that the development of the atomic bomb has altered the whole tempo and scale, and completely overturned the old balances, of war, especially as regards this country. I fear most deeply that once again we are playing the old, old game of thinking of the future in the terms of the past – making, of course, a few concessions to scientific progress, a few atomic guns, perhaps; a bigger and better tank; jet propulsion for bigger and better carriers. We cannot afford to play with our security like that. The last thing I should wish to be is an alarmist, but the blunt fact is that in a future war the stakes for which Britain would be playing would not be merely those of victory or defeat, but, literally, those of life or death.'[36]

The last debate to which he contributed was concerned mainly with defence organization and provided him with the opportunity to express

35. Lord Tedder, Hansard, Lords (12 December 1956), Col. 1082.
36. Ibid. (15 April 1953), Cols 795–6.

his opposition to the idea of having one man speaking for all the Chiefs of Staff – as Montgomery had argued was what was needed when they were colleagues on the Chiefs of Staff Committee, and as Tooey Spaatz believed would be the best way for the US President to deal with the Pentagon. 'What's wrong', he asked, 'with the fact that the Service chiefs have to compromise with each other on defence matters? We all have to compromise, even one man has to compromise before he decides what is the best that can be done'.

In the preceding year he had stated that he was 'sure that once a nuclear weapon has been launched, the deterrent as such will have failed and the floodgate will be opened wide'.[37] He used the occasion of his last speech to re-emphasize the point.

'One cannot differentiate between tactical and strategic nuclear weapons. . . . I must emphasise as strongly as I can from my own experience that strategy and tactics mean different things to different people. The General's strategy may be the Air Marshal's tactics, working to a different scale. The worst of it is that I think the nuclear weapon in a tactical use will inevitably go on to a wider field. I cannot see any possibility whatever of preventing that. You just cannot draw a line across the map in that way.'[38]

Even when he did not participate in a debate, Tedder clearly found pleasure in attending the House of Lords. But he had time for other matters too. He was an active chairman of the board of the Standard Motor Company from 1954 to 1960, and he also served as vice-chairman of the BBC. This was a governmental appointment of considerable importance, for it was during his years as a governor that the BBC had to adjust its operations to prepare to meet the challenge of commercial television.

When he reached his seventies, Tedder started to experience intermittent bouts of illness, and it was only then, from his house to the south of London, that he set about writing his story of the war years. Unfortunately for me it was also a period when academic and governmental affairs left me little spare time, so that I started to see less and less of him. He died in 1967, a year after Toppy. A few months before his death, he wrote to me saying that he was pleased that Leslie Scarman and I were arranging to stay a few nights with him. That is something I still regret we failed to do.

37. Ibid., (3 May 1961) Col. 1317.
38. Ibid., (4 April 1962), Col. 204.

General Carl (Tooey) A. Spaatz

1891–1974

The Single-minded US Air Commander

*   *   *

'Tooey' Spaatz was Commander-in-Chief of all the American air forces that fought in Europe and North Africa during the Second World War – in numbers probably the largest assemblage of aircraft that ever came under one man's direct control. After the German surrender, he was straight away sent to the Pacific theatre, charged with the awesome responsibility of using the newly devised atom bomb. A week after he arrived he became the first, and one may hope the last, military commander ever to use a nuclear weapon.

Tooey was dedicated to the service of which he was one of the proudest of founder members. Of medium build, he was good-looking, with slightly gingery hair. His presence was too unassuming to be described as commanding. He rarely seemed hurried, and he smoked cigarettes endlessly. He was an engaging character with a delightful and quiet sense of humour. He was not an intellectual in any accepted sense of the term. When he was in a serious mood, one could almost hear him thinking. Because he never spoke unnecessarily at meetings, he was sometimes described as taciturn. We took to each other immediately after we met in Algiers in March 1943, and for a time I became a member of his staff.

The Young Spaatz

Tooey was born in 1891 in Boyertown, Pennsylvania, where his German grandparents had settled and whose small newspaper his grandfather had bought. Christened Carl Andrew, Tooey attended local schools until he was sixteen, leaving when his father, the paper's editor and manager, was seriously hurt in a fire. For more than a year Tooey then ran the paper with the help of only a single employee. After his father had recovered, he was sent to military crammers in Washington, DC, as a preliminary to taking up a congressional appointment to West Point. Tooey's father had served as the only Democratic member of Pennsylvania's State Legislature, and

99

had powerful political friends in the nation's capital. West Point, which Tooey entered at the age of eighteen, was for him a way of gaining a college education. He made friends easily but did not try to shine academically, and in 1914 graduated about the middle of a class of 107. That of the following year included two men with whom he was to work closely in the Second World War: – Generals Eisenhower and Bradley.

Tooey's sights had not at first been set on a military career, but soon after becoming a West Point cadet, he decided to make his future in the exciting new world of aviation. After graduating, he had, however, to spend a statutory year in an infantry regiment before being allowed to enter the Army Air Corps School of Aviation. He gained his wings in 1916 and was posted to a pursuit squadron that was attached to a small force which Brigadier-General John Pershing[1] was leading in a punitive expedition against the Mexican, Pancho Villa. In May 1917, the US entered the war against Germany. Urgent steps then had to be taken to increase the size of the minute air force that Tooey had joined. Before leaving for Europe as a captain in command of a new pursuit squadron, he married Ruth Harrison, the daughter of a cavalry colonel.

When he reached France in November 1917, Tooey, as one of America's small band of qualified aviators, was put to work training new airmen, and it was not until September 1918, almost a year later, that he was allowed to see action for himself. Within the space of little more than a fortnight, he downed three German Fokker planes. A few days later – two months before Germany capitulated on 11 November – he was ordered back to the United States in order to help reorganize the system of air training.

During the twenties and thirties Tooey rose steadily in the hierarchy of the small Army Air Corps. He served in pursuit and bomber squadrons, and devised and wrote handbooks on tactics. He also made it his business to make the Air Corps better known to the public, becoming the head of what was called the Western Flying Circus. He encouraged and arranged air races, and in 1929 captured world-wide attention by organizing and commanding an endurance flight of seven days and nights with, of course, in-flight refuelling, which was then in its infancy. He became the Army Air Corps Director of Plans, and was also concerned with the specifications of new aircraft. Above all, he became deeply imbued with the doctrine that the unique function of an air force is to achieve victory over the heads of battling armies by bombing the enemy's homeland – by destroying its cities, its industries, its communications and its ports. In Europe this doctrine was associated with the names of the Italian General

---

1. Later the Commander-in-Chief of the American forces that entered the First World War.

Douhet and the British Air Marshal Trenchard. In the United States it was enthusiastically promoted by Brigadier-General 'Billy' Mitchell, an airman who went so far in its espousal that he publicly denounced the War and Navy Departments for their 'incompetency, criminal negligence and almost treasonable administration of the national defense', and was court-martialled and dismissed from the service.[2] Tooey had served under Mitchell, one of whose strongest supporters was Major Henry Harley Arnold, the 'Hap' Arnold who was to become Chief of the Army Air Forces when the US entered the Second World War. Tooey was one of Arnold's closest friends, and both testified powerfully, but unsuccessfully, on Mitchell's behalf. In 1940, as Lt-Colonel Spaatz, and dressed in civilian clothes, he was sent by Arnold to the UK to report on the Battle of Britain and the German night attacks on London. He returned to the US after four months, having learnt, among many things, about the operational importance of radar, and more confident than any of the other official US observers who had been sent to the UK that the Luftwaffe could not beat the RAF or break the spirit of the British people.

The 8th Air Force

The US Army Air Forces (USAAF) then comprised little more than about two thousand officers and twenty thousand men, and Tooey, soon to become a brigadier-general, was one of its senior members. The truly remarkable build-up of American air power that began in the second half of the thirties had focused to a significant extent on the production of the B.17 Flying Fortress and the B.24 Liberator bombers. Arnold and his trusted lieutenants, Tooey and Ira Eaker, were convinced that these heavily armed aircraft would be able to penetrate the German air defences by day. The RAF's attempts to do so had proved unavailing, and the UK, like the Luftwaffe, had become committed to a policy of area bombing by night. The American air chiefs did not believe that this was the way to implement the Billy Mitchell doctrine. They were convinced that they could carry out precision bombing by day and destroy specific targets, and so succeed where the British and German air forces had failed.

When the US entered the war in December 1941, Tooey was number two to Arnold in the Army Air Forces, which had not yet achieved the status of an independent service, as had both the RAF and the Luftwaffe. Two months later he was appointed head of the Air Force Combat

2. Allen Andrews, *The Air Marshals* (London: Macdonald, 1970), p. 167, and
   S. Copp De Witt, *A Few Great Captains* (New York: Doubleday, 1980).

Command, with the task of transforming it into the US 8th Air Force, which was due to be based in the UK. Ira Eaker was appointed, in the rank of Major-General, as commander of the new force's Bomber Command, and sent to England to prepare the ground for the reception of the whole force. He was soon followed by Major-General Frank Hunter, another of Tooey's old colleagues, who was made head of the 8th Fighter Command. Tooey remained behind in the US for a few months, carrying on with the vast job of recruiting, organizing and equipping his new command. It was not until June 1942 that he moved to England to take charge of the never-ending business of establishing training and operational bases, together with supply and maintenance depots, for the enormous air force that the 8th and its offshoot, the 15th, were to become. He also had to establish relations with the battle-hardened RAF chiefs, a job that was beset with personality problems.

Air Chief Marshal Sir Charles Portal, the head of the RAF, and Air Chief Marshal Sir Arthur Harris, the head of RAF Bomber Command, were convinced that the daylight bombing policy which the American commanders intended to pursue was wrong. So was Winston Churchill. But Arnold and Tooey were not going to be pushed around. The 8th Air Force would fight side by side with the RAF, but it would do so as an autonomous and independent organization. What was more, the 8th Fighter Command was not in England to help the RAF protect the UK. Its job was to operate on its own against the Luftwaffe and to provide fighter cover for the US bombers in their daylight penetration of German-occupied Europe. Co-ordinating air operations in the UK under two national commands was to prove far from easy. There were also wider considerations that had to be borne in mind. When he arrived in the UK Tooey fully supported the Washington view that a cross-Channel invasion of France by American and British troops should take place either in late 1942 or in the spring of 1943. The British Government was convinced that the idea was premature, and instead proposed, with the US finally agreeing, that Allied forces should first take control of the north-west coast of Africa.

Soon after the operation to achieve this aim had been launched, Tedder, as I have already recounted, was made Deputy Commander-in-Chief to Eisenhower, the Supreme Commander, and given charge of all the air forces operating in the Mediterranean Theatre, while Tooey Spaatz became their executive commander under Tedder.

I have also told how it was that at the end of a stint of field-work in the Western Desert, to which I had been sent in order to make a ground survey of the effects of the operations of the Desert Air Force, I was flown to Algiers so that before returning to the UK I could give Tedder and Spaatz an account of what I had learnt. I remained in Algiers for a few days, most of which I spent with Tooey and his staff officers, all of whom seemed eager to learn what it was I had found out. They could not have been more friendly. On my first night I dined in Tooey's mess, and after dinner we all milled around as if we were at a cocktail party. Everyone seemed to know everyone by their first names or by nicknames, and there was no indication that rank mattered in their relationships with each other. Tooey appeared to be Tooey to everybody, neither general nor sir. The only RAF officers whom I remember being there were Hugh Pughe Lloyd and Air Marshal James Robb, Mountbatten's Deputy for Air in Combined Ops, who had been sent out to serve on Tooey's new staff. It was so different from the occasion when I was taken to lunch in a tent outside Tripoli which was the mess of Air Commodore Harry Broadhurst as he then was, the RAF officer who had succeeded 'Mary' Coningham as head of the Desert Air Force. 'So,' he said disdainfully, 'you've been sent out to see what's in a hole' – meaning a bomb-crater. Tooey and his staff wanted to know what effect the holes had had on Rommel, where it was best to make the holes, and with what bombs and what fusing.

I had intended to spend no more than twenty-four hours in Algiers before returning to the UK, but for three days Tooey prevented me from leaving. His mind was entirely on the immediate battle, and I do not recall that any of our conversation touched on the operations of his 8th Air Force in the UK. Tooey made me feel that I was one of his staff, and when I left he said that he would soon have me back. The fact that I was an academic of a kind he had probably never met before seemed to make no difference to him, in the same way as he appeared to take it as the most natural thing in the world that, although a civilian, I had been operating freely and on my own in a battle zone. I had rarely met a man who was so forthcoming in his friendship.

It must have been Robb who some two months later then encouraged Tedder and Tooey to invite me back to North Africa. Tooey had by then moved from Algiers to Constantine, where he had taken over a school as his headquarters. I had spent the night I arrived in Algiers with Tedder, who had me flown next morning to Constantine. I was driven straight from the airfield to Lauris Norstad's office. 'Larry' was now a one-star general – he was a colonel when we first met in Algiers – and was Tooey's Chief Operations Officer.[3] After a long talk about the operations of the preceding two months that had led to the surrender of the Axis forces in North Africa, we drove to the small suburban villa where Tooey was based, and where he and Robb were waiting for us. I was then told that I had been asked back in order to prepare a bombing plan, based on

3. He ended his service career in 1963 as Supreme Allied Commander, Nato.

abortive ones that I had designed when in Combined Ops for the capture of the Channel Island of Alderney, in order to help bring about the fall of Pantelleria, Mussolini's supposedly impregnable island fortress that blocked the way to Sicily. An assault landing on the island by a British division commanded by a Major-General Clutterbuck – whom Tooey insisted on calling Clusterbottom – was due to take place fifteen days later. Tooey was hopeful that I could produce a bombing plan that would make the subsequent landings a walk-over. His friendly confidence made me feel that I would find the job just a routine affair, instead of what it in fact proved to be: the first successful attempt ever to organize a specific bombing plan to achieve so precise a purpose. The combined Navy, Army, Air Force operation was under the command of Eisenhower himself, and Tedder had not been as confident as was Tooey, for whom it was going to be the first, even if small, demonstration of the validity of the Douhet/Trenchard/Mitchell doctrine of air power.

I spent the rest of the afternoon discussing the problem with him, Robb, Norstad and Tooey's chief intelligence officer, George Macdonald. At dinner I then met the regular members of Tooey's small mess, and a nicer bunch of men it would have been difficult to find. Larry Norstad was the youngest, and among the others were two of Tooey's First World War buddies – Ted (Edward P.) Curtis, Tooey's Chief of Staff, and in peacetime a vice-president of Eastman Kodak, and Everett Cook, who I understood was a 'cotton king', and whom they called 'Cookie, the Senator from Tennessee'. I never did discover whether he was in fact a senator. Talk was lively and uninhibited, and after dinner I was driven to a hotel that had been taken over as an officers' mess, where I stayed for two nights before Tooey had me moved to a small cottage close to his villa, which I shared with Larry Norstad. As it was to turn out, I remained a member of Tooey's inner circle after he left Constantine for La Marsa near Tunis, and, as I have said, I stayed with him off and on in the luxurious d'Erlanger villa that became his home until our return to the UK at the end of the year.

The only thing I regretted about being a member of Tooey's mess was that I could not join in the poker games that were regularly played after dinner. After I had watched the first, I realized that the stakes were far too high for me, for within the first ten minutes at least one of the players usually seemed to be a few hundred dollars up or down. Tooey never seemed to mind whether he won or lost. Someone would jokingly say: 'My, Tooey, what's Ruth going to say when she sees that her next pay-packet is down five hundred dollars.' Another light-hearted remark would refer to Tooey's 'strategic conferences' and poker games with Ira Eaker. 'Who's going with you to Gibraltar to make up the party?' someone would ask. Little more than a year after that first night in Constantine the battle had moved to France, and the Germans had been pushed back across the Rhine. Tooey's forward headquarters were then at St Germain near Versailles, where I was occasionally invited to a meal. Dinner one night was followed by the usual poker game, and I sat behind Tooey, following his play. One of the other players was John Hay ('Jock') Whitney, then a colonel with a variety of duties in intelligence, who had flown in from Italy.[4] When Tooey was called to the telephone in the middle of a hand, he passed his cards to me and told me to play out the round. I was terrified. The pot was enormous. Fortunately another 'kibitzer' was 'Bill' Paley, the head of the Columbia Broadcasting Corporation, and then also in uniform. When it came to my turn to raise the stakes or throw in my hand, he had no hesitation in whispering in my ear: 'Throw it in.'

I have told the story of Pantelleria elsewhere[5] and I do not propose to do more here than say that Tooey saw to it that everything I needed was done, including repeated and daily photocover of the island's coastal batteries and airfield, which was furnished with a big underground hangar. The plan I drew up, and which was immediately accepted by Tooey and his staff, specified the targets that were to be attacked each day, with Larry Norstad laying on the required operations and then the follow-up photo-reconnaissance flights, so that the results could be assessed in time to specify which batteries should be the next day's targets. Tooey's confidence in me was unbounded. With the help of a small scratch staff I worked all hours, day and night. On my second day, when he thought that I was already overdoing it, he insisted that I took a few hours off to fly with him to La Marsa to inspect the villa that was going to be his home. We sat on a bench in the garden, just the two of us, smoking and chatting, and looking at the sparkling water of the Golfe de Hammamet. We were already on first-name terms – I was 'Zuck' to him as well as to Larry Norstad. For some unknown reason, Ted Curtis called me Paul, and partly in memory of the stimulating time of those days with Tooey and his staff, that was the name I later gave my son.

A joint air/naval bombardment of the island had been laid on for 8 June, and Tooey and I watched the action from the bridge of one of the destroyers that was engaged. On the preceding day we had flown to Sousse, to confer with the British admiral who was in charge of the naval part of the operation, and with some of 'Clusterbottom's' officers. Tooey had also taken with him Sally Bagby, a young WAC officer on his personal staff. On our way from the airstrip to the admiral's headquarters we had to pass

4. Jock was later to become US Ambassador to the UK.
5. Solly Zuckerman, *From Apes to Warlords* (London: Hamish Hamilton, 1978).

through lines of soldiers who were enjoying the sunshine in various stages of undress, some complete. Embarrassed that Sally was about to be exposed to such sights, Tooey took hold of one of her arms with one hand and covered her eyes with the other as he steered her through the camp. That was Tooey, the sensitive family man.

Tooey's comment on the next morning's operation, when our destroyer opened fire after we had come within range of the shore batteries, was: 'What the hell kind of damage do they think these small shells will do?' A few minutes later, a large formation of B.17s flew towards the island to unload their bombs on the two coastal batteries that had been designated as their targets. The detonation of the bombs obscured the whole coastline in front of us. After two more days in which the coastal defences were bombed, the Italian commander capitulated – before the assault force had even set foot on the island.

Tooey's belief in the unique significance of air power had been given a terrific boost, all the more so because Robert Lovett, the Assistant Secretary of the Army, had flown from Washington to spend a few days with him in order to follow the progress of the operation. Tooey was exultant, Lovett and Eisenhower impressed, and 'Mary' Coningham disdainful because heavy bombers had been brought in to do a job which he felt should have been left to his fighter-bombers, in his view the only force that knew about Army/Air co-operation.[6] Only Tedder worried lest the wrong lessons would be drawn from what he rightly regarded as an experiment. He feared that the operation would lead to the wrong conclusions: the Army would never move before the enemy forces in front of them had been battered by heavy bombers.

A couple of days later Tooey presented me with an official 'commendation' for the part I had played.

'Mary' Coningham's reaction was at least partly due to his dislike of the fact that the reorganization of the Mediteranean Air Command had placed him under Tooey's direction. He was, of course, not the only seasoned RAF field commander who resented finding himself under the command of 'inexperienced Americans', but 'Mary' was probably more open in indicating what he felt about the situation than were others. Before the invasion of Sicily in July of 1943 there was an occasion when, as commander of Tooey's tactical air forces, he had lunched with him in La Marsa, to which Tooey had by then moved, and when his behaviour made a lasting and unfortunately hostile impression on Tooey and on those of his staff officers who shared his mess in the d'Erlanger villa, where I was then quartered. The story is worth repeating.

6. Orange, *Coningham*.

'Mary' enjoyed a rightful reputation as a brilliant and hardened tactical air commander. Unfortunately, however, he had little respect for the less experienced Spaatz under whose command he had been placed. One day after the lunch at which 'Mary' had been a guest, we had moved into a side-room that looked on to the garden. Tooey then started to discuss some tactical matter that had cropped up. Without a word 'Mary', who had been listening disdainfully, suddenly got up and walked into the garden, where he could be seen picking blossoms from a hibiscus bush. On his return he bent down on one knee and presented the flowers to Tooey, saying: 'Master, I bring you these.'

Tooey was not amused. He knew well enough that the gesture was 'Mary's' way of indicating that he had nothing to learn from an American general who had been in the war for less than a year. Vincent Orange, in his biography of Coningham, refers to an incident which led Tooey to send Air Marshal James Robb, his RAF deputy, to tell 'Mary' that 'he should correct his attitude'. I do not know whether it was the same incident as the one that I had witnessed.[7]

That was my first experience of Anglo-American relations taking a wrong turn at a high level of command. It was not the last. General Brereton, who had been in charge of the small US air force that had been based with the Middle East Royal Air Force since the middle of 1942, and who at first had got on well with Coningham, refused to serve under him when he was appointed in 1944 as forward commander of the Tactical Air Forces for the assault phase of the invasion of France. Tooey's inability to get on with Leigh-Mallory was of course more important, and a major test of the formidable task that Eisenhower and Tedder had in suppressing personality and national problems when they moved to the UK as Supreme Commander and Deputy Supreme Commander respectively for the

7. Coningham and Spaatz never got on together. According to the former's biographer, Vincent Orange, Tooey had created 'a highly-secret communications network, known as *Redline*, manned exclusively by Americans and used to bypass Coningham. Officers were to be trained to take over at a moment's notice as soon as Spaatz got permission to separate his forces from those of the RAF'. In late September, Coningham's American deputy, Lt-General John Cannon, complained to 'Mary' that he was receiving direct operational orders from Tooey's HQ. As a result, 'Mary' wrote Tooey a 'stiff letter', in which he said: 'Either my exercise of command is satisfactory, or it is not. In the latter case, the remedy is to change. But as commander, I cannot be responsible for the force and at the same time have my superior headquarters cut across and undermine my authority. This leaves me no alternative but to request to be relieved and that would not only be deplorable in this happy and closely integrated force, but to me personally would be a disastrous act. I feel so strongly on the matter, however, that it would be my duty.'

Normandy invasion. Of the two, I should think that the burden of dealing with personality differences was heavier for Tedder, since he knew that, despite the total confidence which Eisenhower had in him, and whatever the command organization may have looked like on paper, Spaatz, Brereton and other senior US air commanders could bypass him and discuss their problems directly on a personal basis with their American colleague – and contemporary – who now happened to be the Supreme Commander.

Working with Spaatz

After Pantelleria, and encouraged by Tedder, Tooey was only too ready for me to continue to play a part in the choice of bombing targets in the preparatory phase of the invasion of Sicily, which was scheduled to take place a month later. Apart from the enemy's airfields and ports, which had often been bombed, air attacks had not followed any precise or coherent overall strategic plan. My advice was that the bombing offensive should from then on focus on the nodal points of the rail network through which the Axis forces in Sicily received their reinforcements and supplies. Tedder and Tooey agreed. After Palermo had been captured by Patton's Seventh Army – a bare fortnight after it had landed in the west of the island on 10 July – a detailed analysis, in which the Palermo railway officials played a major part, was made of the daily records of rail movements in the preceding months. It showed that the more that bombing attacks had concentrated on the rail centres that regulated traffic, and which were also responsible for the maintenance and marshalling of rolling stock, the greater were the returns in terms of the dislocation of the movement of troops and military supplies. Indeed, both the Sicilian and southern Italian rail systems had become to all intents and purposes paralysed by the end of July as a result of attacks on only six rail centres, of which the most northerly was Naples. Before endorsing the conclusions to which the analysis was leading, Tedder, as I have related, flew to Palermo to see for himself how the work was progressing and what it was revealing. The acceptance of my conclusions by Tooey was particularly significant in the light of the arguments he had with Tedder about the best use of the Strategic Air Forces after he resumed command of the 8th Air Force on his return to the UK.

At the time Tooey could not afford to let his attention stray far from the immediate course of the Mediterranean campaign. He was none the less much concerned about what was happening in the strategic air war against Germany, and particularly about the difficulties into which the 8th

Bomber Command had run in its efforts to undertake daylight raids against targets in western Germany. Losses had mounted, and the need for long-range fighter escort for the heavy bombers had become ever more obvious. He and Ira Eaker kept in close touch – Gibraltar was not the only place where they met – and together they planned what was intended to develop into a programme of 'shuttle bombing' of Axis targets. Aircraft based in the UK would attack specified targets in Germany and then fly on to North Africa or southern Italy, where the crews, having rested, and their aircraft having been rearmed and fuelled, would turn round and attack other targets on their way back to the UK. The first and only one of this particular kind of long-distance shuttle mission took place in August 1943, with one division of bombers attacking ball-bearing plants in Schweinfurt, some 100 kilometres to the east of Frankfurt, and a second, aircraft factories at Regensburg, about the same distance north of Munich. The plan was for the first division to return to the UK after it had dropped its bombs, and for the second to fly on to North Africa. The whole operation was the deepest penetration into Germany yet attempted by the 8th Bomber Command. Despite long-range fighter support, the losses were considerable. Sixty out of a total force of some three hundred B.17s and B.24s failed to return.

Apart from the knowledge that large numbers of aircraft had definitely been shot down, the general situation was not immediately clear, and Ira Eaker decided to fly out to La Marsa to confer with Tooey and with Colonel Curtis LeMay, who had flown out in order to re-form those of his bombers as had managed to reach North Africa. During the afternoon of the day that Eaker arrived, he and a few others moved to a side-room that opened out of the main hall of the d'Erlanger villa and started a poker game, with Tooey chain-smoking cigarettes and Eaker continuously rolling a cigar from one corner of his mouth to the other. There was tension in the air and very little talk except for the poker calls. Brigadier-General 'Pete' Quesada, who had been one of Tooey's young pre-war aviator colleagues and a member of the crew of Tooey's seven-day flight-endurance test, and who was now deputy chief of Tooey's Coastal Command, manned the telephone, every now and then announcing excitedly that more of the bombers which had got through were again operational. Tooey and Eaker would look up, their faces impassive, and then go on with the game. I felt I knew what they were thinking, especially Tooey, about the failure to beat the German defences and about the young crews who had been lost. Despite all that had happened, I was also sure that both were none the less determined to continue the strategic air war by way of daylight bombing. That was the doctrine they had helped establish. That, to them, was the only way that Germany was going to be defeated.

Overlord and Independence

Italy had surrendered before Tooey returned to England at the end of the year, and the British and American armies, although well established in southern Italy, were still fighting hard against fierce German resistance. In the preceding two to three months, Arnold, Tooey and Ira Eaker had been discussing ways of reorganizing the US bomber forces that were already in Europe in order to improve the effectiveness of their operations against Germany. One outcome was that Doolittle's 12th Bomber Command, together with the US fighter forces in North Africa and the Middle East, were reconstituted as the 15th Air Force, with its main base in the Foggia area of southern Italy. In addition to providing support in the land battle, the main function of the new air force, which Arnold decided Ira Eaker was to command, was the bombing of targets in the Balkans, Austria and southern Germany. To this end, arrangements had been made with the USSR for the establishment of air bases on Soviet soil, to allow shuttle bombing.

Eaker had argued strongly but unsuccessfully against Tooey and Arnold about the need to create this new force, both because he preferred to remain in command of the 8th, and also because of the difficulties he foresaw in setting up the supply and maintenance organization which the new command would require.[8] It was therefore much against his wishes that he left England at the end of the year to take over from Tedder the post of C-in-C of all the Allied air forces in the Mediterranean Theatre, with Air Chief Marshal Sir John Slessor as his deputy, and with Tooey resuming command of the 8th Air Force. As it turned out, the 15th Bomber Command was unable to bomb targets in Germany itself until towards the end of the war, by when the Reich's air defences had been all but whittled away.

Arnold had also long wished that all the Strategic Air Forces ranged against Germany – British as well as American – should be under 'unified command'. When the 8th Air Force was being formed in the UK he had worried lest the RAF would try to subordinate it under its command. The boot was on the other foot by the end of 1943, with US forces in the UK fast outnumbering the British. Arnold again raised the question of unified command, having at the back of his mind the idea that Tooey should be overall commander of all Allied bomber forces. Harris, Portal and Chur-

8. H.H. Arnold, *Global Mission* (New York: New York Times Company and Arno Press, 1972).

chill would have none of it. Portal, like Tedder, believed that Tooey 'had little capacity for high command'.[9] Arnold then created a new command for Tooey, the United States Strategic Air Forces (USSTAF), consisting of the 8th and 15th as well as the 9th Air Force of medium bombers and fighters that was also stationed in the UK. Portal was made responsible to the Combined Chiefs of Staff of the US and UK for co-ordinating the bomber operations of the RAF with those of USSTAF. But Tooey still had his direct line to Arnold.

He took up his new command in England concerned not only to intensify the bombing of Germany, but to outdo Harris in the effort to bomb Germany into submission. He was also determined not to surrender an ounce of his independence, even though Eisenhower, to whom he was subordinate, and who was to be in supreme command of the invasion of France that was now projected for the middle of 1944, had the right to call, as and when he needed, on any or all the Allied air forces to help in his operations.

The struggle to assure his independence revealed Tooey at his most pertinacious, and obstinate to the point where at times it almost seemed that not Germany but the projected invasion was the real enemy, for by then Tooey had changed his mind about the need for the cross-Channel operation that he had favoured when he first took command of the 8th Air Force. Like many in RAF Bomber Command, he had now come to believe that the invasion was both what some bomber commanders called an unnecessary boating expedition, and also a highly hazardous venture that had every chance of failing. On the one hand the Allied invading forces might be pushed back into the sea, while on the other, Germany could be subjugated by bombing alone.

Tooey knew that the idea behind the AEAF plan to disrupt the railway network of north-west Europe had its basis in what had been learnt in the Mediterranean, and that I had been responsible for putting it to Leigh-Mallory and then for writing the first draft of what was known as the AEAF overall air plan. Tedder, with whom I was in constant touch, approved what I was writing and, so at first did Tooey, whom I was also then seeing frequently. Knowing that I was to a certain extent a free agent, he at one point even suggested that I should work with him at his HQ rather than with Leigh-Mallory, an invitation which I obviously had to decline.

Like those of the Air Ministry, Tooey's representatives on a planning committee that Leigh-Mallory had set up were also at first in favour of what was being planned as, in a quiet way, was Portal. Some three weeks

9. Orange, op. cit., p. 174.

before our return to the UK, when Tedder had got me to explain to him the results of air attacks on the Italian railway network, Portal's comment was 'so we were laughed out of Hamm', a reference to the ironical accounts that used to appear in the press when, in the early months of the war, it was reported that yet another successful attack had been made by the RAF on that particular German railway centre – attacks in which few bombs had ever fallen anywhere near their target.

Argument soon started. In mid-January Harris sent a powerful minute to Portal, in which he denounced the whole idea of directing his bombers against railway centres and coastal batteries. If we do that, his minute ended, 'we shall commit the irremedial error of diverting our best weapon from the military function for which it has been equipped and trained, to tasks which it cannot effectively carry out. Though this might give a specious appearance of "supporting" the Army, in reality it would be the gravest disservice we could do them. It would lead directly to disaster'.

The Air Ministry planners soon swung into line behind Harris. Tooey then became acutely concerned that Harris was going to be allowed to continue with area attacks on enemy cities, so possibly bringing Germany to its knees before *Overlord* could be launched, while he, being subordinate in the US command hierarchy to Eisenhower, would be ordered to implement the AEAF plan.

Early on in the controversy that followed, I had invited him to spend a night in Oxford to dine with me at my college, Christ Church. There was a large turnout of members of the High Table, and Tooey was a great success and enjoyed the dinner enormously. He also made the occasion memorable. In the common-room after dinner, after the port had circulated a couple of times, I heard him proclaiming loudly that Bach sounded better when played on a guitar than on a church organ. If only he had his guitar with him, he said, he would show them; he was much interested in music and had become a proficient guitarist when at West Point. Someone then said, well, at least we have an organ – the cathedral in Oxford is part of the fabric of Christ Church. So all but two of the company trooped out, the cathedral was opened and the college organist proceeded to play. I was one of the two who remained in the common-room, for I had a feeling that my guest, who had partaken freely of the college's excellent wine, was getting out of hand.

After a while they all returned, with Tooey still proclaiming that Bach as played on the organ was not a patch on Bach when played on a guitar. The conversation round the table then resumed, some, including Tooey, having a further drink or two. When I later helped him to bed, he switched to the subject of the AEAF plan, to which he said he was not opposed in principle. What worried him was that Harris was going to be allowed to go on bombing Germany into submission while he was directed to hit targets in preparation for an invasion that might never take place, since by then RAF Bomber Command might well have succeeded in its so-called strategic objective. All I could do was say that I was sure there was no question that Harris would be allowed to divorce himself from *Overlord*. I waited till he was safely in bed before leaving.

Harris's alternative to the AEAF plan was simply to continue his night bombing of German industrial cities. Tooey, on the other hand, while insisting that attacks on aircraft plants – with which he included those that produced ball-bearings – had overriding priority, set his staff to work to put forward a specific 'strategic' plan in place of the AEAF's transportation plan, and one that could be implemented by the US 8th Bomber Command in precise daylight attacks. The one that they proposed, and which Tooey accepted, was a programme of attacks on German synthetic oil plants, the argument being that if these were destroyed before D-Day, the results would be far more catastrophic to the German High Command than the bombing of the rail network which, he was informed, had so much spare capacity that, whatever damage was done, there would always be enough left to deal with military movements. Transportation targets, his advisers declared, should only be 'targets of last resort'. It is interesting that the pre-war UK bombing plans prepared for the RAF had also designated 'oil' as a desirable target, but in general second to the German rail system.

Contrary to what David Mets has written in his biography of Spaatz,[10] I am sure that at the start Tooey was less concerned with the substance of the arguments about the relative merits of bombing railway centres or oil plants than he was in finding himself under Leigh-Mallory's command. The promotion of synthetic oil plants as strategic targets of highest priority for the 8th Bomber Command was a means of assuring the independence of his forces. The trouble was that Tooey and Leigh-Mallory neither understood nor liked each other. As Tedder put it in *With Prejudice*[11] Spaatz had 'made it abundantly clear that he will not accept orders, or even co-ordination, from Leigh-Mallory'. To the Americans Leigh-Mallory's manner was very 'British' and stand-offish, which some took for overweening confidence and conceit, and others interpreted as a cloak for, as one put it, 'nervous self-defence'. L-M, as he was called, never sought out Tooey to try to reconcile their differences in a friendly way, nor did Tooey seek him out. General Hoyt Vandenberg, an airman who had been on General Marshall's staff in Washington, had been posted as Leigh-

10. David R. Mets, *A Master of Air Power: General Carl A. Spaatz* (Novato, Calif.: Presidio Press, 1988).
11. Ibid., p. 508.

Mallory's deputy before becoming C-in-C of the 9th Air Force. 'Van' could not have been a nicer or easier man to deal with, but while he learnt both to respect and to like his RAF boss, he failed utterly to improve relations between the two men. Nor indeed, did he succeed in making Leigh-Mallory's AEAF headquarters a happy place in which to work. We were supposed to be a fully integrated HQ, but the suspicions entertained by the more senior RAF and USAAF officers about each other's intentions usually worked their way down the line.[12]

At a meeting in mid-February, Tooey made his opposition to Leigh-Mallory's having any say in the targeting of the 8th Bomber Command bluntly clear. Leigh-Mallory had called all the air chiefs together to consider an updated draft of the AEAF plan. Harris was outspoken in his opposition, Tooey less so, but insisted that the AEAF plan conflicted with the *Pointblank* directive to attack specific targets in Germany which Roosevelt and Churchill had agreed at their Casablanca summit in January 1943 and which he was trying to implement, and in accordance with which air superiority had to be achieved by bombing aircraft factories and ball-bearing plants within the Reich. He ended by asking for the date when Leigh-Mallory proposed to take control of the strategic bomber forces. Although fully conscious of the hostility around him, Leigh-Mallory unhesitatingly answered, 1 March – which was only a fortnight away. 'That's all I want to know.' responded Tooey. 'I've nothing further to say.'

Starting well before D-Day, and for some weeks after the landings, all the air barons used to meet formally under Leigh-Mallory's chairmanship (for what some styled 'morning prayers') in order to assess the military situation and to agree the following day's air operations. About a fortnight before D-Day Tooey arrived, accompanied by Brigadier-General Cabell and another of his one-star generals. Leigh-Mallory opened the meeting tactlessly by asking the two to leave, saying that their presence was not required. When the meeting ended, Tooey asked me to lunch – our relations were as friendly as ever despite my responsibility for the controversial part of the AEAF plan – and during the short drive from Leigh-Mallory's headquarters at Stanmore to Tooey's home at Bushey Park we discussed the plans that he had in mind for his air forces. Before we sat down to lunch, the main topic of conversation among the members of his mess was Cabell's ejection from the meeting. Cabell was still incensed. Tooey closed the subject by indicating what he thought of Leigh-Mallory. 'Now Cabell,' he said, 'that's not burning you up, is it? You start worrying when I throw you out.'

In those days Tooey's relations with Harris also seemed distant and

12. E.J. Kingston-McCloughry, *The Direction of War* (London: Jonathan Cape, 1955).

cool. Harris had admired Ira Eaker's efforts to build up the 8th Bomber Command and, as he put it to me during an evening I spent with him immediately after my return from the Mediterranean, he regarded the transfer of Eaker to Italy as a disaster, especially since Spaatz, so he said, did not appreciate the vital importance of the strategic bombing of Germany. I doubt whether the easy-going Tooey ever got on close personal terms with the dominating and confident Harris, who regarded attempts to hit precise targets, such as ball-bearing and synthetic oil plants, as 'panacea bombing'. For Harris, what mattered above all was the area bombing of German cities.

According to David Mets, Tooey came away from the meeting that was called by Portal and Eisenhower towards the end of March to settle the dispute about the role of the Strategic Air Forces having 'suffered one of the toughest defeats of his official life'. This observation is, I fear, a piece of historical romance. In fact Tooey had immediately reported to Hap Arnold that he accepted the decision that the transportation plan came before what he called 'the oil scheme'. As he put it in his message, 'the decision reached was justified based on all factors involved, which are predominantly the absolute necessity to insure the initial success of Overlord . . . the time has arrived now when the most essential thing is the fullest coordination of the air effort in support of Overlord'.[13] Ira Eaker, who had flown over from Italy to confer with Tooey, was in London the day of the meeting, and joined Tooey when it ended. 'I have never seen him so jubilant and overjoyed,' Eaker recorded in his diary. 'He had won out completely on the command set-up', and Tooey was 'not too displeased' that the 'communications plan had won out over the oil plan'.[14]

Although the two were to have many an argument afterwards, the fact was that Tooey had no objections to serving under Tedder's nominal command. He had already done so with a fairly loose rein in the Mediterranean for all but a year. It was Leigh-Mallory whom he was not prepared to have anywhere near his line of command. What also mattered to Tooey was the need to justify his belief that Germany could be made to surrender as a result of strategic bombing alone. This was his paramount objective. At the same time, and for a few months after rail centres had been accorded a higher target priority than synthetic oil plants, he still had an open mind about the way the Billy Mitchell doctrine of air power was to be achieved – despite the fact that the word 'oil' had by now become a symbol of the doctrine of USSTAF independence. 'You may well be

13. Spaatz to Arnold, 26 March 1944 (V. 60193).
14. James Parton, *Air Force Spoken Here* (Bethesda, Md: Adler & Adler, 1986), pp. 378–9.

proved right,' he said to me one day. 'Destroying the rail network might well turn out to be a much more important objective than going for the oil plants.'

Unfortunately the controversy had engendered a great deal of bitterness in 8th Air Force staff circles, where there was little enthusiasm to help in the implementation of a plan whose purpose had been decried as being only tactical. It therefore fell to RAF Bomber Command to execute the greater part of the pre-D-Day programme of attacks on railway centres of France and Belgium, with the 8th Bomber Command coming in towards the end by directing most of its effort against those targets in western Germany that had also been designated in the plan. Tedder had found it prudent to exercise his co-ordinating responsibility lightly and not to press too hard on Tooey.

Since they were directly responsible for the operations of their respective commands, Tooey and Harris could in any event decide for themselves when conditions were less favourable for an attack on a specified rail centre than for a night-time area raid on a German city, or a daylight operation against an aircraft factory or synthetic oil plant. Tooey could also deal directly with Eisenhower, and there was always Arnold ready to back his decisions. Indeed, with Tedder's agreement, the 8th Bomber Command had made a few attacks on synthetic oil plants during May – that is to say, before D-Day on 6 June, with more following later that month, and then continuing throughout the period up to September, when the Supreme Commander ceased to have control over the heavy bomber forces. It was Tooey's job to co-ordinate the attacks made on oil plants by the 8th Bomber Command with those carried out from Italian bases by the 15th Air Force against the Romanian oil refineries.

The results of these attacks were often impressive but in no way decisive in so far as causing a German collapse. Moreover, Tooey's argument that the Luftwaffe would fight hard to defend oil plants but not rail centres, and that such attacks would therefore help maintain air superiority, proved to be wrong. Despite the fact that there never was a concerted programme of attacks on oil plants before D-Day, no air battles took place over the beaches as British and American troops fought their way ashore. Tedder had been correct when he ended a pre-D-Day argument between Tooey and Leigh-Mallory about which targets the Luftwaffe would defend, when he said that no one could know in advance what would make the enemy come up and fight. In any event, hitting oil plants in Germany could not have affected what happened over the beaches. At the time the Luftwaffe had ample stocks of fuel available both in the Low Countries and in France, and indeed in western Germany as well.

The staffs of both the UK and US Bomber Commands never, however, ceased to feel that attacks on targets that immediately affected either the land battle or the 'pads' from which, soon after D-Day,[15] the Germans had started to launch flying bombs at the UK, were diversions from what they regarded as their basic 'mission' – to attack targets in Germany, as specified in the *Pointblank* directive that had been issued to the Allied bomber forces in June 1943, and which had been reissued as late as January 1944. For Tooey, the primary objective called for by this directive was the destruction of the German aircraft industry and of the Luftwaffe, something that had to be done if the German military and industrial system were to be destroyed and the will of the German people to resist 'fatally weakened' – all this in fulfilment of the classical concept of strategic air war.

It soon turned out, however, that the doctrine was not all that easy to implement. In late February, about a week after Tooey had asked Leigh-Mallory for the date when he proposed to take command of the Strategic Air Forces, about a thousand US heavy bombers attacked a number of German aircraft plants, which were then subjected to similar but smaller attacks for the whole of the following week. But the jubilation inspired by photocover pictures of destroyed aircraft factories was short-lived, for it was soon learnt that, instead of falling, the output of German fighters continued to rise. In late June the whole of the 8th Air Force again attacked aircraft factories and oil plants in southern Germany, but once more to no significant effect. The output of German aircraft in the final quarter of 1944 was still more than twice what it had been when the year started. The June attack took place before the Normandy beach-head was secure, and in part was a show of independence on Tooey's part. Neither Leigh-Mallory nor Tedder had been formally told that it was going to take place. Whether Eisenhower was in the picture I never discovered.

Area Bombing, Oil and Transportation

After Germany's capitulation, Harris claimed that the main reason for the failure of his area attacks to end the war in the second half of 1944 was due

15. Heavy bomber attacks were carried out by RAF Bomber Command to assist Montgomery in his efforts to break out beyond Caen at the eastern end of the Allied front, while the 8th Bomber Command did the same to help Bradley in his thrust beyond the St Lô–Périers line in the west. Coningham continued to argue against the use of the 'heavies' in such operations, not because he was concerned about the way the 'strategic' air war was going, but because he regarded their use as an intrusion into his field of responsibility as the 'tactical' air commander.

to the diversionary calls on his forces that were made by *Overlord*. For Tooey the main reason, other than *Overlord*, why the 8th US Bomber Command did not succeed in destroying the critical targets on which the German war economy and military machine depended was that poor weather prevented his bombers from making precision attacks by day. The results of those that it was possible to carry out were in any event never as catastrophic as was anticipated. Germany did not crumble under the bomber assault on cities and industrial targets, mainly because of the extraordinarily successful programme of industrial dispersal and repair which Albert Speer's Ministry of Armaments had set in train.

It was all very disappointing. The British Chiefs of Staff and their opposite numbers in Washington had agreed that as soon as the Allied forces had succeeded in securing a firm foothold in France, the operations of the two bomber commands should no longer be under Eisenhower's control. Indeed, as early as the third week of July Portal had suggested to Tedder that the time had come for the control of the heavy bomber forces to be returned to the Joint Chiefs of Staff. Tedder and Eisenhower disagreed, and it was not until September that the change was made, with Arnold and Portal deputed to act as joint co-ordinators of the strategic air war, and with Tooey and Air Marshal Sir Norman Bottomley, Portal's Deputy Chief of Staff, in executive charge. The responsibility for advising about targets was entrusted to a Combined UK/US Strategic Targets Committee, which straight away recommended that synthetic oil plants should be designated as the first priority targets for the heavy bombers, with rail centres, ordnance factories and motor vehicle plants bracketed together in second place. In practice, however, the two commands still operated independently. Harris resumed his area attacks while, mainly because of bad weather and the difficulties of making deep penetrations, it turned out that the US 8th, during the first three months when it was under the new command set-up, that is to say in the last quarter of 1944, again failed to carry out as many precise bombing attacks on oil plants as it wished, and therefore had to direct more of its effort, mostly under blind and radar-bombing conditions, against rail centres.[16] When weather conditions pre-

16. The term 'precision' or 'pinpoint' bombing was a euphemism. As Edward Field, a navigator in the 8th Bomber Command has recently reported, 'pinpoint bombing did focus on particular targets, but equally could be described as area bombing, since only the lead navigator of the squadron of planes focused its bombsight on the target. We who followed simply dropped our bombs when we saw the lead plane's bombs falling, with the result, we were told, of the bombs falling in a pattern of a square mile around the target' (*New York Review of Books*, Vol. 37, No. 11 [1990], p. 61). As a US air general was to put it much later, precision bombing meant the area bombing of precise targets.

cluded attacks on oil plants, they were also unsuitable for attacks on other small targets such as ordnance depots. As week followed week, the 'knock-out' blow that the bomber chiefs had promised failed to materialize.

By late October, American troops had managed to thrust into Germany across part of the front that they covered, and preparations were well in hand to continue the advance. Then came a setback. Towards the end of December the German army, well supported by the Luftwaffe, mounted its powerful counter-attack through the Ardennes. Once again it became obvious that, despite the even more strenuous effort that Hitler was having to make to hold the Soviet advance in the east, strategic bombing had not denied him the means that he needed to launch a powerful counter-attack in the west. Claims that had been made from about October onwards that a few more weeks of attacks on oil targets would immobilize the German Army and the Luftwaffe had proved groundless.

But contrary to these continuing claims, Tooey had sent Arnold a message three days before the opening of the German counter-attack in which, without any reference to oil targets, he stated that there was 'increasing evidence that the attacks on rail communications and industrial areas' indicated that 'the breaking point may be closer at hand than some of us are willing to admit'.[17] Tooey may well have spoken to Tedder before he sent this message, but whatever piece of intelligence it was that had impressed him about the effects of the attacks on the railway system, he, like Harris, continued to argue that bombing in accordance with their plans – not of transportation targets, as Tedder continued to urge – could, and would, end the war. When Arnold sent him a message expressing his disappointment that the Allies, with a five-to-one numerical superiority in the air, were failing to deliver the fatal blow, Tooey replied that he no longer believed in 'the chimera of one air operation that will end the war'.[18] None the less, pressure to launch a knock-out blow continued to grow, and in January of the new year plans for a major onslaught against Berlin and other cities in eastern Germany were being prepared, the assumption being that such an offensive would not only cause chaos but help the Russians in their advance, since the cities in eastern Germany were important communication centres whose destruction would impede the movement to the eastern front of German reinforcements from the west and from Italy.

Tooey and Bottomley were party to the drawing-up of this plan, which was put to the Russians at the Yalta Conference at the beginning of February 1945. They, for their part, indicated only Berlin and Leipzig as

17. Mets, p. 270.
18. Ibid., p. 273.

targets that they would like to see hit. As usual, however, it was left to the operational commanders – Harris for the RAF and Doolittle for the 8th – to decide, depending on prevailing operational conditions, which cities on the target list that had been issued by the Combined Strategic Targets Committee should be attacked. On the night of 13 February, Harris dispatched eight hundred of his bombers against Dresden, on what proved to be one of the most devastating area attacks of the war. On the following two days, and then after a gap of a few days, on a third, and despite the fact that a burning and smouldering city made 'precision' bombing impossible, Doolittle dispatched some three hundred of the 8th Bomber Command's aircraft in attacks supposedly directed against the city's railway centres. A sense of outrage spread in the UK when the news of the indiscriminate destruction that had been wreaked became known, and little more than a month later Churchill, who had been among the first to urge that attacks should be made on eastern German cities, turned round and condemned the destruction of Dresden as 'terror bombing'. Harris was outraged. The two bomber commands had only been following plans that had been endorsed by higher authority.[19] Tooey was more cast down by what had happened, and particularly the killing of thousands of innocent civilians, than he was by the political rebuke.

The choice of bombing targets became ever more limited as the Russians pushed on from the east, and as US and UK forces reached the Rhine. Tedder had never stopped urging that railway centres should continue to be bombed in accordance with a coherent policy. He had put forward a plan to isolate the communications that linked the Ruhr with the rest of Germany. Instead, at the end of February, and contrary to what he was urging about the need to concentrate attacks on rail centres and critical viaducts, nine thousand US aircraft made a daylight and low-level sweep over practically the whole of a now defenceless Germany, attacking rail targets far and wide, and anything and everything that moved. In a second sweep, some political embarrassment was suffered when inexperienced pilots bombed cities in Switzerland, among them Basle and Zurich, having incorrectly assumed that they were over Germany. Tooey and Ted Curtis, in civilian clothes, had to take a couple of days off to go to Switzerland in order to make formal and official apologies. German archives now show that the two massive demonstrations of US air power achieved practically nothing that was militarily useful. The dispersed and slight damage that was inflicted on rail installations was quickly repaired.[20]

19. Churchill later circulated a textually amended second message that failed to mollify the bomber chiefs.
20. Mierzejewski, *The Collapse of the German War Economy*.

The Pacific and the Atom Bomb

The Russians had overrun Romania by the last week of August 1944, and as they continued their push through the Balkans it was not long before the Germans were denied the supplies of oil that their forces on the eastern front had also been getting from Hungary. By March the Russians were in Austria, and in April their armies linked up with the Americans in Czechoslovakia. In mid-April Tooey therefore called a halt to his forces' operations, and declared that the strategic air war against Germany was at an end. Not until 7 May, however, a week after Hitler's suicide on 30 April, and after the Russians had taken over Berlin, did Germany finally capitulate.

By the time this happened, plans were being drawn up to send some of Tooey's aircraft to the Pacific, where Arnold had wanted Tooey to become C-in-C of all land-based aircraft for the final weeks of the war against Japan. General Douglas MacArthur, Supreme Commander in the Pacific, disagreed. So did Admiral Nimitz, C-in-C of the naval forces in the theatre. In particular, MacArthur was not prepared to assign to Tooey the considerable land-based air forces which General George Kenney, his top airman, commanded. He was prepared to have either Kenney or Arnold himself as overall air commander, but not Tooey.[21] Tooey was therefore sent out in command of the 8th Air Force, which by then had only started to be redeployed from the UK, and of a fleet of the new Superfortress bombers, the B.29s. In addition, he had something that the other commanders in the theatre did not have: the atom bomb. After attending the formal signing of the Articles of Surrender in Berlin on 9 May, Tooey set out, by way of Washington, to take over his new command.

It was then that he learnt for the first time about the atom bomb. Arnold had not been a member of the restricted circle that had been charged by President Roosevelt with the task of seeing that the weapon was developed. He had, however, realized from snippets of information that something momentous was afoot.[22] General Leslie Groves, the executive head of what became the vast and dispersed atom-bomb organization of scientists and engineers that had been code-named the Manhattan Project, was so skilful in maintaining security about the work which he administered that those in one compartment of the project knew little or nothing

21. D. Clayton James, *The Years of MacArthur*, Vol. II (Boston, Mass.: Houghton Mifflin, 1975).
22. Arnold, *Global Mission*.

about what was happening in the next. By August 1944 Arnold had, however, been told to arrange for a small unit of Superfortresses to be adapted for a special task, and after he had been fully briefed about what was going on, he and Henry Stimson, the Secretary of the Army, who was in political charge of the project, decided which four Japanese cities should be targets for atomic attack, given that the test of a prototype bomb were to prove successful. Tooey was then put into the picture. Groves explained to him the nature and destructive power of the new weapon, and Arnold then gave him the list of suggested targets, as well as written orders (which Tooey demanded) to bomb whichever city he selected, depending on operational conditions. He was, however, told not to take action without further presidential authorization.

When Tooey reached the Pacific on 1 August, his first job was to brief General MacArthur about what was likely to happen and, after him, Admiral Nimitz and General Kenney. Tooey later told his family that MacArthur had listened to the news in an offhand way, and that at the time he seemed more interested in the design of some new army barracks.[23] A week later Hiroshima was obliterated, and then, after two days, Nagasaki. Tooey was back in the US in early September. It is not surprising that his wife described him as coming back dog-tired.

Final Years of Service

Now that the existence of the atom bomb had been revealed to the whole world, it was obvious that the USSR, which it is known had had to shelve the bomb project on which it was about to embark when the war started, would follow in the wake of the USA. Soon after his return, Arnold therefore put Tooey in charge of a small team, which included Larry Norstad and Hoyt Vandenberg, to consider what impact the bomb and other new developments such as rockets would have on the future of war and on American security. The concept of air power into which Tooey's team tried to fit all these new technical unknowns was obviously the only framework of which they knew – that of the past four years of war. Within less than ten years developments in missile and nuclear technology were to make the conclusions that they reached obsolete.

Soon after Tooey had submitted his report to Arnold, he was made his

23. It is worth noting that neither MacArthur in his *Reminiscences* (London: Heine-mann, 1964) nor William Manchester in his monumental *American Caesar* (London: Hutchinson, 1979) makes any reference to Tooey's arrival in the Pacific to give the order for the destruction of Hiroshima and Nagasaki by atom bombs.

successor as Commanding General of all US Air Forces – Hap Arnold was by now a very sick man. The enormous task of demobilizing the US's wartime forces was already moving apace, and during the two years that Tooey occupied the top US Air Force post he had had to fight hard to muster political support for the maintenance of a strong air force and, what was every bit as important, a force that was to be as autonomous a service as were the Navy and the Army. He succeeded in this latter endeavour, but not in his advocacy that now that peace had come, the US needed, if not as vast a fleet of aircraft as it had built up during the war years, a standing air force that comprised a minimum of seventy 'combat groups'.

With the war over, I saw Tooey for the first time some three months after he had taken Arnold's place. When I telephoned on my arrival in Washington, he suggested that I came straight over to the Pentagon, and when I got there – it was the middle of the afternoon – I found him waiting for me outside his office. 'Let's go to my house. We can talk undisturbed there,' he said. He was then living in quarters in Fort Myer, just outside Washington, and we drove there by way of Alexandria in Virginia, where he wanted to show me the house which he and Ruth had had to leave when he moved into his official quarters. As I was to discover, while waiting for me to turn up he had telephoned and asked her to lay on a dinner party. When we got to Fort Myer, we chatted for an hour or so over drinks about what had happened since the end of the war, about the probable intentions of the USSR, and about the way events seemed to be unfolding in Europe. I do not remember that we so much as referred to the arguments that had raged in 1944 about transportation versus oil as strategic target systems. It was what was happening now that mattered. One of his remarks, which stuck in my mind, is that in trying to rebuild itself, the UK had to learn that motor vehicles, meaning tractors and the like, no longer had to follow a man carrying a red flag. The British worker had to learn to move as fast as the tractor. It was Tooey's way of saying that, compared with the USA, the UK was still living in the past.

At dinner, for which we were joined by Hap Arnold, Jimmy Doolittle and his wife, and Brereton and his (I wondered how Ruth had managed to whip up the meal at such short notice), talk continued along the same lines, about what was happening in Europe, speculation about the future of US relations with its wartime allies, and what so-and-so was now doing, and so on. It was late when Hap Arnold drove me back to my hotel. He seemed deeply worried about the implications of the development of the atom bomb.

Tooey did not indicate to me what his immediate reaction had been to the destruction of Hiroshima and Nagasaki. The bomb now existed, and that was that, and it was obvious that other countries, in addition to the UK and the USSR, would now try to become nuclear powers. He asked me to visit Curt LeMay in order to help make him understand that atomic bombs would be vastly more effective agents of destruction in strategic air war than conventional weapons. I do not believe that Tooey was joking when he asked me to do this. LeMay, who, in a fire-bomb raid on 10 March 1945 had laid waste to 15 square miles of the Tokyo complex and killed an estimated 84,000 people, was not yet the nuclear firebrand that he was to become. I declined the suggestion.

Tooey took it for granted that the USSR was the enemy of the future, and that the US would have to be the guardian of the peace of the world, if possible through the agency of the United Nations, which he, together with other top US air generals, envisaged as being provided with an international air force which an American airman would command. It was a naïve idea, if for no other reason than that it did not reckon with the USSR's power of veto in the Security Council.

When he visited Tedder in June 1946 to obtain his agreement to adapting a few airfields for the handling of Superfortresses, Tooey could have had little if indeed any idea about what was going to happen in the US nuclear weapons field. A public debate was in progress about the desirability of Congress taking nuclear technology out of the hands of the military and of creating a civilian authority, an Atomic Energy Commission, that would be charged with the responsibility of dealing with the subject, both in its military and civil aspects. All that Tooey could be sure of was that the US would almost certainly continue to produce atom bombs, while all that Tedder was aware of was that, since the Anglo-American wartime collaboration in the development of the new weapon looked like ending, the British Government might well decide that the UK should develop its own bomb. That political and highly secret decision was in fact not taken until October, three months after Tooey and Tedder had had their talk. Whatever else, neither could have realized that what they then agreed would become a quasi-permanent arrangement, that an organization called Nato would be formed some three years later, and that it was only then that the British Government would legalize what they had decided on a 'personal basis', by signing a formal agreement that allowed the stockpiling of American nuclear weapons on British soil. Quite innocently, the two had taken the first step that would turn the UK into the US's 'unsinkable aircraft-carrier'.

Retirement

Tooey's deal with Tedder, and arranging for the adaptation of airfields in the Pacific Theatre for the handling of atom bombs, were probably the only moves that he made in the nuclear field during the two years that he was the Chief of Staff. Needless to say, however, the nuclear issue continued to exercise his mind after his retirement in 1948. He then became military correspondent of the journal *Newsweek*, a post he held for nearly ten years. Read today, forty years after they started to appear, most of his articles merely seem to reflect conventional military thinking in the first decade of the post-war East-West arms race. One of his themes, however, was the need to replace the Joint Chiefs of Staff organization by a general staff headed by a single presidential military adviser. This Tooey saw as the only way to eliminate the inter-service battles for resources which always led to the distortion of what the US really needed to assure its security. Another of his constant themes was the continuing import-ance of air power, a topic he had already elaborated in an article that appeared under his name in the April 1946 issue of *Foreign Affairs*, but which reads very much like a 'staff paper'. In this article it was admitted, as Tooey had done in his final despatch at the end of the war, that victory had been an achievement in which all three services had shared. But the final sentence of the article none the less revealed Tooey's continuing faith in the Billy Mitchell doctrine. Time, he declared, had not allowed the US to build an air force during the Second World War of sufficient strength to show what otherwise was possible. 'Another war, however distant in the future,' so the article declared, would probably be decided 'by some form of airpower before the surface forces were able to make contact with the enemy in major battles.' That, to Tooey, was ' the supreme military lesson of our period of history'.

When in 1949 it became known that the USSR had succeeded in de-veloping the bomb, Tooey wrote that what the US now had to do was improve its air defences and increase its stock of atom bombs. Simul-taneously, however, he warned that the 'peace objectives' of the world could be assured only through the United Nations. He argued powerfully against the concept of a 'preventive nuclear war', and was opposed to suggestions that the atom bomb should be used in the conflict in Korea – although not against China if it openly entered the war. When a world-wide campaign for an end to nuclear tests developed in the mid-fifties, Tooey wrote that the testing of H-bombs should cease – the weapons that had already been developed were destructive enough – but that the testing of small atomic bombs should continue, since these might be required in 'bush-fire' wars. He clearly did not have in mind just how destructive 'small' atom bombs, smaller than those that had destroyed Hiroshima and Nagasaki, could be, or to what their use might lead, but he certainly realized that an all-out nuclear war could very well mean the end of civilization. If a third world war was to be avoided, he wrote, it would be only through 'the strength and determination of the United Nations'.

Tooey did not find writing easy. His technique was to agree the lines that his articles would take, and then leave the drafting to a staff writer. Ira Eaker is also said to have had a hand in some of the pieces that appeared under Tooey's name. But he always edited the final version, and, I am reliably told, so did Ruth.

In addition to his connection with *Newsweek*, Tooey became a member of the board of Litton Industries, the conglomerate which had many defence contracts. A friend who was associated with the company as one of its executives has told me that Tooey was not always as moderate in his strategic views as some of his *Newsweek* pieces implied. He recalls a board meeting during the period of the Vietnam war when things were obviously going very badly, when, in reply to a question a fellow board member put to Tooey before the meeting began its formal business, the answer repeatedly given was 'Bomb them, bomb them', which happened to be the futile policy which the USAF was then pursuing.

Tooey and Ira Eaker both co-operated in the move to establish the Air Force Academy which today stands so proudly in Colorado, the sister institution of the Army's West Point and the Navy's Annapolis. The two men remained close friends to the end, and each year spent a few weeks, usually alone, in a fishing lodge they had built in a remote spot in Oregon. There were also annual parties which Jock Whitney laid on at his estate in Georgia for Tooey, Eaker, Ted Curtis, Cook and others of the old group, shooting by day, drinking and playing cards at night. I suppose that inevitably tales about past battles came up, talk about old friends – and old enemies. I was sad that on an occasion when I was in Washington I had to decline an invitation to join them.

On my frequent visits to the US I did, however, usually either see Tooey or speak to him on the telephone. Sometimes he would take me to lunch in the Army and Navy Club; occasionally I would go round to his house for a drink in a little study whose walls were covered by photographs, mostly of Air Force colleagues. As I cast an eye over them, I always gained the impression that there were no RAF faces among them. Perhaps if I had looked closer I might have found a few, for, after the war, Tooey remained on friendly terms with several RAF commanders with whom he had had dealings.

The last time I remember going round to see Tooey was when I wanted him to check a manifestly incorrect idea that had got into Dickie Mountbatten's head when he was master-minding a TV series of programmes about his life. Mountbatten, who was in attendance at the Potsdam Conference, thought that he was the only field commander to be told about the atom bomb before it was used. I told him I was certain that he was wrong, and that as I was about to visit Washington I would inquire. It was then that Tooey told me about the briefings that he had had to give MacArthur, Nimitz and Kenney about the likely use of the new weapon.

Tooey died aged eighty-three in 1974. In the years before then, he devoted himself to his family and his many grandchildren. He had also become an ardent bird-watcher. My own interests had greatly diversified by then, and I had become much involved in UK governmental affairs. But I was basically a biologist, and I still regret that I never spoke with Tooey in those last years of his about the new interest that had filled his declining years – ornithology.

Sadly the antipathies that existed during the war between US and UK members of the Allied staff commands, and which were never too far from the surface, started to colour even the earliest historical accounts of what had happened in the years of conflict. They continue to do so. Published records of Montgomery's argument with Eisenhower about how the final western push into Germany should be made had led to a total breach between the two men. Tooey published reviews of Montgomery's autobiography, and also the one published by Field-Marshal Lord Alanbrooke, the British Army Chief of Staff during most of the war, and a man who strongly supported Montgomery. 'How the Allies managed to win the Second World War,' so one of the two reviews began, 'handicapped as they were by American generals, is a mystery.' Tooey, however, said that he was not interested in 'might-have-beens' – whether if so-and-so had been in command, or it would have been better if we had done this rather than that. He declared that he had not bothered to read what the post-war US Bombing Survey Unit had written about the strategic air war. Tedder, who died in 1967, had published his autobiography *With Prejudice* the preceding year. I never did ask Tooey what he felt about Tedder's book, or even if he had read it.

TWO ADMIRALS

*   *   *

Admiral Earl
Mountbatten of Burma

Admiral Hyman G. Rickover

Admiral of the Fleet Earl Mountbatten of Burma

1900–1978

The Man of All Ambitions

* * *

Admiral of the Fleet Earl Mountbatten of Burma was the quintessential admiral: he was tall, handsome and radiated confidence. Admiral Rickover, the father of the American nuclear navy, was the antithesis of this. Where Rickover never set out to please, except for a chosen few, Mountbatten invariably did, the humble and lofty alike. Where Rickover did not hesitate to shout and abuse, Mountbatten masked determination with charm, finesse and, when needed, guile.[1] And where Rickover had only one goal in mind, a single-minded determination to build and control a nuclear navy, Mountbatten, in addition to his greatest ambition to achieve the highest command in the Royal Navy, always had many. Their dissimilarities were legion. Where the two were alike was that, apart from being the same age, both possessed endless drive and stores of energy; that they respected each other; and that in their different ways they succeeded in making enemies. The Second World War proved the springboard that launched both into worlds of experience of which they could never have dreamt before.

Dickie Mountbatten was a 'Royal'. His connection with the British monarchy derived from the marriage of Queen Victoria's daughter, Alice, to Grand Duke Louis IV of Hesse, whose daughter Victoria had in turn married Dickie's father, Prince Louis of Hesse. Dickie was thus one of Queen Victoria's great-grandsons. Prince Louis's father, Alexander, had married a commoner and had been accorded by his nephew, Duke Louis, the title Prince of Battenberg.

Dickie's father, Louis, was Alexander's eldest son, and with a strong desire to follow a naval career, he was allowed by Queen Victoria to

---

1. But according to John Barratt (John Barratt with Jean Ritchie, *With the Greatest Respect*, London: Sidgwick & Jackson, 1991), who was Mountbatten's secretary and personal general factotum for some fourteen years, his employer frequently lost his temper with his domestic staff over the most trivial matters.

131

assume British nationality and to enter the Royal Navy, of which years later, and essentially through professional merit, he became its head – in those days a position styled First Sea Lord. It was a sad day for the family when, shortly after the start of the First World War, public pressure forced him to resign office because of his German origins. The family name was then changed from Battenberg to Mountbatten, and Prince Louis became Marquess of Milford Haven.

He had two daughters and two sons, the elder George, the younger Louis, known to his family and friends as Dickie. One of Dickie's sisters became the second wife of King Gustaf of Sweden, the other married Prince Andrew of Greece, and their son, Prince Philip (Dickie's nephew), in due course married the future Queen of England, Elizabeth II. One of Prince Louis's sisters, and so Dickie Mountbatten's aunt, married Tsar Nicholas II, and shared his fate after the Russian Revolution in 1917. Both George and Dickie – who was styled Lord Louis Mountbatten when the family name changed – followed their father into the Navy, and George, the senior by eight years, served throughout the First World War. He died in 1938.

The Playboy and the Professional

Dickie entered the Royal Naval College, Osborne, as a cadet at the age of twelve, three years after Patrick Blackett. From Osborne, where he was tormented because of his German connections and his father's forced resignation from the Royal Navy, he moved to the more senior naval college at Dartmouth, and from there to the Navy's engineering college, out of which he passed top of his class. In 1916 he was posted as a midshipman to Admiral Beatty's flagship, the battle-cruiser *Lion*, in which he had his first taste of action at sea. The *Lion* was not hit, but two of her accompanying destroyers were sunk. Dickie was then moved, first to the *Queen Elizabeth*, and from her to a two-month stint in a submarine. Finally, as a sub-lieutenant, he was posted to a torpedo-boat of which he was given command as the war came to an end.

Like Patrick Blackett, Dickie was one of four hundred naval officers who in 1919 were sent to Cambridge because their education had been interrupted by the war. But unlike Blackett he was there for only some six months, during which he spent little time at lectures. He took part, however, in many debates, including some in the Union, and he is also reputed to have become mildly left of centre politically, largely as a result of the influence of a fellow-undergraduate, Peter Murphy, whose close friend he remained until the latter's death in 1966. Dickie once told me that he had read Karl Marx, but I took this with a pinch of salt. When in India in 1920 during a tour with his second cousin, the Prince of Wales, he became engaged to Edwina Ashley, who was staying with the Viceroy, the Earl (later Marquess) of Reading. Dickie and Edwina had met frequently before and had long decided to get married, so that their engagement came as no surprise to anyone. Lady Reading, however, wrote to Edwina's father to say that she had hoped his daughter 'would have cared for someone older, with more of a career before him'. Edwina was the granddaughter of Sir Ernest Cassel, an immensely rich Jewish banker who had been Edward VII's financial adviser, and through whom she inherited a considerable fortune, a large London house, the Broadlands Estate in Hampshire, and Classiebawn Castle in Ireland. According to Philip Ziegler, Dickie's official biographer,[2] he then had a personal income of about £600 a year, half of which he earned as a naval officer.

After his marriage, and until the start of the Second World War in 1939, Dickie divided his time between rich living and his career as a sailor. Publicly, as Ziegler writes, he was regarded as a polo-playing playboy, a man who enjoyed fast cars, travel and entertaining, and who was fascinated by Hollywood where, among others, he made friends with Charlie Chaplin and the Douglas Fairbanks family. Marriage with Edwina had its ups and downs, but regardless of a host of diversions, Dickie never allowed his luxurious life and marital troubles to jeopardize his professional career. He served in a number of ships, and when given command of an old destroyer called the *Wishart*, he transformed her into the most efficient ship in the Mediterranean fleet. His officers and men were devoted to him – unlike, as is noted later, what happened to Rickover when he tried to brighten up the *Finch*, the only ship that he was ever to command. For some years signals became Dickie's speciality. He taught for a short spell at the Royal Navy's signal school and in the early thirties became chief wireless officer in the Mediterranean fleet. Dickie loved gadgetry and he set about improving a 'station-keeping' device invented by the French to help ships keep their distance apart when sailing 'in line abreast'. An old naval friend of mine, into whose ship Dickie's improved version of the equipment was first fitted, told me that Dickie himself supervised every step of the installation.

2. Philip Ziegler's comprehensive biography of Mountbatten was published in 1985 (*Mountbatten*, London: Collins). Mountbatten's story has also been told by Richard Hough (*Mountbatten*, London: Weidenfeld & Nicolson, 1980) and by Alden Hatch (*The Mountbattens*, New York: Random House, 1965). Antony Lambton's *The Mountbattens* (London: Constable, 1989) presents a picture of Dickie's early years which is dominated by the theme that Dickie was on the one hand deeply bruised by the 'disgrace' suffered by his father when he was forced to resign as First Sea Lord, and on the other by an obsession about his royal status, and in particular, about the genetic superiority of the Hesse blood.

Between 1936 and 1939 Dickie was a member of the Naval Air Division of the Admiralty and helped in the political manoeuvring to create a Fleet Air Arm independent of the RAF. During this period of headquarters service he also launched the Royal Naval Film Corporation. Cinematography was one of his passions, and one of his contemporaries told me that in those days it was his strongest naval interest. Being based in London, he found it easy to meet and make friends with prominent politicians of the day, among them Anthony Eden, whose critical views about Neville Chamberlain's 'appeasement' policies towards Hitler he fully shared.

More important, his shore job allowed him to oversee the final stages of the building of the destroyer *Kelly*, of which he was slated to take command. When war broke out a year later, he was given command, with the rank of captain, of the destroyer flotilla to which the *Kelly* belonged, but his performance as a flotilla leader led his superiors to judge him as lacking in 'sea sense'. Whatever it was that he lacked, it was certainly not courage. He sought battle wherever and whenever he could. The *Kelly* was mined, torpedoed and all but sunk in the North Sea. After he had managed to get her to port, and while waiting for her to be repaired, he saw equally dramatic action as head of another destroyer flotilla, which it is also said he handled with greater dash than tactical skill. His new ship *Javelin* was hit by torpedoes, its bow and stern blown off, and some fifty of her crew killed. After the *Kelly* had been repaired, he was posted to the Mediterranean, again in command of a destroyer flotilla. In a fierce action during the withdrawal of British and Australian troops from Crete, the *Kelly* was blown apart by bombs. Half her crew went down with her.

Dickie handled all these mishaps with the panache of a man who did not know how to lose control. His men had unflinching confidence in him. He was the last to leave the *Kelly*, and having managed to reach one of the ship's rafts, he swam around to pull to safety poor swimmers and sailors who, because of injury, could barely keep afloat – all this while German aircraft were strafing them. He and the other survivors were picked up by another of the flotilla's destroyers. After he had been landed at Alexandria, he arranged to see Air Chief Marshal Sir Arthur Tedder, who had to explain to him how it was that the RAF was not around to beat off the German aircraft that had caused his ships so much damage.

When back in the UK, Dickie was offered, and accepted, command of the aircraft-carrier *Illustrious*, which was then undergoing repairs in the United States, where Dickie was sent, together with Edwina, on what proved to be a highly successful propaganda tour, one in which he wooed both the mighty, including President Roosevelt, and the less mighty. Without any warning, he was then ordered back to the UK, to head up the Commando organization that Winston Churchill had established after the fall of France, and whose first chief, Sir Roger Keyes, a fearless First World War admiral, Churchill dismissed summarily in late October of 1940. In appointing Dickie, the Prime Minister set out for him as the new CCO (Chief of Combined Operations) the duties he would have to discharge in harassing German positions, but under the 'general direction of the Chiefs of Staff' – whom Keyes, when CCO, had always tried to bypass. Dickie became a junior member of the Chiefs of Staff Committee.

Chief of Combined Operations

I met him for the first time some six months after his appointment as CCO, when he invited me to join his staff at Combined Operations Headquarters (COHQ) as a scientific adviser. By then he had transformed the organization, and it was easy to sense that one personality dominated the whole building which we occupied: Dickie's. Professional officers mingled with wartime officers, as well as with socialite figures, for some senior members of the staff were old personal friends of his. There was the Marquis de Casa Maury, whom he made head of intelligence. Casa Maury was a wealthy member of Dickie's pre-war playboy set. The organizer of *matériel* was Sir Harold Wernher, a rich, good-looking man and a brother-in-law of George, Dickie's brother. Wernher and George had married sisters. In the shadows was Peter Murphy, with whom he had always kept in touch.

I was placed with two other scientific advisers under Captain Tom Hussey, who headed a division that looked after all technical innovations, from the most trivial, such as a spring-loaded walking-stick designed by Sir Malcolm Campbell, the racing driver, to test the hardness of the sand of a beach, to vast undertakings such as *Mulberry*, the artificial harbour, and *Pluto*, the cross-Channel underwater oil pipeline, both of which were to prove critical for the invasion of France in 1944. Hussey was another of the Combined Operations' staff who had long been a friend of Dickie. He told me he had been one of the officers charged with the task of seeing that Dickie and his cousin the Prince of Wales did not 'get into trouble' during the course of the world tours they had made in the twenties.

Geoffrey Pyke, the first scientific adviser whom Dickie appointed, was a highly cultivated man with a quick mind and boundless imagination. He was not a professional scientist and had been introduced to Dickie by Leo Amery, a First World War cabinet minister, who will be remembered in the history books as the man who, after the humiliating withdrawal of British forces that had landed in the spring of 1940 in northern Norway, called upon Neville Chamberlain to resign the prime ministership, using the memorable words of Cromwell to the Long Parliament: 'You have sat too long here for any good you have been doing. Depart, I say, and let us have done with you. In the name of God, go.'

As well as Pyke, Dickie decided to recruit professional scientists who were already engaged in war work. He approached Sir Henry Tizard who, in addition to being scientific adviser to the Chief of the Air Staff, was then the chairman of an unofficial group of 'top' scientists who were working in the service departments. Tizard suggested that he should invite Desmond Bernal, the Cambridge crystallographer with whom I was then working in the Ministry of Home Security in the analysis of the destruction caused by German bombs, he focusing on the physical aspects, I on casualties and social effects. In replying to Mountbatten, Bernal proposed that since he and I were working as a team, he should invite the two of us, a suggestion which Dickie accepted. Our appointments were not full time, both of us carrying on with the work we had been doing for the Ministry of Home Security.

What struck me when I was ushered into Dickie's office a few days later was not just his good looks and bearing, but his absolute lack of 'side' – there was nothing stand-offish about him and none of the aura of self-importance I had encountered in some senior officers with whom I had been asked to discuss the analyses I had made of the effectiveness of different types of bomb and shell. However much Dickie took pride in his royal connections, and whatever use he made of them, Geoffrey Pyke was not far off the mark when he penned these words about Dickie as Chief of Combined Ops:

> Snobbery – by which in such a case is meant what the Americans call 'snootiness' – is a violation of his [Mountbatten's] vitality . . . to him an hour with an enthusiastic mechanic, or for that matter a stevedore, or scientist, or barrister, who will expand his personality by giving him an insight into their subject, their trade union or professional organisation, even their individual ambitions and fears, is more attractive than an hour of the laborious artificial laughter which constitutes so much of the social life of all of us. . . .[3]

He added that Mountbatten, while 'so quick in thought that few can get there before him . . . is almost, though not quite, inhibited from contemplation'.

Dickie paid the closest of attention to everything that went on in his HQ: the planning and organization of small cross-Channel raids, the training of Commandos at their base in Scotland, and the development of new weaponry and gadgetry for which Tom Hussey's department was responsible. He was in total command, enthusing everybody, and making

3. Quoted in David Lampe, *Pyke: The Unknown Genius*, (London: Evans, 1959).

even those who were doing the most trivial things feel that what they were doing was essential to the success of Combined Ops. He was tireless. One evening when I was summoned to his small office I found him rocking on his feet with fatigue but still as interested and enthusiastic as ever. I seem to remember that he had spent the previous night in a train coming down from Scotland, where he had been dealing with some problem that concerned landing-craft. His flag-officer or naval aide, a Royal Naval Volunteer Reserve officer by name the Earl of Antrim – Ran to his friends – was with him. The train was crowded, but a small compartment with two bunks had been reserved for the CCO. Ran had gone out to the loo and returned with a smile on his face, saying that he had just squeezed past a 'brown job', as sailors referred disparagingly to soldiers, 'a brown job major-general who it is nice to think will be standing in the corridor all the way to London'. No he won't, said Dickie, you will. Send him in. Ran, whose lack of awe for his master was usually amusingly evident, was still a little affronted when he laughingly told me the story the following day. Combined Ops was a happy place, and friends one made there remained friends for life.

What Pyke did not note about Dickie as CCO was that the war had erased the pre-war image of the rich-living playboy. Nor did he note that when it came to technical gadgetry, Dickie's sense of priorities, like his own, was inclined to go astray. His fascination with exotic ideas was boundless, and while he was rarely, if indeed ever, their originator, he was certainly the driving force behind all the technical developments for which Combined Ops became responsible. For example, the idea of artificial harbours had been under investigation well before he became CCO, and many were to have a hand in the development of what became the immense breakwaters of block-ships and concrete caissons which for more than two months became the artificial harbour through which reinforcements and supplies were sent to the Allied forces that had landed on the Normandy coast early in June 1944. But without Dickie's enthusiasm, the disparate parts that made up the *Mulberry* harbour probably would not have been got ready as rapidly as they were.

One grandiose idea by which Dickie was carried away was the notion that giant aircraft-carriers could be built out of ice. This project was the most monumental of Geoffrey Pyke's brainchildren. Pyke's mind was of a kind that instinctively attracted Dickie. He had already invented a fast snowmobile to deal with the snows of northern Norway, on the assumption that British forces would return there after their disastrous withdrawal in 1940. When in Canada with Tom Hussey supervising some work on this project, Pyke sent Dickie a fat report entitled *Habbakuk* in which he set out the idea of building a giant aircraft-carrier, the hull of which, made of reinforced ice 30 feet thick, would be about half a mile long – big enough to accommodate several squadrons of aircraft. No torpedo could sink the vessel, and even though it would cruise at only a few knots, it would be virtually impregnable. Pyke's report included a few pages on which he had written witty messages to Dickie who, having scanned it, passed it to Major-General Wildman-Lushington, a Royal Marines officer who was his Chief of Staff, with a request that, after he had read it, it should be passed to Bernal. As Bernal was away from the office it was handed to me. I returned it with the comment that my own experience did not permit of any opinion other than the general one that the idea of a vast ice-ship, if ever it could be implemented, was probably more suitable for times of peace than of war. Bernal read it, and he reported favourably. Dickie then felt justified in approaching Winston Churchill, whom he had no difficulty in infecting with his own enthusiasm for the idea.

A highly secret Habbakuk Committee was set up, and Dickie told me that I was to be a member. I attended only the first meeting. Apart from a few regular officers, among the others who were present were Lord Cherwell, Churchill's personal scientific adviser, Bernal, and Charles Goodeve, a physical chemist who was Deputy Controller for Research and Development at the Admiralty. Pyke was in America at the time. Neither Cherwell nor Goodeve showed any enthusiasm for *Habbakuk*, and Goodeve's dampening comments angered Dickie considerably. He would, he said, put in a complaint to Goodeve's superiors.

When the meeting broke up, I asked to be excused from the committee. I was, however, invited to take part in one more meeting. In order to speed the investigation of the properties of fortified ice, Bernal had recruited Max Perutz, a brilliant young refugee scientist who had worked with him in the Cavendish Laboratory at Cambridge and who, like him, was interested in the structure of molecules. Perutz's achievements in this field were later to win him a Nobel Prize. By the time Pyke returned from North America, a considerable amount of work had therefore been carried out to further his idea but, as usual, he was dissatisfied. He was then living in a friend's flat, and being ill in bed with jaundice, he insisted that a meeting should be held in his room. I have memories of a most extraordinary conference with Dickie, Wernher, Tom Hussey, Bernal and myself all seated round the foot of Pyke's bed. Dickie tried to assure him that work was proceeding as fast as it possibly could. Pyke was not satisfied. 'Without faith,' he kept protesting, 'nothing will come of this project.' 'But I have faith,' replied Dickie. 'Yes,' said Pyke, 'but have the others got faith?', and, turning to Harold Wernher he asked solemnly: 'Have you got faith, Brigadier?' Poor Wernher did not know what to say, but before he could utter a word, Dickie had chipped in: 'Wernher's on my staff to see that I am not over-lavish with my own faith.'

In spite of a considerable expenditure of resources, the project came to nothing. It did, however, take up more and more of Bernal's time. He was in attendance at the Quebec Conference in the summer of 1943, at which Dickie gave a striking demonstration of the properties of Pykrete, as the reinforced ice was by then called. Having shown the Combined Chiefs of Staff that a block of Pykrete, unlike one of ice, could not be shattered with an axe, he drew a pistol and fired first at a block of ice, which the bullet penetrated, and then at the Pykrete, off which the bullet bounced, fortunately not hitting any of the distinguished company. Bernal, at Winston Churchill's request, then had to demonstrate to President Roosevelt that Pykrete melted far more slowly than ice when put into hot water.

But if the President became convinced by all this, his Chiefs of Staff remained sceptical. They were accordingly instructed to prepare a paper setting out the precise nature of their objections. After his return to London from the conference, Dickie told me that, realizing that the American chiefs were not fully informed about the pros and cons of the project, Bernal had offered to help their staff in drafting the paper, and that his offer had been accepted. Bernal usually – though certainly not always – knew both sides to a question. But his initiative on this occasion was brought to Winston Churchill's attention. He was not amused. 'Next time you come with me to a high-level conference,' he told Dickie, 'you come without your scientific advisers.'

Years later, after both Pyke and Bernal were dead (Pyke committed suicide not long after the war ended), Max Perutz asked me whether I knew why enthusiasm for the *Habbakuk* project had waned. I told him that in my opinion it had started waning from the moment Dickie had left Combined Ops to become Supreme Allied Commander South-East Asia. When I later told Dickie about Perutz's question, he said that the reason was that Portugal had made the Azores available to the Allies as a staging-post, and that iceberg carriers were no longer needed. Knowing Dickie as I did, I still think the answer I gave Perutz was the right one. Had Dickie continued to serve in London, he would have gone on pressing for *Habbakuk*. It was too grand an idea for him to abandon.

As a non-technically minded biologist I was no help to Dickie with the 'hardware' side of Combined Ops. I was first asked to estimate the number of nights in a month when the phase of the moon, the tides and the wind would permit of small Commando raids across the Channel. I collected what data there were about past weather conditions, and then, with help from my Oxford staff, started calculating. It took a month – there were no electronic computers in those days – and I then reported to Dickie the useless conclusion that there would never be a night suitable for a small raid. I was put on to the job of devising compressed and dehydrated rations, and was asked to enquire how night vision could be improved. He then got me to take part in the training of a small group of Royal Marines who, under the command of Major 'Blondie' Hasler, were preparing to make a hazardous canoe raid on enemy shipping in the Gironde, north of Bordeaux. Other than Hasler, I never saw any of them again. Launched from a submarine close to the mouth of the Gironde, disaster struck from the start. Some were drowned, others were captured and shot on the spot (this was one of the war crimes that emerged at the Nuremberg trials), and only Hasler and one Marine managed to find their way to Spain and from there back to the UK.[4]

Neither Bernal nor I had anything to do with the planning of the much bigger and disastrous Commando raid on Dieppe, an operation in which Canadian forces suffered grievous losses. Dickie never ceased to feel deeply about the disaster. It was one thing for him to share the perils of the sea with his men. It was another to be held responsible for a plan that was not wholly the product of Combined Ops, and for a shambles in which he himself had not fought. As a member of the Chiefs of Staff Committee, he none the less shared the responsibility for the operation.[5] He organized a comprehensive enquiry to see what lessons could be learnt from the operation, of which the basic, and in retrospect obvious one was that a frontal assault on a defended harbour on the north coast of France was not a way to secure a beach-head for the reoccupation of mainland Europe. The purpose of the post-mortem, Dickie said, was 'not tears, but lessons learnt. We have lost nothing if we have learnt these lessions, everything if we have not'. He had refused a request from Bernal and me to watch the operation from one of the ships that were engaged. When we protested that journalists were being allowed to do what we wanted, he merely said that they could be more easily spared than his scientific advisers. We were given minor parts to play in the post-mortem, Bernal reporting on the vulnerability of landing-craft, and I analysing the nature of the injuries suffered by the wounded and of such dead as were returned, so as to determine which enemy weapons had caused most casualties.

Not long after Bernal and I joined him, Dickie had issued an order which said that he had 'decided that the two Scientific Liaison Officers, Professor Bernal and Professor Zuckerman, should be allowed to act as Scientific

4. The story of this daring and tragic raid has been told by C.E. Lucas Phillips in a book called *Cockleshell Heroes* (London: Heinemann, 1965). It was also successfully made into a feature film.
5. The history of the Dieppe raid is still a matter for dispute. The total responsibility is laid on Dickie's shoulders in a recent book by B.L. Vella (*Unauthorised Action: Mountbatten and the Dieppe Raid*, Oxford: OUP, 1990) who, as the title implies, claims that the operation was laid on without proper authority.

observers at the meetings of the planning syndicates, each taking a different operation in turn. This is an experiment to which I attach great importance as I am anxious to link up the scientists from the very beginning of operational planning so that when their scientific knowledge is required, they may be completely in the picture'.

Bernal was far too busy with *Habbakuk* and other hardware projects to participate in this kind of work. The first call made on me by Dickie was to devise a bombing plan for a Commando operation he was planning for the temporary reoccupation of the Channel Island of Alderney – there were reasons other than its proximity to Cherbourg for not considering its permanent recapture. The proposed operation was condemned by the Chiefs of Staff as one of Dickie's impractical and wilder ideas, and was fortunately cancelled. Probability calculations based on the figures I had been given for the bombing accuracy of the aircraft that were going to be employed indicated that barely a handful of bombs would hit the island itself, let alone the guns that had to be silenced. Planning for the operation was reinstated some months later, by when I had refined the methods I had used to calculate what a given force of bombers whose accuracy of bombing was known could achieve when they aimed at precise targets. It, too, was cancelled. But the methods were not. They were used about a year later in the planning of the Pantelleria operation, to which I have already referred.

Then at the end of 1942 Dickie sent Bernal and me to the Middle East. As though it were a straightforward task, he wanted us to find out why the Desert Air Force had failed to destroy Rommel during his retreat from El Alamein! There were also a number of other matters into which it was thought we could inquire. As it happened, Bernal was whisked off a few days after we reached Cairo. Dickie had sent a message asking him to go to Canada to deal with some problem related to *Habbakuk*. Left on my own I was able during the two and a half months that I was away to carry out a number of studies, in particular the one I did of the effects of our air attacks on Tripoli.

Dickie was much interested in all that I had to tell on my return and, like Tedder, particularly in my account of the difference between what intelligence sources had been saying about the results of our bombing of Tripoli and its harbour when it was a supply centre for the Axis forces, and what had actually happened. He began to see me as a planner, and not as a 'nuts-and-bolts' man, and so got me to write an account of the role that the air should play in combined operations.

Before many weeks had passed, he received a signal from Air Marshal James Robb, who had left COHQ, where he had been Deputy CCO for Air, to join Tedder and Spaatz in Algiers, saying that I was wanted back urgently. Dickie did not tell me why, but over lunch at his house with him and Edwina he advised me that, if one were offered me, I was not to accept any rank in the Royal Air Force. They wouldn't make you more than an air vice marshal, he said, and then you'd have to address air marshals as sir, adding, you don't even call me sir. This was the first time we were together on a personal and friendly basis, and the first of the few times I met Edwina.

We next met at the start of the Allied invasion of Sicily. He had flown out to witness the launch of the operation and had spent a night in Tooey Spaatz's villa at La Marsa. Tooey, as I had said, had 'adopted' me as a member of his mess, and with Tedder's encouragement had involved me in the planning of the air operations for the invasion. Dickie left the dinner early, taking me to his room for a long talk.

He was no longer in London when I returned from my second tour in the Mediterranean. He had left for Ceylon as Supreme Allied Commander South-East Asia, keeping both Bernal's and my name on his books as scientific advisers. Bernal paid one visit to Ceylon, but I never joined him. The proposal did not seem as exciting as my involvement with Tedder in the planning of the air operations associated with the Allied landings in Normandy, and in the subsequent battles that led to the defeat of Hitler's Germany.

The Years Between

The next time I met Dickie was in the summer of 1946, when he was given an honorary degree at Oxford. We had run into each other during the course of the day, and I was at the traditional dinner that is given by Christ Church as the finale to the day's ceremonies. When the after-dinner speeches had ended, he beckoned to me and asked whether I could slip away to the room where he was spending the night. I first took him to a friend's house immediately opposite the main gate of the college, but after ten minutes or so I saw that meeting a new lot of strangers bored him even more than the dinner had seemed to do. We went to his room where we talked long into the night, about the war, about the enormous problems that it had left behind, and about what his future was to be. He wanted to return to the Navy, but other ideas had been mooted, such as his becoming Governor-General of Australia. The one job that he felt that he could have done was that of prime minister, but that office had been closed to him because of his royal connections. He and Edwina would have known how to handle the settling of ex-servicemen, and so on and so on. He talked as though there was nothing that he could not do. Anyhow, Attlee was already Prime Minister and that was that.

A few months later Dickie was appointed successor to General Lord Wavell as Viceroy of India, with the formidable task of bringing Britain's responsibility for the subcontinent to an end by the middle of 1948. I wrote to congratulate him and to offer my best wishes. He acknowledged my note saying that if he were to succeed he needed the good wishes of all his friends.

The next time I remember our meeting was in 1951, at a cocktail party given in Admiralty House by the First Lord of the Admiralty (as the minister in charge of the Royal Navy was still called). Dickie was then serving a stint as a member of the senior naval staff, and was in charge of transport and supplies. My main Whitehall concern at the time was the Government's Advisory Council on Scientific Policy. He drew me aside, and we had a long talk about many things, but particularly about the sorry state of the country. Because of ill-health, Ernie Bevin had been replaced by Herbert Morrison as Foreign Secretary, and he, said Dickie, was no good. Attlee, the Prime Minister, was sick, and Aneurin Bevan, the Minister of Health, who had been daggers drawn about public expenditure with the Treasury – in particular about a proposed increase in the defence budget and a decrease in that of health – had resigned. Dickie was immensely worried, and I was not surprised when he again said that with all his political experience, he might have made a better job of leading the country than had Attlee, whose government neither of us guessed was just about to fall. Another thing that worried him was the rumour that the US was about to test a 'super-bomb' in the Pacific, and he was fearful lest a 'chain reaction' would be triggered in that vast ocean. I assured him that it was inconceivable that any such test would be contemplated if there were even the remotest possibility of that happening.

In 1954, after another spell at sea, Dickie, not the most popular choice among his peers, was appointed First Sea Lord, the post that his father had been compelled to relinquish in 1914. One day in 1957 he asked me to call on him. He had something he wished to discuss. It turned out to be what he styled 'broken-back warfare'. There would be a nuclear war; there would be immense destruction; how could the UK be provided with the supplies it needed from overseas if it lacked a strong navy? A government paper on defence that was in preparation was going to suggest that, were a global nuclear war to break out, there would be no point in having a navy. Would I go away and think about the problem. I did, and had no answer. I did not start to delve into the subject of nuclear conflict until a year or two after this talk.

The four years that Dickie served as the Royal Navy's Chief of Staff were stormy. There was the disastrous Suez operation, in which he would have been expected to have followed the orders of Anthony Eden, the Prime Minister, instead of arguing against the operation both on military and political grounds. Ziegler quotes a letter that Dickie sent Field-Marshal Sir Gerald Templer, his opposite number in the Army and who was all for action, in which he wrote that military force was of no avail in a conflict against an invisible enemy. One cannot 'fight ideas with troops and weapons. The ideas and the problems they create are still there when you withdraw the troops'. Dickie felt this deeply. He had the experience of the partition of India behind him. Gerald Templer, a forthright general with a brilliant fighting record, thought he knew better. He had put down a lengthy and dispersed insurrection by communists who were trying to take over Malaya. In so far as Eden insisted that the Suez operation should go ahead, Templer's views prevailed against those of Dickie.

But Dickie was right. Suez turned out to be a military shambles and a political disaster. Being proved right, however, did not endear him to his fellow Chiefs of Staff, who were aware that, because of the use he made of his social position, ministers other than Eden had been informed about his misgivings. When the ships were already at sea, he wrote to Eden urging him to order the assault convoy back. He also drafted a letter of resignation but, as a serving officer who had to obey orders, he knew that it could not be sent at the time. Ziegler writes that Dickie fully expected that his defiance would lead to dismissal. But within a few days of the start of the actual assault, it was Eden who had to resign. He had had to bow to international pressure and call a ceasefire.

While I can well imagine that the outcome of the Suez operation may have enhanced whatever respect his fellow Chiefs of Staff may have had for Dickie's political judgement, it also sharpened their fears that whenever he wanted he could operate behind their backs. This became very evident when Harold Macmillan succeeded Eden as Prime Minister and appointed Duncan Sandys Minister of Defence, with specific instructions to cut defence expenditure, to reduce service manpower, and to end the independence of the services by bringing them together executively under the Ministry of Defence. The UK's defence policy from now on was not to fight wars but to deter them through the threat of nuclear retaliation, and in particular retaliation by means of ballistic missiles. The day of the manned bomber was to be ended.

Obviously none of the Chiefs of Staff wanted to see his service decimated, and in his efforts to protect the Navy in the subsequent inter-service battle for resources, Dickie succeeded in intensifying the suspicion in which he was held by his colleagues. Gerald Templer is recorded as having said: 'Dickie, you're so crooked, if you swallowed a nail you'd shit a corkscrew.'[6] Dickie was the only one of the Chiefs of Staff who saw

6. According to Denis Healey (*The Time of My Life*, London: Michael Joseph, 1989) the remark was made by Templer to Sandys.

virtue in integration, but integration was to get nowhere during Sandys's term as Minister of Defence.

Chief of the Defence Staff

In mid-1959 Dickie left the Admiralty to become Chief of Defence Staff. At the time I was spending a few months at the California Institute of Technology and was taken aback when I received a letter asking whether I would consider becoming the Chief Scientific Adviser (CSA) to the Ministry of Defence. Dickie was apt to say that the idea was his. In fact the suggestion that I should be approached was made by the permanent secretaries of the War Office and Air Ministry. I was reluctant to surrender the freedom I then enjoyed as a university professor, and months passed before I agreed, but on terms that allowed me to combine my academic and scientific activities with my duties as CSA. Dickie frequently told a story – once at a public luncheon – that I accepted the invitation only after I had gone round to his house for a latish supper, and that when I still refused to say yes, he took hold of one of my hands and Edwina the other when we were standing on the pavement outside their front door, tugging away until I agreed. The tugging certainly took place, but it was not because of that that I finally agreed. It was all very flattering, with Edwina saying that Dickie needed me if he was to make a success of his job as CDS. But neither Duncan Sandys, then Minister, nor the university, had yet agreed (which in the end they did) that I could fill two full-time jobs, even if I took a salary from only one.

When I joined the Ministry of Defence in January 1960, Dickie had already been there for some six months, and Harold Watkinson had replaced Sandys as Minister. Dickie's previous post as First Sea Lord had been taken by Admiral Sir Charles Lambe, a close friend from the days when they were boys at Osborne. Lambe was also one of the few to whom he listened, but unfortunately he was a sick man and was seldom around, dying of a heart attack some six months later. The two other Chiefs were Templer – always suspicious of Dickie – and Air Chief Marshal Sir Dermot Boyle, the head of the RAF, who was equally so.

Ziegler writes that soon after becoming CDS Dickie invited the three Chiefs of Staff to his country house, Broadlands, for a weekend in order to persuade them that the Ministry of Defence needed a full-time director of plans to chair a Joint Planners Committee. Templer was opposed, and Dermot Boyle bluntly told his host that he considered his appointment as CDS 'the greatest disaster that has befallen the British Defence Services within memory'. Dickie was trying 'to substitute the authority of a single man for the collective responsibility of the Chiefs of Staff'. Boyle may well have been echoing Tedder's views on the subject.

Small wonder it was that when Air Chief Marshal Sir Thomas Pike succeeded Boyle, he too was always suspicious of Dickie. Dickie was, however, more fortunate in Templer's successor, General Sir Francis Festing, an amiable giant of a man. Festing had been a divisional commander in South-East Asia when Dickie was Supreme Commander, and admired him greatly. When Lambe died, his place was taken by Admiral Sir Caspar John, a son of Augustus, the painter. Ziegler writes that while Caspar John had got on well with Dickie in the Admiralty, and while generally agreeing with him on matters of policy, he not only disliked Dickie's 'theatricality' when he became CDS but found his 'tactics often devious, if not dishonest'.[7]

Dickie quite unnecessarily added to the wariness with which he was regarded as CDS when he raised the question of his rank. During the war, when he was CCO, his status had been that of a temporary Vice-Admiral. As head of a combined service organization, he had also been accorded honorary and corresponding rank in the Army and the Royal Air Force. As CDS he felt that he should be promoted to five-star rank not only in the Navy but in the other two services – he should be a Field-Marshal and Marshal of the Royal Air Force as well as an admiral of the fleet. The Army and RAF would have none of it. One hostile minute which the Permanent Secretary of the War Office penned to his minister not only advised strongly against what Dickie wanted, but described him as 'probably the most mistrusted of all senior officers in the three services'. In due course Dickie was, not unexpectedly, promoted to five-star rank in the Royal Navy, but both the Army and the Royal Air Force saw to it that his other ambitions came to nothing. Years later, on the occasion when the statue of Dickie that stands in St James's Park was being unveiled, and thinking that he knew the story, I reminded the long-retired Field-Marshal Lord Harding of what had happened. Harding, who had been Templer's predecessor as head of the Army, pretended that he had never heard the story. 'Why,' he said, 'if I had been there I'd have led the cavalry down Whitehall to prevent any such thing happening.'

When Charles Lambe died, Dickie began to treat me as his confidant. He needed someone whom he liked, someone he could trust, with whom he could argue, and on whom he could rely for an honest opinion of encouragement or discouragement about whatever enterprise on which he had it in mind to embark. I think the need intensified after Edwina's death

7. For my own part, I got on easily with Caspar John, who regarded me as a fellow-Bohemian.

in Borneo early in 1960 when as President she was on a tour on behalf of the St John's Ambulance Brigade Overseas. He used to say to me that we had to engender 'the spirit of the hive' in the Ministry, a reference to Maurice Maeterlinck's romantic picture of the way the social life of bees is organized. 'The spirit of the hive' had presumably operated both within his personal staff when he was Supreme Commander South-East Asia, and in his viceregal staff in the difficult days that led up to the partition of India. But no spirit of the hive animated the Chiefs of Staff organization of which he had become the head. Yet this could never have been deduced from the orderly and gentlemanly proceedings of the formal Chiefs of Staff meetings, which Dickie invited me to attend as a matter of course, nor from the informal Chiefs' meetings which staff officers and officials did not attend.

It was not just his wish to centralize power that made his colleagues suspicious of his motives and methods, and what they saw as his irresistible love of intrigue. When Dickie wanted something to happen, big or small, he would use all his wits, his guile, in whatever way seemed appropriate, to get it done. He was not averse to saying to a Chief of Staff, 'I happened to discuss the matter yesterday with the Queen, and she was heartily in favour' of whatever it was that he was after. Ziegler also records an occasion when he tried to scare Sir Ronald Melville, a well-liked Permanent Under-Secretary in the Civil Service, because the task of enquiring into the question of 'functionalizing' the services was not being discharged with the zeal that Dickie thought necessary. He told Melville that he had just seen Harold Wilson, who had become Prime Minister, and whom he had reminded that the responsibility for speeding up the work of 'functionalization' was Melville's, implying that he was not doing his job properly. Melville rang up his Civil Service colleagues in the Prime Minister's private office to see if this was true. It was not. It had been days since Dickie had seen the Prime Minister. This was just Dickie's way. Harmless, almost childish, one might say, but sinister to those who suspected he was up to something they did not like.

I should think that at one time or another, and with the possible exception of Festing, all the Chiefs of Staff who served when Dickie was CDS had reason to believe he had done something behind their backs which he should not have done without their joint assent. In his official biography of Harold Macmillan, Alastair Horne writes that 'On several occasions Dickie reported decisions of the Chiefs of Staff to the Minister of Defence in terms quite contrary to what had actually been decided.' Knowing Dickie as I did, I feel this is a bit of an exaggeration. He was too subtle for that. But that he sometimes gave his colleagues cause for alarm, I had every reason to know.

For example, during the period that he was First Sea Lord, the Royal

Navy had embarked on a vastly expensive project to build a giant aircraft-carrier, but this time not of ice as when he had been CCO. After he became CDS, the Chiefs suspected that he was still promoting the project, despite the fact that, were it to proceed, it would have made an impossible demand on the defence budget. Peter Thorneycroft, who became Harold Watkinson's successor as Minister of Defence in late 1962, had already decided that the project was simply not affordable, and what little money may still have been spent on producing drawings was formally stopped by Denis Healey when he succeeded Thorneycroft. But the suspicion that Dickie had not abandoned the idea persisted. The Army chief might then believe that Dickie was supporting a costly Army project. When it in turn was cancelled, it was all Dickie's doing even if it then transpired that the cancellation was a ministerial decision about which he had barely been consulted.

Perhaps the worst of his troubles about armament concerned an RAF venture to build a strike and reconnaissance aircraft code-named the TSR2, which was in competition with a parallel, but not as sophisticated a design whose development for the Fleet Air Arm was already much further advanced. It was no secret that Dickie favoured the naval project, and that he was a friend of the retired naval officer who was the project manager in the company that had been awarded the contract to produce the machine. Dickie wanted the RAF to accept a modification of the naval aircraft – a perfectly reasonable suggestion if it were technically possible and less costly. The RAF would have none of it. Because of this, I kept well clear of him when I was asked by Watkinson to make an independent review of the two projects. My conclusion was simple. Given that the RAF's operational specifications could not be changed, their project had to stand. But if the operational requirements could be relaxed, which I suggested they might well be, then there was no point in wasting hundreds of millions of pounds on two aircraft when a common design was feasible. The RAF was furious, and unjustifiably suspected collusion between Dickie and me. There had been none. Development of the RAF machine continued, but in the end the TSR2 did not go into production. The money simply was not there. But the Navy got its Buccaneer.

There was another RAF project which undeservedly caused trouble for Dickie, when the fault, if fault there was, was entirely mine. By that time, however, our names had become linked in the press as the 'Zuckbatten Axis', as though the two of us were all-powerful behind the scenes in determining defence policy. Dickie therefore had to share in the trouble into which I ran.

The matter related to the question of which service – the RN or the RAF – was to be the custodian of the UK's nuclear deterrent. Duncan Sandys had based the UK's deterrent policy on a ground-launched nuclear ballistic missile codenamed *Blue Streak*, which his successor, Watkinson, was about to cancel for technical and financial reasons. Those were the days when ideas for new strategic nuclear weapons were springing up in the US like weeds in a neglected garden. By 1960 the US Navy had started to produce nuclear-powered submarines that could launch Polaris nuclear missiles from the deep. The US air forces wanted a nuclear-powered bomber that could launch a nuclear Skybolt from the skies. In early 1960 Harold Macmillan, the Prime Minister, had extracted a promise from President Eisenhower that, as a replacement for Blue Streak, the UK, in order to retain its status as a nuclear power, could purchase either Polaris or Skybolt. Macmillan preferred the latter, since the UK had already invested vast sums in a fleet of heavy bombers which had been designed to carry free-falling nuclear bombs, but which could also be adapted for the air-launched ballistic missile – at that time no more than an R&D programme in its earliest stages. Neither the President nor the Prime Minister knew much about the status of either system, but a provisional agreement was reached that the UK would buy Skybolt if the project were to reach fruition.

The US Air Force chiefs kept feeding those of the RAF rosy news about the progress their project was making. As the Ministry of Defence's chief scientific adviser, it was my responsibility to keep abreast of what was happening, and the information with which I was being provided by the Director of Defense Research and Engineering in the Pentagon, and by his deputy, who was directly responsible to the US Defense Secretary for the project, was far from encouraging. I had a second source of information in Jerry Wiesner, the President's science adviser, and he, like my Pentagon friends, was sure that Skybolt would never materialize. The project was not only highly doubtful technologically but strategically redundant in the light of the rest of the US's vast nuclear weapons programme.

I visited the States several times to see how things were going, and copies of the minutes that I sent back – first to Watkinson and then to Thorneycroft – were passed not only to Dickie, but to Tom Pike, the Chief of the Air Staff. Rumours started to circulate that I was trying to get the US to cancel the Skybolt project so that the UK could buy Polaris for the Royal Navy, the assumption being that Dickie wanted that to happen. In fact he had no part in what was going on, and it was only when he came to realize that the US was likely to cancel Skybolt for their own reasons that he sent me an urgent message (I was on one of my Skybolt visits to Washington) asking me to use my contacts to find out whether the US would sell the UK two Polaris submarines, complete with thirty-two missiles, for £200 million! The Royal Navy had never attempted to find out how much a Polaris fleet would cost, and the figure was utterly unrealistic.

The truth was that neither when he was First Sea Lord nor when he became CDS did Dickie pay any consistent attention to the question whether the Royal Navy rather than the Royal Air Force should be responsible for the maintenance of the UK's status as a strategic nuclear power. Indeed, he had expressed doubts about the wisdom of the UK becoming one. In September 1958 he had joined with Templer in tabling a paper in which they stated that they 'absolutely' opposed the concept of an independent UK nuclear deterrent. Dickie had also declared that an independent British nuclear force would be 'neither credible as a deterrent, nor necessary as part of the Western deterrent'.[8] At the time both were concerned lest Sandys's emphasis on nuclear deterrence would lead to a dangerous run-down of the UK's conventional defences.

Nuclear matters had in fact been remote from his area of responsibility when Dickie was first posted to a major position on the Admiralty staff in 1950, the year when design studies were embarked upon to produce a propulsion plant for the nuclear submarines which the Royal Navy proposed to build. Little progress had been made before 1955, when Admiral Rickover, the head of the US nuclear submarine programme, had spontaneously, but without legal authority, offered to help the RN admiral who was then in charge of submarines.[9]

The part played by Dickie personally in securing Rickover's help in the British nuclear submarine programme is not at all clear, and he certainly did not make it any clearer in some of his later accounts. Dickie had first met Rickover in London in 1956, when he was still First Sea Lord, and in January 1957, a year later, he told Duncan Sandys, the Minister of Defence, that the UK was making so much progress with its own design of a nuclear propulsion plant – Rolls-Royce were the contractors – that the need for 'US help is largely past'.[10] At the end of the year, however, he changed his tune. According to Ziegler a meeting had then taken place between Dickie and Rickover, and the two had struck a deal within 'five minutes', with Rickover agreeing that the UK could buy a complete American plant as a prototype for what the Royal Navy needed. The two men, so Ziegler writes, immediately joined a meeting where all the more senior members of the British nuclear propulsion project team were gathered, in order that Dickie could tell them about the happy conclusion of his five minutes' talk with the American nuclear admiral.

8. Ziegler, op. cit., p. 561.
9. A detailed account of the development of submarine propulsion for the Royal Navy has been provided by Vice-Admiral Sir Ted Horlick (*Proceedings of the Institution of Mechanical Engineering*, Vol. 196, No. 7 [1982]).
10. Ziegler, op. cit., p. 558.

It is difficult to fit this story to the facts. To make the sale possible necessitated the amendment of the US Atomic Energy Act of 1954. The congressional hearings to consider whether this should be done took place in 1958, and the amendment was not passed until July of that year. In the course of his two appearances before the Congressional Committee, Rickover only once referred to Dickie, saying that he understood that Admiral Mountbatten had already told Admiral Arleigh Burke, then the US Chief of Naval Operations, that he was satisfied with the amount of information about nuclear propulsion that the UK was obtaining from the US. In order to prevent his own and his staff's time being taken up by the UK's enquiries, Rickover also informed the committee that early in 1958 he had suggested that the UK should make a 'commercial arrangement' with a US company to buy a complete propulsion plant.

Clearly Dickie could not have concluded the five-minute deal with Rickover in December 1957, six months before Congress made it legally possible for the US to sell the UK the plant it wanted. Rickover was a stickler for the rules, and would certainly not have endangered his relations with Congress because he was impressed by Dickie.[11] Even less does the record substantiate an extraordinary story of Dickie's that was later broadcast in a BBC TV programme. The purchase was allowed, so it was said, because Dickie had prevented the demolition of a house in London in which Eisenhower had stayed in the pre-*Overlord* days of 1944. 'Ike was furious, when I told him,' said Dickie, 'but I prevented it and so we got the propulsion plant.' In the later part of Dickie's life, fancy about the past had a strong tendency to replace the reality.

When the Skybolt débâcle ended at Nassau in December 1962, with President Kennedy agreeing that the UK could purchase the Polaris missile, Dickie had to deal with the silent anger of RAF chiefs who were also still wondering what he was up to about the TSR2, and who, without any justification, saw the whole unhappy Skybolt affair as some deep-seated plot to transfer to the Royal Navy a strategic responsibility which on paper had been theirs. Air Chief Marshal Sir Charles Elworthy (better known as

---

11. This did not prevent him from pulling Dickie's leg. In 1958 Dickie visited the US submarine base at New London and was shown over the *Skipjack* nuclear submarine, as well as over some of Rickover's other installations. At the end of the day, Dickie noted in his tour diary that Rickover in his goodbye had said: '"I can never thank you enough for today's visit. You have shown all my team that there is an Admiral who really does understand nuclear propulsion, can ask intelligent and stimulating questions and is capable of inspiring us on. Couldn't we fuse the USN and the RN into one Service with you as the International Chief?" I thanked him and gently pointed out how impracticable this suggestion was, but told him that I would always be glad of his candid advice and help for British Naval nuclear propulsion.'

Sam) had by then succeeded Pike as CAS. Sam had been one of the first 'unified' commanders to be appointed after Dickie had managed to arrange that all forces deployed overseas should be under one command. One day Dickie came into my room saying: 'Can you believe it, Sam came in to see me, and I said sit down, but he replied, No Sir, and then started to complain about something where he assumed I had gone back on my word. If he had had a cap on, I truly believe he would have saluted.' What Dickie did not tell me is that Sam, according to Ziegler, had called him to his face 'a liar and a cheat'.[12] In due course Sam, a charming man much cleverer than Pike, and not given to losing his temper, became CDS.

Despite the aura of intrigue which he engendered in his dealings with the Chiefs of Staff, Dickie succeeded, where others would have failed, in bringing about a number of far-reaching and valuable changes in the management of defence. A one-star officer was appointed to his staff as Director of Defence Plans. With Watkinson's backing, he succeeded in persuading his colleagues to agree that the officers in command of those forces which the UK still deployed overseas should cease reporting separately to the heads of their services in Whitehall – the Navy chiefs to the Admiralty, the Army commanders to the War Office, and the Air Force commanders to the Chief of the Air Staff. From now on they were to come under unified command, with the regional commanders-in-chief reporting to the Ministry of Defence. One of Dickie's main opponents in this move was General Sir Richard Hull, then the Army commander in the Far East and who, at the end of 1961, succeeded Festing as head of the Army staff. Until Dickie ceased being CDS in 1965, I always had the feeling that Hull would oppose Dickie whenever he could. The two were simply not made for each other. Hull, the son of a general, had begun his Army career in a smart cavalry regiment and, like Caspar John, was not the least bit impressed by Dickie's style.

The establishment of unified commands in overseas theatres was only the prelude to Dickie's main administrative achievement as CDS: the integration of the three services under a single Secretary of State.

The idea behind this far-reaching change was hardly new, but every previous attempt to implement it had failed. During the Second World War, Winston Churchill, following the precedent established by Lloyd George in the Great War, made himself chairman of the Cabinet's Defence Committee and, in effect, the country's generalissimo. Attlee, his successor, deprived the three service ministers of the seats they had traditionally enjoyed in the Cabinet, and appointed one of his Cabinet colleagues as Minister of Defence, to whom they reported, at least on paper. At the

12. Ziegler, op. cit., p. 616.

time, however, this proved to be a futile move, since it did not deprive the services of their right to negotiate their own budgets with the Treasury. In 1957, Harold Macmillan formally announced that Duncan Sandys, the Minister of Defence, was from then on going to have full executive power. He would be authorized to decide all matters that affected the shape, size and deployment of the forces. As it turned out, however, the small ministry over which Sandys presided simply did not have the staff to exercise the authority with which he had been endowed. He did, however, set up a Defence Council, a body that I do not recall ever engaging in any significant discussions of defence policy. As Harold Macmillan noted in his memoirs, what Sandys managed to achieve still meant that 'the system was to remain basically one of co-ordination', with the Chief of Defence Staff having 'no control of his own'.

Dickie was determined that another effort should be made to succeed where Sandys had failed. He waited until Sir Robert Scott had replaced Sir Edward Playfair as the Ministry's Permanent Secretary. Playfair had moved to Defence from the War Office, where he had come to share Templer's suspicions of the changes that everyone knew Dickie had in mind. Scott, on the other hand, had no service loyalties. He had been Commissioner-General in South-East Asia between 1955 and 1957, and, like Dickie, was not averse to flouting tradition. Nor was Peter Thorney-croft, Watkinson's successor as Minister. I, too, could not have been readier for what Dickie had in mind. Some two years before joining the Ministry I had chaired an independent government committee that had been asked to advise on the control of government R&D, and our report had commented adversely on the fact that the existing administrative machinery of government made it impossible to co-ordinate the demands of the three services as they fought for a share of an ever-decreasing supply of R&D resources. The Defence Research Policy Committee, the inter-service organization that I had to chair when I became the Ministry's chief scientific adviser, was impotent in preventing waste and duplication. As I saw it, the only possible cure, if a cure were ever going to be possible, was for authority on defence expenditure to be vested in a single Minister of Defence. That was what Dickie also wanted.

He set his staff to prepare a paper that laid out the broad lines of the organization that would be needed in order to achieve the executive integration of the services. He then started to discuss the subject with the Chiefs of Staff, who to begin with tried to dissuade him by commenting that the idea of integration was all very well but that it would never work with any CDS other than himself. 'They tried to flatter me,' he told me bitterly. 'They don't realize that I am above flattery.'

As soon as the staff paper was ready, Thorneycroft arranged that it should be discussed with the Prime Minister. The meeting took place on a Sunday evening in December 1962, with Thorneycroft, Dickie, Rob Scott and myself present. When it ended Thorneycroft was instructed to push ahead under full steam, Macmillan later warning him not to tolerate any opposition and not to be defeated in the way Sandys had been. 'Anyone who raises any objection can go, including ministers.' Over drinks at the end of the meeting, the Prime Minister teased Dickie because of his single-minded concern about the powers that a CDS should have, the PM telling him that there was more to the matter than the bickerings of Chiefs of Staff. 'Why,' he said, 'speaking as an old Grenadier, the good soldier doesn't bother about you people at the top. You'd be lucky if he knew the name of any officer above that of his company commander.' Dickie was not amused.

Later Dickie used to say that the five of us met on successive Sundays to discuss progress and plans. I myself have no recollection of any further meeting, nor have I been able to find any record of any. What I do know is that a great deal of work had to be put in hand, with the Chiefs of Staff commenting both separately and jointly on successive drafts of the paper that the Ministry was preparing for Thorneycroft to lay before Parliament. The Prime Minister then arranged to have it closely studied by two retired generals who had been on Churchill's staff during the war. This done, Parliament debated the proposals in July 1963, and on 1 April 1964, not quite a year and a half after our meeting with the Prime Minister, a new Ministry of Defence came into being under a Secretary of State who was endowed with full executive authority over all matters relating to defence. Thorneycroft remained in charge until October of that year, when the Government was defeated at the polls. Since Dickie retired in July 1965, he had little more than a year in which to enjoy the new regime that he had been so instrumental in bringing about. But again it was not a happy year for him.

Denis Healey, a powerful character whom Dickie had barely met before, had been appointed Secretary of State for Defence when the Labour Government took over. A limit of £2,000 million a year for defence was set by the Cabinet, and Healey had little room for manoeuvre in dealing with the political and industrial problems that this low figure implied. He was also determined to decide his own priorities and to put his own mark on defence policy. On the other hand, Dickie, with less than a year's service ahead of him, was convinced that what had so far been achieved in the reorganization of defence was only a beginning. He wanted Healey to move straight away to the next administrative step, the so-called 'functionalization' of the services to which I have already referred – for example, the establishment of a single intelligence organization for all the services instead of three separate ones (in the end intelligence was the only 'functionalization' that did come about while Dickie was still CDS). Healey, however, was not to be deflected. He set in hand a far-reaching review of the UK's military commitments, focusing on the cuts he would have to make, among them the cancellation of the ill-fated TSR2 fighter-bomber reconnaissance plane on which the RAF had set its heart, and what trivial amount of money as was still being spent in structural designs of a giant aircraft-carrier. Dickie did not understand Healey. He had been accustomed to getting his own way with defence ministers. On occasion he would, for example, say to Watkinson or Thorneycroft: 'About that matter we were discussing, here is a draft of a minute I shall be sending you, and here is one of the reply I should like you to send.' He had no hesitation in using this ploy even in the presence of the Permanent Secretary and myself. Healey would have none of it.

Dickie was then moved from the scene. The Prime Minister asked him to tour Commonwealth countries to persuade their leaders to help stem the strong tide of black immigration that was taking place into the UK. Healey encouraged him to go, and Dickie was away for almost three months. By the time he returned he had barely a month left as CDS and was therefore unable to play any significant part in the defence review which was nearing its end, and which, in the pursuit of economies, elaborated as general policy what was called an 'island strategy', the idea that many of the overseas responsibilities of the RN could in future be discharged by the RAF – given, of course, that the UK had the island bases from which to operate and the aircraft to fly, neither of which condition ever materialized.

On the publication of the review, Christopher Mayhew, the Navy minister, who on one occasion had sparred seriously with Rickover, Admiral Sir David Luce, Caspar John's successor as Chief of the Naval Staff, and Admiral Sir Frank Hopkins, one of Luce's deputies, resigned. I, too, disagreed strongly with what was being proposed, but my differences with Healey merely led to my moving from the Ministry of Defence to the Cabinet Office, where I already had a base, having been appointed by Harold Wilson Chief Scientific Adviser to the Government as a whole as well as to Defence. Aghast at the review, Dickie, although retired, wanted to enter the fray by attacking Healey in what would have been his maiden speech in the House of Lords. With an election looming, I strongly advised him not to do so, since speaking would have involved him in a public argument on a matter that had become an issue of party politics. He accepted my advice, and satisfied himself by sending the Prime Minister a copy of the speech that he would have made.

Nuclear Misgivings

But it was not his arguments with the Chiefs of Staff, nor the major institutional reform of the Ministry that he instigated (reforms go on being made on the foundation that was laid in 1964), nor his reaction to Healey's defence review, which in my opinion made Dickie's tour as CDS enduringly memorable. It was his gradual realization that Nato's nuclear policies were both misconceived and dangerous. Nato's dogma had it that tactical nuclear weapons could be used to redress a presumed inferiority of the conventional forces of the Western Alliance when compared with those of the Warsaw Pact powers. At first, but without having devoted any critical attention to the matter, Dickie had accepted the doctrine, which in fact was no more than *post hoc* rationalization. The story of his conversion is a long one, and I can do no more than give a brief summary of it here.

It began when, with his encouragement, I set in hand the detailed and critical 'war-game' studies to which I have already referred, and which were based on actual Nato plans. They had shown that since the USSR could reply in kind to Nato's nuclear fire, the result of a nuclear battle in Europe would be associated with enormous losses of civilian life, with vast areas transformed into radioactive waste and, what was most important from the view of tactics and strategy, with no military advantage to either side. These were the studies which I had discussed with members of the US President's Science Advisory Committee, as well as with the scientific directorate of the Pentagon. They were also studied by Dickie and his staff as well as by the Chiefs of Staff. Dickie had no hesitation in agreeing the conclusions to which they led. Nor had Caspar John. Pike, and then Sam Elworthy, were more or less neutral – their main interest was focused on strategic nuclear policy. Festing was mildly interested, but Hull, his successor, took the view that my conclusions were based on sentimental feelings about the horrors of destruction. He could not see, or pretended not to see, that any battle in Europe in which both sides used nuclear weapons would grind to a halt within a few days, and in such a state of disorganization that would leave neither side able to conduct controlled military operations.

Convinced that I was right, Dickie encouraged me 'to go public' with my heterodox views at the 1961 annual conference of the military chiefs of the Western Alliance. From then until his retirement in 1965, he continued to challenge Nato nuclear policy. Being Dickie, the man who bore himself like a Caesar, an ex-Supreme Commander of Allied Forces, and a man whose courage and leadership under fire had become part of war history, he was listened to with respect by the other members of the Nato Military Committee. But, and this he could never understand, nothing changed. Nor did anything change when he pointed out that the Cuban missile crisis of 1962 had exposed the fact that the advent of nuclear weapons had made the UK defenceless.

Throughout the week of the Cuban crisis our ambassador in Washington, David Ormsby-Gore, had been keeping Harold Macmillan informed about the exchanges that were going on between President Kennedy and Khrushchev. In the Ministry of Defence business continued as usual until the approach of the weekend when, if the Russians did not agree to remove the warheads and ballistic missiles they had installed in Cuba (at the time there was no certainty that they had sent warheads as well as missiles), the US had made it clear that it would resort to military, and possibly nuclear, action. On the fateful Saturday before the deadline, Thorneycroft summoned Dickie, Rob Scott, the Ministry's Permanent Secretary, myself and the Chiefs of Staff to meet him at nine o'clock the following morning, by when the deadline would have expired. By the time we arrived, Khrushchev had, however, announced on open radio that the Soviet missiles would be removed. We looked at each other across the table, not knowing what to say. Then Dickie spoke up. 'What would we have done if the Russians had not caved in?' he asked. No one answered. 'We've got to work this out,' he went on. 'If nuclear war were ever to break out, what would we do?' He was the only one to put the question, which still remains unanswered. Years later a speech he delivered in Strasbourg on the subject started to make people sit up and to realize what was implied by the concept of nuclear war.

Retirement

Up to the day Dickie retired as CDS at the age of sixty-five, his life had been one of action. He rarely stopped even for a second to ask himself what was next on the day's agenda. It was always full. And so it was to continue after he had retired, but with a big difference. What he had done as a naval officer, as CCO, as Supreme Allied Commander South-East Asia, as Viceroy of India, and as Chief of the Defence Staff, had been determined by the nature of the jobs themselves. To fill his days, he now had to set his own priorities. But although the two of us grew even closer after his retirement than we had been before, I often found them hard to understand, even though I realized how difficult it was for him to reject invitations to appear at functions or to refuse to do jobs he was asked to undertake on behalf of the Government. For example, late in 1966 the spy

George Blake had made a spectacular escape from prison, and Roy Jenkins, then Home Secretary, asked Dickie to head a commission to look into prison security. Dickie said he would take on the job provided that I would help him. Jenkins telephoned to warn me that I would be getting a call from Dickie about an inquiry into prison security he had asked him to undertake, and hoped that I would say yes to whatever request Dickie would make. I had to tell him that I was far too busy with other matters to agree any such thing, but Jenkins then said that I could at least help to get the enquiry off the ground. When Dickie telephoned, I told him the same thing. He protested, but I satisfied him when I undertook to recruit for him a scientist who was much better qualified for the job than I was. I attended the first meetings of his commission and then dropped out. When in due course Dickie presented his report, he expected action to follow. Very little did. Like the immigration enquiry he had taken on during his last year as CDS, the exercise was very much a matter of public relations in which his distinguished name was being used.

Dickie had also started to worry about money.[13] After Edwina died, he suspected that the Broadlands Estate was being run at a loss, and knowing that I had once been chairman of an independent government committee that had concerned itself with agricultural economics, and having told me what was worrying him, he asked me to put him in touch with the best man I knew to advise how to make the estate pay for itself. I did, and presumably good advice was provided, for by the time he retired, Broadlands was, I believe, financially viable. But Dickie still worried about money. A member of the Institution of Electronic and Radio Engineers, an organization in which he had long been interested, persuaded him that the UK needed a national electronics research council. Dickie leapt at the idea, despite my warning that if he managed to attract industrial sponsors, the last thing they would do was share their R&D secrets with each other.

To gain support he invited to dinner the chairmen of some of the larger industrial companies that were concerned, and also the permanent secretaries of the then Ministry of Technology and of the Ministry of Defence. Some of his guests were attracted by his idea, and for a short time he also managed to get the Ministry of Technology (and its successor department) to provide both funds and services. I attended the dinner but declined to participate in his new council. What was more important, I also helped dissuade him from having anything to do with a suggestion that he should be given a large stipend for his services as chairman. It would look terrible, I told him, if it were said that you had set up the National Electronics Research Council just to help line your pocket.

13. According to Barratt, op. cit., money matters had always worried him.

Vice-Admiral Sir Ronald Brockman, a senior military aide who had been with him ever since India, said the same. Dickie accepted our advice. Most of the industrialists who had attended the dinner had done so because of a combination of professional and social interests. They were not going to be left out of a body that might provide some advantage to their competitors and customers. Two of them telephoned me several times after that first dinner meeting to say, please, please, get your friend off my back.

The council survives to this day, but in an attenuated form. During its active days it succeeded in doing some useful things. For example, it managed to arrange that electronic engineering should become a school subject, and it also organized courses for would-be electronic engineers. An annual Mountbatten Lecture was established in 1978. Dickie gave the first. The second, which I delivered the following year, was all but a memorial speech. Dickie had been murdered three months before.

Another of the main ventures that occupied his time and into which he tried to draw me was the United World Colleges, a charity he had set up in order to collect money to establish multinational teenage schools in different countries. In order to persuade me to help, he arranged a small dinner for me to meet some of the people who were already involved, among them the headmaster of St Donat's College in Wales – the core institution of the whole scheme. He also got me to spend two days at the college. But I was not persuaded. As Ziegler records, I wrote to Dickie saying that I was dismayed by the poor level of teaching of science and mathematics. 'This must all be very depressing to you,' I said, 'but I see no point in pulling my punches. . . . Frankly I have a fear that from the point of view of education, Atlantic College [as it was then called] falls between two stools.' It was indeed a depressing letter, retorted Dickie, but science teaching was already good and was rapidly improving. 'It is depressing that one of my greatest friends should have so completely misunderstood what we are doing at St. Donat's.'[14]

I do not think that I did misunderstand. As a professional academic, I judged that the best that Dickie's colleges could achieve would be totally overshadowed by the vast national educational programmes that were under way in all the advanced countries of the world – and in some of the less advanced ones too. I was also dubious about the value of deliberate efforts to produce the 'rounded man', the 'leaders' of the next generation. Cecil Rhodes had set out to do the same thing and on a much grander scale, and I had always felt that the small proportion of Rhodes scholars who had made their mark after their time at Oxford would have done so had they never been there at all. Whatever part of the world from which

14. Ziegler, op. cit., p. 665.

they came, Rhodes scholars were the most outstanding of their generation. But Dickie dismissed all my comments and travelled the world using
his immense prestige to prise money out of any Midas he could persuade.
One with whom he failed was Jock Whitney, whom Dickie had got to
know in his pre-war playboy days, and then when Jock became US
Ambassador to the UK in 1957. Jock was one of a company of rich men
who were invited to a dinner at the White House which Dickie had got the
President – I believe it was Nixon – to arrange. When not long after I saw
Jock, he asked with a smile: 'What's Dickie up to? Trying to regenerate the
Herrenvolk?[15] I gave nothing.' Perhaps I may be proved wrong, and the
United World Colleges, of which I believe there are now six, will one day
produce the world leaders he hoped they would.

Basically what I felt was that, with his unique political and military
experience, the energy that Dickie expended after his retirement on ventures such as the National Electronics Research Council could have been
used for far more significant social and political good. Ziegler's book
reminds me that I once asked Dickie to take on something (at this distance
in time I do not remember what it was) and that he refused. He wrote to
say that I did not realize what his life had become. He had 'a private staff
of four who are kept fully stretched. I often do thirty, forty, sometimes
fifty letters a day and often make three or four and sometimes even five
speeches a week'. As I saw it, the trouble with Dickie was that he usually
devoted as much attention to what was unimportant as to what clearly
was the opposite. He accepted invitations to appear at insignificant gatherings, at the same time as he was impulsively interested in almost any
suggestion that looked as if it might lead him back to the national stage.
Early on in his retirement he was close to accepting a hazardous invitation
from the Government to visit Rhodesia to parley with Ian Smith about that
country's imminent unilateral declaration of independence. Fortunately
the Prime Minister had second thoughts. But I think that in the end Dickie
would have declined anyhow.

The Cecil King Affair

This incident occurred soon after Dickie had retired, and some six months
before the end of Harold Wilson's first administration. The course of the
second did not run smoothly, with the UK economy in bad shape, and
with the left and right of the Labour Party constantly at odds with each

15. A reference to Hitler's belief that a 'pure' Germany would represent a 'super
race'.

other. Almost the entire press was anti-Labour, and cries that 'Wilson must go' started to ring out, even in Cecil King's *Daily Mirror*, the only national daily that was normally loyal to the Labour Party. Rumour then also had it that some members of the Government's intelligence organization, MI5, had formed themselves into a secret 'dirty-tricks' coterie in order to discredit Wilson and to bring down the Labour Government.[16] It was also rumoured that there were a few extreme right-wing retired senior military men who were organizing a coup against the Government.

One Sunday in May 1968, Hugh Cudlipp,[17] then Cecil King's right-hand man, called on Dickie at Broadlands, where the talk turned to the sorry state of the country and to King's view that it was essential to replace Wilson's administration by a 'government of national unity'. Cudlipp told Dickie that King wanted to meet him and that he would arrange for the two to see each other the following day. Later King was to say that it was the other way round, and that Dickie had asked for the meeting.

That same Sunday evening Dickie dined with Patricia, his daughter, and John Brabourne, his son-in-law, and told them about the forthcoming meeting, and about the suggestion that he should play a part in a new national government. John tried to persuade him to cancel the meeting but, having failed, suggested that at the least I should be there, presumably to put a brake on Dickie if necessary. Next morning both John and Dickie telephoned to urge me to be at the meeting that afternoon, but without telling me why. The story of what happened next is now widely known, but since it illustrates Dickie's impetuosity it is worth retelling briefly.

When I arrived at Dickie's flat, King and Cudlipp were already there, but apparently nothing had yet been said. As soon as I had sat down, Dickie told King to start, which he did by painting a picture of a demoralized Britain, of public order disintegrating, of the likelihood of bloodshed in the streets and of the need to bring Wilson down. A new national government was wanted to restore order, with Dickie as its central figure. Dickie was nodding his head as King spoke, as though he agreed. He then turned to me, saying that I had not opened my mouth so far. What did I think, he asked? I immediately got up and walked to the door, saying that I was not going to listen to such treasonable nonsense, and that neither should he. Throw them out, I said. Dickie tried to stop me at the door, but

16. See Stephen Dorril and Robin Ramsay who, in their recent book *Smear* (London: Fourth Estate, 1991), write of a number of anti-Wilson plots in which different groups of people were involved. In his notorious book *Spycatcher*, Peter Wright purported to give details of a particular MI5 plot, but under interrogation admitted that the plot that he was talking about was a figment of his imagination.

17. Later Lord Cudlipp.

I kept on saying 'Throw them out', which Dickie duly did soon after I had left.

The story broke some years later when Cudlipp published an account of the meeting. Dickie, to whom Cudlipp had sent the relevant pages of his typescript, first tried to get him to suppress the story, but in the end rested content when Cudlipp agreed to a few minor factual amendments of his text. Rumours had, however, already started to appear in the press about Dickie's presumed part in an abortive coup to unseat Wilson. Questions were asked in Parliament, where it was made clear that Dickie had not played any part in any anti-Government movement. But the story has proved to be too good to die and has been resurrected more than once since Cudlipp's book appeared.

That Dickie was intrigued by what King had suggested is highly likely. That was the way he was, sometimes, as Ziegler writes, cherishing 'Walter Mitty dreams of himself leading the country from the Slough of Despond'. But whatever dreams he may have had, I am certain that Dickie knew nothing about supposed MI5 rebels, nor about the group of retired fire-breathing officers who were said to be planning a military coup. The rumours with which his name had become associated were no more credible than are recent allegations that he was a homosexual Soviet spy. Since his death, 'debunking Dickie' has become a profitable pastime for some journalists.

The King incident was, moreover, totally out of keeping with the tenor of a speech that Dickie delivered in Strasbourg a few months before his murder in August 1979. The Stockholm International Peace Research Institute (SIPRI), a body that is sponsored by the Swedish Government, had been awarded a prize by a French charitable foundation, and Dickie had been asked to accept the prize on its behalf, his being the most prestigious name on the list of the organization's council of scientific advisers. I had introduced Dickie to SIPRI, and he had accompanied me to one of its meetings in Stockholm. Dickie wrote asking me to draft for his Strasbourg appearance 'a really tough speech which will shake the conscience of the world'. I wrote a piece to which he then applied his personal touch. Few people were present when he delivered the speech, and there was no subsequent press comment. Dickie was deeply disappointed and wrote to tell me that 'it simply was a damp squib'. He was wrong. A year later a debate was initiated in the House of Lords to draw attention to the speech. That was the beginning.

A central part of what he said went as follows: 'As a military man who has given half a century of active service, I say in all sincerity that the nuclear arms race has no military purpose. Wars cannot be fought with nuclear weapons. Their existence only adds to our perils because of the illusions which they have generated.' He then went on to say that he found the idea that nuclear weapons 'could be used in field warfare without triggering an all-out nuclear exchange leading to the final holocaust' more and more incredible. Nuclear weapons, he said, cannot be 'categorized in terms of their tactical or strategic purposes . . . as a military man I can see no use for any nuclear weapons which would not end in escalation . . . nuclear devastation is not science fiction – it is a matter of fact.'

The passages that I have quoted were picked up by the CND movement with no reference to Dickie's additional statement that East and West had to live with a balance of strategic nuclear forces. An exchange of letters in *The Times* then followed, in which it was made clear that Dickie had not set out to espouse the cause of CND but to explain that the idea of using nuclear weapons was madness, and that a state of mutual deterrence between East and West could be maintained after a balanced reduction of nuclear and conventional forces. Once this had been made clear, several other top military men came out publicly to support what he had said, and on both sides of the Iron Curtain one started to hear the same message: that while the existence of nuclear weapons is a deterrent to war, their actual use carries the risk of total disaster.

Dickie's speech had brought about the reaction which he wanted. Today its theme is a critical part of the negotiations about reductions in nuclear armaments that are still taking place between East and West.

Dickie on Himself

In reply to a light-hearted remark I once made that I might write a piece about him after he had died, Dickie wrote to me saying 'of course no one knows me better or can expose my weaknesses more effectively, because there is no good having a picture without the warts'. Whether I did know him better than anyone else, I do not know. By the time we had become close friends, he had completely discarded the playboy image he had displayed in the twenties and thirties. The Dickie I knew was a man immersed in world affairs, and according to his own lights concerned only to do good. He was fully aware of his major warts, which some people found amusing and others highly irritating – that is to say, his vanities, his zeal in collecting orders and decorations, and the pleasure it gave him to show off his collection of swords – each with some personal significance – or of silver cups he had won at polo, or his many uniforms and academic gowns that came with his honorary degrees. He was a stickler for correctness in the wearing of decorations. Once at the annual banquet of the Royal Academy in the days when white ties, orders and decorations were *de rigueur*, he spotted that Patrick Blackett was wearing his badge of a

Companion of Honour rather than that of the higher Order of Merit. He flicked the badge with his finger, saying, 'You shouldn't be wearing this', to which Patrick with some embarrassment replied: 'Sorry, I just wanted to give it an airing.' He knew that there were officers who had been affronted when Antony Head (Viscount Head), the Minister of Defence at the time of Suez, had stood aside to make it easy for him to become Colonel of the Life Guards, the Household Cavalry regiment in which Head had started his service career. To parade on horseback behind the Queen at the annual Trooping the Colour ceremony, dressed in his magnificent scarlet uniform and plumed helmet, gave Dickie enormous pleasure. He knew, too, that his not entirely successful effort to have the family name of the monarchy changed from Windsor to Mountbatten-Windsor was unpopular, even though it marked the fact that Prince Philip, the father of the Queen's children, was a Mountbatten on his mother's side.[18]

Since his death, what has drawn most criticism about Dickie was his tendency to rewrite the history of events in which he was concerned, to enlarge upon his own role, and to claim credit where credit was not his. No man could have had less reason to do any of this. His own achievements needed no embellishment. But as Ziegler has written, after his retirement from public service Dickie was wont to confuse what he would have liked to have happened with what actually did happen. He could justifiably boast that *Mulberry* harbour and *Pluto* were the work of Combined Ops, but occasionally he would enlarge on the achievement by speaking as though Combined Ops was responsible for the planning of the whole of the Normandy invasion. He liked to believe that he was the only one in the know about some matter, or that he was the first to be told about some important impending event. A lengthy series of TV programmes about his life was produced a few years after his retirement, with Dickie participating not only in the preparation of the scripts but in the shooting. One programme told of his presence at the Potsdam Conference in 1945, at which he learnt that an atom bomb was likely to be dropped on Japan, and that this would bring the Pacific war to a speedy end. 'I was the only commander', he said to me, 'who was let into the secret at the time.' I had to tell him that this was impossible and that, among others, General Spaatz must also have been briefed. After all, Tooey had just left his command in Europe to move to the Pacific where, provided that the presidential order was given, it was to be his responsibility to drop the

18. The change that Dickie wanted raised constitutional issues, and according to Alastair Horne, Harold Macmillan's biographer, a declaration in 1960 decreed that the name Mountbatten-Windsor will not come into use until the generation of the Queen's great-grandchildren.

bomb. Spaatz had to know, I said. No, replied Dickie. He wasn't there and he wasn't told. As I was about to visit Washington, I said that I would see Spaatz and put the question to him. The answer was what I expected, and I was given a list of the various commanders in the Pacific, starting with General MacArthur, who had had to be 'in the know'. I passed the information to Dickie and the necessary change was made in the script. Had Dickie really thought about the matter, he would have realized that he had been wrong. But because of the way his mind worked, it was he who had to be the first to know. Sometimes his stories indicated little sense of humour. His anecdote about the UK being allowed to buy an American nuclear propulsion plant because he had prevented the demolition of a house which Eisenhower had once occupied would have been funny had he told it as a joke. The likelihood, however, is that at the time he believed it, in the same way as he recorded as a serious matter Rickover's sly remark that Dickie should command the American as well as the British navy.

He also failed to see why people were sometimes amused by seemingly innocent remarks of his. One story which I like concerns a stopover he had to make in London on his way back to South-East Asia from the Potsdam Conference. Among the people he had to see was M. Massigli, whom General de Gaulle, now back in Paris, had sent to London as his ambassador. France had not been represented at the conference, and Dickie had to tell the Ambassador that the Allied leaders had decreed that, on the capitulation of Japan, his command was to become responsible for the time being for overseeing French interests in Indo-China. A member of his staff telephoned Gérard André, who after years as a POW had become Minister in Massigli's small embassy, to inform him that Dickie wanted to see the Ambassador next morning at eight o'clock 'That won't do,' said Gérard (he was to make history as the longest serving member of the diplomatic corps in London as Minister to successive ambassadors, and he also became one of my close friends). 'M. Massigli cannot be here till eight-thirty.' 'Then make it eight-thirty,' said Dickie's messenger.

Next morning Gérard turned up early to check that the charwomen had finished their cleaning and was surprised when Dickie turned up ten minutes ahead of time. 'I'm afraid I'm a bit early,' said Dickie. 'My first three appointments this morning took less time than anticipated.' Gérard still raises a laugh when he tells the story.

The exaggerations that marked Dickie's post-retirement years have proved easy game for journalists. They have even inspired hostile comment from at least one important member of the staff he had under him. 'He fabricated what he wished to remember' about his role in the partition of India, said the historian Professor Sir Cyril Philips, who at the time was on Dickie's staff. He was interested only in polo, said Sir Cyril, but he thought that he himself had devised the plan for partition. Others have said that instead of spending all his time dealing with the tumultuous and bloody events that marked partition, he sat up late at night – like Nero fiddling when Rome was burning – working at the genealogy of the Hesse family.

In the case of India, what people now forget is that it was neither Dickie nor the Government in London but its Hindu and Muslim populations who decided that partition into India and Pakistan was to be the consequence of British withdrawal. Dickie's predecessor, Wavell, and for decades other viceroys before him, had failed to find a way of sorting out India's social, economic, racial and religious problems. What Dickie brought to India was not a predetermined and peaceful solution to its problems, but the courage to accept unhesitatingly whatever was to happen once London had decided to end its imperial power. Dickie could not have prevented the bloodshed. He had to see it through. Working at night on the genealogy of his family was probably his way of putting out of his mind the horrors that surrounded him during the day. Other viceroys, other commanders, had different ways to relax. Spaatz played poker, Tedder sketched, and Rickover read.

Dickie's warts were inseparable from his achievements. Harold Macmillan said of Dickie that he was 'a strange character . . . who tries to combine being a professional sailor, a politician and a royalty. The result is that nobody trusts him'. And Ziegler concluded his official biography by saying that Dickie's 'vanity, though child-like, was monstrous, his ambition unbridled. The truth, in his hands, was swiftly converted from what it was to what it should have been. He sought to rewrite history with cavalier indifference to the facts to magnify his own achievements. There was a time when I became so enraged by what I was beginning to feel was his determination to hoodwink me that I found it necessary to place on my desk a notice saying: REMEMBER, IN SPITE OF EVERYTHING, HE WAS A GREAT MAN'.

Despite the way he bore himself, the apparent certainty in his manner, Dickie sometimes did not seem to understand how he fitted into the company around him. He wanted to be liked, but could not understand why his peers so often failed to comply. He disliked knowing that disagreeable things were said about him behind his back. He once asked me to try to explain to him why he and I, with our totally different backgrounds, got on so well together. My answer, I fear, was a very feeble one. I said I just liked him, and that I took his trust in me for granted. When he rejected my advice, that was his affair. I did not mind.

Ziegler did not try to explain Dickie's warts. It would have been as difficult, and as sterile, a task as trying to explain his strengths. I view

Dickie's life as a long saga made up of disparate and isolated events strung together by the force of his personality along a never-broken thread of ambition. He was a man of action, and, as Geoffrey Pyke wisely remarked, not one given to contemplation. Unlike Rickover, he did not read books. Even documents and minutes he read slowly. 'I envy you the way you read so quickly,' he once said to me. 'My mother taught me to read line by line, and I can't get out of the habit.' Sometimes as he read his lips moved as if he were reading the words aloud. Whatever pretentions he had about himself, he never regarded himself as either a deep or an original thinker, nor, while he lived surrounded by beautiful objects, by magnificent pictures and silver, was he interested in the serious world of the creative arts. If Dickie had read works on modern history or biographies of modern greats, had he, like Tedder, viewed what he had done against the broad canvas of history, he would have realized that his exaggerations would reduce the credibility of his real achievements. But Dickie did not read, and his life had been so full of great events that it provided him with all the material he needed to fill his years of retirement with romance and glory.

Ziegler could not have concluded his biography in any way other than the one that he did, except by saying that for all his faults Dickie *was* a great man. No one can deny that he was a great historical figure. He may not have determined the historical events with which his name is associated – not the Allied invasion of Europe in 1944, not the defeat of Japan, not even the integration of the three armed services. He took on the supreme commandership of South-East Asia even though he knew he would inevitably run up against the opposition of the C-in-Cs under him who happened to be much his senior in substantive rank. He played the critical part that he did in transforming the service departments because, as Horne says in his official biography of Macmillan, the Prime Minister knew that Dickie 'was the only serving officer with the power and prestige to put through the reforms he had in mind' – and Macmillan, with 'amused detachment', had 'nothing against Mountbatten predictably grasping all the credit for them'.

Dickie's achievement was to play the part that he was given in all these events with the courage, the dash and even the impetuousness that they demanded, and, come what may, with the determination to succeed. It is because of this that he belongs to the heroic figures of history. If he was not great in the sense that an Einstein or a Beethoven was, or great in the sense that Winston Churchill and Thomas Jefferson were, or even the equal of military figures such as Wellington and Nelson, Dickie was great because he had the courage to take on and discharge responsibilities at which lesser mortals quailed. Experience was to teach him that ideas and national aspirations could not be fought with weapons, and equally that weapons whose destructive power was infinite and uncontrollable were not military weapons.

After his death I often asked myself whether he would have achieved what he had if he had not had any royal connections, and if he had not married into great wealth. My answer has always been yes. I do not believe that it was his particular complex of Hesse genes that made him what he was – a considerable military figure. All successful men of arms who reach the top must have the ambition to do so, and the genetic make-up necessary to fulfil their ambitions. Dickie would have had the same commanding presence whatever his ancestry. He would have had the same courage by which the quality of leadership has to be sustained. He would still have been as avid for new ideas as he was when he was CCO. He may have been too impetuous to be given command of a grand fleet, but he was a man who always sought out the enemy and there was no one better to take over the command of Combined Ops from the elderly admiral by whom he was preceded. Dickie, too, may not have been the first choice as Supreme Allied Commander South-East Asia. Sholto Douglas's name had been canvassed, but he was disliked by the Americans. Tedder's name had also been proposed, but Eisenhower felt that he could not spare him. When Churchill then nominated Dickie, he knew that with the record he had established as a driving force in Combined Ops, and despite his relative youth, he would invigorate the C-in-Cs of the three services who were then facing the daunting task of containing the Japanese armies that were threatening India. Nor do I believe that Dickie would have been chosen to be the last Viceroy of India had the Government in London not decided that it was a job that needed someone with Dickie's determination to see the job through, come what may. Above all, with everything that Dickie had achieved by 1945, his subsequent rise in the naval hierarchy and to the post of CDS would have been inevitable. Only service prejudice could have prevented that from happening.

It was not in Dickie's character to fade away anonymously, as did Rickover when, dying, he withdrew his name from the educational foundation he had set up. Although Dickie had to have security protection when he went to Classiebawn, he obviously could not have foreseen that his end would be as dramatic as his life had been – death from an IRA bomb. But he had prepared for it by spelling out in detail the grandest funeral he could envisage. And that is what it was. During the service in St Paul's Cathedral, I could not take my eyes off the bier on which his enormous coffin rested, as I thought, well Dickie, your death, like so many chapters of your life, has certainly reverberated round the world as you wanted it to do. I only wish I could have given you a better answer than I did when you asked me why the two of us got on as well as we did.

Admiral Hyman G. Rickover

1900–1986

The Father of the American Nuclear Navy

* * *

Admiral Rickover was as different from any stereotype of a naval officer as it is possible to imagine. He never carried himself with the self-assured air that one associates with military men of his rank. From the time that he first became known outside naval circles, he was hardly ever seen in uniform. The Rickover I first met was a slight figure with closely cut white hair, dressed in a nondescript blue suit. His prominent nose was not exactly hooked, but was certainly not straight. His look was determined. When silent he seemed deep in thought, and sometimes a veil of sadness would pass across his face, and then a smile, as he made some amusing, usually cynical remark, or related some funny story in which he figured to the embarrassment of others. Passing him in the street, one could have taken him for a schoolteacher, or even, like his father, a tailor – anything but a naval officer. No one could have guessed that he was one of the most outstanding military technologists of his age, and at the same time one of the most disliked officers who had ever graced the US Navy. For more than half the sixty years that he spent in the service, he wrestled with single-minded fervour against the naval hierarchy, hardly ever missing a chance to show up his superiors as men tied to outworn tradition that obstructed progress. Riding headlong against opposition was something that came naturally to the 'father' of the nuclear navy.

By changing the way that naval power can be projected across the globe, Rickover's achievement was enormous and undoubtedly helped set the course of East-West military relations during the opening decades of the nuclear age. Yet now that he is dead, I find myself asking why it was that he had to pay the price he did, a deep-seated dislike by so many of his peers, for realizing a purpose in which they also shared.

I knew him well for over twenty years, particularly that side of him which he wanted me to know. Rickover made his own rules. Shortly after we met in the early summer of 1962, when I was chief scientific adviser to the British Ministry of Defence, he decided that I, not as it should have been, the naval department concerned, was to be his channel of communication both with the Royal Navy and the British Government for all matters relating to nuclear propulsion. Over a long period he paid what I believe were annual visits to Holy Loch in Scotland to inspect the US submarines stationed there. Usually with minimal notice, I would get a telephone call, saying that he was flying over on such and such a day, usually a Friday, and that he would like to spend the Saturday night with me. Could I see that an aircraft was laid on to fly him from Glasgow to Birmingham or Norfolk, depending on where I was that weekend, and see to it that he got to Heathrow Airport on the Sunday evening in time to catch a flight that would get him back to Washington in time to be at his desk first thing on Monday morning? I would pass the message on to the Ministry of Defence and leave it to the officials there to make the necessary arrangements. So far as I know, he never bothered to inform the US naval authorities in the UK that he was making an inspection, nor did he ask them to help with his travel arrangements. Twenty years later, when he was eighty-two, and just before he was clumsily edged out of the US Navy, several previous conventional moves to get him to retire having failed, he sent me a formal letter covering his two final reports on radioactivity levels in the US nuclear submarine base in the Holy Loch. He continued to use me as his link with the British Government long after I had officially retired.

It was Rickover who engineered our first meeting, and my introduction was as odd as was the course of the strange friendship that followed. I was in Washington and staying with Sir Michael West, the general who was then in charge of the British Military Mission to the United States. One day when at lunch, Sir Robert Scott, the permanent secretary of the ministry in which I worked in London, and who was also on official business in Washington, came in, apologized for interrupting, and asked me to leave the table for a moment to meet Rickover, who had refused to come in with him. Rickover was sitting in a car with Gerard Smith, a senior member of the State Department with whom he and Scott had been lunching. The journal *Foreign Affairs* had just published an article of mine under the title 'Judgment and Control in Modern Warfare', in which my theme was the futility of imagining that nuclear weapons could ever be used in field warfare. 'That was a fine piece of yours. Keep it up,' said Rickover. 'We military are not made to think. Keep in touch.'

We did. In 1982, twenty years later, and about six months after he had been ousted from his official posts, he sent me a letter saying that he had been reading the same article (he made no reference to the fact that he had done so when it first appeared) and that it was both 'thoughtful and illuminating', but that I should not expect my unconventional views to be adopted by our present military leaders, who were neither 'the best brains in the country' nor able to break away from 'conventional thinking'.

The Beginning

The Rickovers were one of the thousands of Jewish families which at the end of the nineteenth and early years of the present century were fleeing to the United States from the ghettos and pogroms of eastern Europe. They came from Poland. The father arrived first, in 1899, and having set himself up as a tailor in New York, sent in 1904 for his wife and two children, a daughter aged eight, and Hyman four. In 1908 the family moved to Chicago. Hyman was now aged eight (ten, according to his school record), and worked hard at school. Out of hours he added to the family's meagre fortunes by doing paper rounds and by serving as a Western Union messenger boy. Many children of Chicago's Jewish immigrants of those years were to make their names in the professions. A few became national figures. Hyman Rickover emerged from his Orthodox and presumably Yiddish-speaking background into a category of his own.

He was already a vice-admiral when we first met. Over the years we saw each other frequently, but even though we got to know each other well, he rarely spoke about his early years. When I asked why he had chosen a naval career, all that he would say was that it was the only way open to him to get a college education. From the various biographies that have already been written about him[1] I do, however, now know that he graduated with distinction from his High School in Chicago early in 1918 – that is to say, just as the First World War was nearing its end. His out-of-school job as a Western Union messenger had brought him to the attention of Adolph Sabath, a Jewish Congressman who represented the Chicago district in which the Rickovers lived. And Sabath, exercising his statutory right, nominated Rickover as a midshipman to the Naval Academy at Annapolis. After some two months of solitary cramming in preparation for a stiff entrance examination, Rickover entered the academy in June 1918.

At Annapolis his relations with his fellow-midshipmen were a foretaste of what was to come as he climbed the ladder of promotion. He was one of seventeen Jews in a class of 955, and in 1922 passed out 106th of the

1. Clay Blair Jr's *The Atomic Submarine and Admiral Rickover* (London: Odhams, 1954); Richard G. Hewlett and Francis Duncan's *The Nuclear Navy* (Chicago, Ill. and London: University of Chicago Press, 1974); Patrick Tyler's *Running Critical* (New York: Harper & Row, 1986); the exhaustive, critical biographical study written by Norman Polmar and Thomas B. Allen, *Rickover: Controversy and Genius* (New York: Simon & Schuster, 1982), a book that was much disapproved of by its subject; and Francis Duncan's *The Discipline of Technology: Admiral Rickover and the Naval Nuclear Propulsion Program 1957–1982* (Annapolis, Md: US Naval Institute Press, 1989).

539 who graduated. 'Hazing' was an accepted part of life at Annapolis, and Rickover, an impecunious foreign Jew and a 'grind' who disliked and was no good at sport, was a natural victim. Years later he is said to have admitted that he had to endure far more than his fair share of bullying because he was Jewish. One other student of his year seems to have been persecuted more than he was – a fellow-Jewish midshipman, Leonard Kaplan by name, who was 'sent to Coventry' from the beginning of his four years in the academy (from which he passed out second in his class). Except, presumably, for the few other Jewish 'middies', it was regarded as an offence for anyone to talk to Kaplan. But even had Rickover been accepted socially, he was far too poor to engage in the social life of the academy. He appears to have made no friends, and such time as was not taken up by formal classes he spent with his books.

His first posting was to a destroyer, where he found himself one of five ensigns in a complement of eight officers. Not surprisingly, the life of the ward-room was not for him. When not on duty, he spent most of his time either reading or in the ship's engine-room. Three years later he was transferred to the battleship *Nevada*, in which he served for two years – again, almost entirely in home waters – in a company of seventy-five officers, of whom thirty were ensigns. True to form, and even though for a time serving as the ship's electrical officer, he rarely joined in the social activities that are part of a naval officer's life. In 1927, after five years of sea duty, he returned to Annapolis for a year's post-graduate study. This was followed by a year at Columbia, where at the age of about thirty, and now a full lieutenant, he gained his master's degree in engineering.

At his own request, and because it provided the best opportunity that he could envisage for using his training as an electrical engineer, Rickover's next posting was to the submarine branch of the Navy. He served for three years, again in home waters and the Panama zone, as one of four officers in a small submarine. It was during this tour of duty that he married Ruth Masters, a graduate student in international law whom he had met at Columbia. Despite his Orthodox Jewish upbringing, the marriage took place in an Episcopalian church.

Rickover was now in his mid-thirties and had every reason to expect that his seniority entitled him to the command of either one of the Navy's older submarines or, at the least, a minesweeper. Instead he was posted in 1933 to a humdrum shore job as an inspector of supplies. It was not an exacting assignment, and once again, and in the company of his studious wife, he immersed himself in books. The Rickovers apparently lived in a self-sufficient world of their own. During this period Rickover published an article criticizing the method by which enlisted men were chosen for promotion, and another, under his own name, but clearly influenced by his wife's interests, entitled 'International Law and the Submarine'. Both appeared in the Navy's professional journal, *The Naval Institute Proceedings*.

In 1935, he was once again posted to sea duty in home waters, and this time as assistant engineering officer in the battleship *New Mexico*. Legend has it that in his effort to achieve economies in the use of fuel, he went so far as to reduce the supply of fresh water in washrooms. The crew and even officers complained, but Rickover paid no attention. On the rare occasions he went ashore, he went alone.

Two years later, he was sent to the Far East with the rank of lieutenant-commander to take command of the *Finch*, an ancient minesweeper that was then being used to ferry supplies and tow targets. It was the least impressive ship of the American contingent in the international naval force that was helping to protect European and American interests during the Sino-Japanese War. Rickover became a martinet as he strove to improve the condition of his ship. He invented endless duties for his crew, and punished backsliders. His effort to impose discipline and raise morale all but led to mutiny.

Before three months were up, Rickover was relieved of his one and only command. In the realization that there was no future for him as a 'line officer', he then asked for a transfer to the naval category of Engineering Duty Officer (EDO). EDOs are responsible for designing and supervising the building and repair of ships and are inferior to line officers in the naval hierarchy. Few ever reach the rank of rear-admiral, let alone full admiral, as Rickover was eventually to do. As an EDO he was first posted to Cavite in the Philippines, where for two years he behaved with his customary zeal as he tried to improve the efficiency of the main Navy Yard. His wife had accompanied him to the Far East, and when not on duty, Rickover preferred to spend his time on excursions with her rather than join in the social life of the base. *Pepper, Rice and Elephants* is a record that Ruth Rickover published of a tour that they made to Indonesia and Thailand.

At the Bureau of Ships

Rickover's first real opportunity to reveal his abilities came in mid-1939. He was posted to the US Navy's Bureau of Ships in Washington. War was looming in Europe, and 'BuShips' had been charged with a vast new shipbuilding programme, one that grew ever bigger after Pearl Harbor. Rickover was made head of the electrical section, a division of the bureau that was responsible for designing a ship's electrical system in its entirety, from general lighting to the power supply for the radar and guns. Instead of treating his job as a purely administrative one, he made himself personally responsible not only for the construction but for the performance of all manner of electrical equipment. He himself selected his industrial contractors and worked directly with the responsible official in each of his chosen suppliers. To Rickover, responsibility meant a ruthless understanding of everything that came under his charge. According to Polmar and Allen, his single-mindedness again failed to endear him to many of his naval colleagues. He worked seven days a week, all hours of the day and night, and expected those under him to do the same. He learnt how to bypass normal channels. He was outspoken; he shouted abuse at officers or ratings whose work he found wanting; he brought in civilians to replace naval personnel; senior officers found themselves working under their juniors. Rickover seemed to have a constant need to denigrate the naval bureaucracy. Yet his strange ways did not prevent him from organizing what was acknowledged at the time as the most technically competent section in the whole Bureau of Ships.

Early in 1942 he was promoted to the rank of Commander, and some months later he became a temporary Captain. Towards the end of 1944 he was moved from the electrical division and given the responsibility of reorganizing one of BuShips' vast supply depots. After that he was sent to Okinawa to establish a ship-repair base which, no sooner had it been completed, was destroyed by a typhoon. But this hardly mattered. The war was at an end.

Rickover was in his forty-sixth year when he returned from Okinawa to the States, where his first job was to help in the 'mothballing' of ships. Critical questions were then being asked about the strategic significance of navies in the nuclear age that had just opened. Dr Ross Gunn, a nuclear physicist who worked in the Naval Research Laboratory, had before the war suggested that nuclear power could be used to propel both submarine and surface vessels. A nuclear-power plant did not need oxygen. In theory, therefore, nuclear-propelled submarines could remain submerged for months, as opposed to days or hours as was the case with conventionally powered boats. With Philip Abelson of the Carnegie Institution, Gunn had set to work to see whether usable nuclear fuel could be extracted from uranium ore. The process that they devised proved sufficiently promising for it to be used in the Manhattan Project's huge Oak Ridge separation plant in Tennessee.

No sooner had the war ended than many, not just Gunn and Abelson, urged that work should be started without delay to develop a naval nuclear reactor. The US Navy, however, had not played a major part in the Manhattan Project, the organization which, under the executive direction of Major-General Leslie Groves, had produced 'the bomb', and had no facilities of its own with which to try to develop the reactor it wanted.

Nor did it have more than a handful of men who knew anything about nuclear physics. It was therefore arranged that a small team of naval engineers from BuShips should spend a few months at the Oak Ridge separation plant to learn the fundamentals of nuclear technology. The bureau also placed a few contracts with commercial firms to investigate problems that would be encountered in the development of a nuclear propulsion plant. Rickover had been chosen to work with the General Electric Company, with which he had formed a close association when he was head of the bureau's electrical division. He was, however, immediately switched to the Oak Ridge team, despite the fact that the head of BuShips, Vice-Admiral Mills, was well aware that on past form Rickover was bound to antagonize some of his new colleagues. What mattered to Mills was that Rickover could get things done. This transfer was the critical turning-point in Rickover's career, the step that was to make his a household name.

The Nuclear Engineer

Three of the party of eight whom Mills sent to Oak Ridge were civilian engineers, and of the three only two had any grounding in nuclear physics. Although Rickover was new to the subject, he soon made himself *de facto* leader of the whole group. He was senior both in years and rank, and under his direction the eight were soon working as a coherent team in assessing the nature of the engineering problems that would have to be resolved if nuclear propulsion were ever to become a reality. Rickover was also the man who could be relied upon to solve the administrative problems that arose in dealing with the new Atomic Energy Commission (AEC), the body that Congress had now charged with the responsibility of overseeing the exploitation of atomic energy, whether for military or civil purposes.

As was only to be expected, the new commission's first priority was nuclear weapons, but Rickover was insistent that the second should be the design and production of a reactor to power submarines. Other officers, many well above him in the hierarchy, and including Admiral Nimitz, then the Chief of Naval Operations (CNO), were urging the same thing. A division of BuShips to deal with nuclear matters was therefore established under Captain Mumma, an officer who had been active in the nuclear field well before Rickover entered it. Despite this move, Rickover was determined that he, and no one else, was to be the Navy's kingpin for nuclear propulsion, and all that he could associate with it. 'His' Oak Ridge team had the advantage that they were becoming more familiar with the subject than any of their fellow-officers. They had also got to know AEC officials who would inevitably be involved were a nuclear propulsion R&D project to be launched. The team had also visited all the Manhattan Project nuclear establishments that the new commission had taken over, as well as the Westinghouse and General Electric plants which the bureau had commissioned to do work relevant to reactor design.

Rickover bypassed Captain Mumma and sent reports of the progress 'his' team was making at Oak Ridge direct to Mills, whom he in turn bypassed when he got two submariners on Admiral Nimitz's staff to urge the need to develop a naval reactor. There had been many in Washington who did not want him back at BuShips at the end of his four-month stint at Oak Ridge, but Rickover, who had never stopped pressing his case, got Mills to appoint him the bureau's liaison officer with the new AEC. Mills was fully aware that Rickover would continue to make enemies in his new appointment, but he also knew that, once given a free rein, Rickover would not allow anything to get in his way. 'He would outwork, outman-oeuvre, and out-fight the Commission, its laboratories and the Navy.'[2] In order to separate Rickover administratively from Captain Mumma, Mills therefore decided to create a nuclear power branch in the research division of the bureau. Rickover, its head, immediately recruited as many of the other members of the Oak Ridge team as could join him, and also saw to it that all naval personnel who were working either in AEC laboratories or on nuclear R&D projects in industry, reported directly to him. He wasted no time in showing who was in charge.

Six months later, in January 1949, the AEC set up a division of reactor development under Dr Lawrence Hafstad. So as to avoid unnecessary trouble, Hafstad wisely decided that Rickover's nuclear power branch in BuShips should also serve as the AEC's naval reactor branch. As an official of the bureau, Rickover could now write to the AEC demanding some piece of action, and then, as an officer of the AEC, draft the reply which Hafstad, his AEC superior, would send to the head of BuShips.

The Man with Two Hats

At that time Rickover knew far less about reactors than did many of the professional staff of the AEC, and he failed to understand why they were reluctant to launch a crash programme to develop the reactor he wanted. He even crossed swords with Robert Oppenheimer, the brilliant theoretical nuclear physicist who had directed the scientific work of the Manhattan

2. Richard G. Hewlett and Francis Duncan, *Nuclear Navy, 1946–1962* (Chicago, Ill. and London: University of Chicago Press, 1974), p. 142.

Project, complaining that there were too many scientists in the nuclear business and not enough engineers. As Rickover saw it, the reactor problem was 90 per cent engineering and only 10 per cent science. You did not wait till you had all the facts before you set about making the bomb, he is said to have protested to Oppenheimer. Oppenheimer replied that he already had all the facts, but that that had not been the problem. Rickover's meetings with the General Advisory Council of the AEC, of which Oppenheimer was the chairman, did not endear him to its scientific members. Rabi, one of its members, could never understand why, as he bluntly put it, I wasted time with so intolerable a man.[3]

Later, long after Rickover and I had also become friends, I found it odd to read in Polmar and Allen's biography that Rickover had turned to William Borden, executive director of the Joint Congressional Committee on Atomic Energy, to help in his campaign to get work started on a naval reactor, and that Edward Teller, the head of an AEC committee that was looking into reactor safety, was also an ally. It was Borden who precipitated the public inquiry into Oppenheimer as a security risk, and it was Teller's testimony that was critical in having Oppenheimer condemned. It would seem that Rickover would have supped with the Devil if that had helped his purposes.

Things moved swiftly. In August 1949 the Navy informed the AEC that a nuclear reactor had to be ready by 1955 for installation in a submarine hull. Rickover decided that Westinghouse, helped by the AEC's Oak Ridge laboratory, should be made responsible for the development of a small pressurized water reactor (PWR). It was the idea of Alvin Weinberg – the director of Oak Ridge – that pressurized water should be used as a 'coolant' for the reactor. Simultaneously, and as a back-up project, a contract was placed with General Electric for the development of a sodium-cooled reactor, the company to be helped by the AEC's Argonne laboratory. The contract for the submarine hulls into which the two reactors were to be installed, was placed with the Electric Boat Company.

Both the Navy's and the AEC's budgets were, however, severely stretched at the time. In an effort to obtain congressional funds for the reactor project, Rickover appeared in January 1950 before the Joint Congressional Committee for Atomic Energy, whose chairman, Brien McMahon, must have been told by Borden how remarkable a man Rickover was. Rickover performed in his most persuasive way. The money was voted,

---

3. I reviewed Hewlett and Duncan's book on Rickover when it appeared in 1974 and sent Rabi a copy of what I had written. In acknowledging it, he reaffirmed his unfavourable opinion, adding that Rickover 'now looms large' but as a technologist 'somewhat devoid of meaning', an example of how one scheming face can influence people 'bent on upheaval'.

and the meeting proved to be the beginning of a relationship with Congress which was to provide him for ever after with a platform from which to castigate, as necessary, the Navy, the AEC, or the Secretary of Defense. After congressional money had been voted for the reactors, funds for the submarine hulls were included in the shipbuilding programme. In June 1952 President Truman did the honours at the keel-laying ceremony of the first nuclear submarine, the *Nautilus*, with Gordon Dean, chairman of the AEC, singling Rickover out for special praise. Rickover was there, but in the background, in civilian clothes. Only when ordered by the Secretary of the Navy did he wear uniform.

Rickover had already started to organize educational and training programmes for the naval and civilian personnel who were to man the nuclear navy he was going to create. He called for big changes in the Annapolis curriculum. Potential officers in nuclear-powered ships needed a proper grounding in mathematics, science and engineering. From the start of the nuclear programme in 1950 until his retirement some thirty years later, he made himself personally responsible for the selection of the officers and ratings who were to become members of his élite nuclear corps. It is said that he himself interviewed more than fifteen thousand candidates. They were strange and brutal interviews, as I once saw for myself.

Those who wanted to join 'his' navy first had to spend a year learning about the intricacies and dangers of nuclear technology. They then had to take a rigorous written examination before they were interviewed by members of Rickover's staff. Then came their final interview in Rickover's office, with the Admiral doing his best to incommode them, asking strange questions and then shouting abuse on hearing their answers. He is said to have played practical jokes on them, sometimes making a candidate sit on a chair, one of whose legs had been shortened so that he could not sit still. After giving a foolish answer, a candidate would sometimes be sent to wait for hours in a small store-room that adjoined his office. He once gave me a small card on which was printed a quotation to the effect that the best leader is one for whom a man would 'cheerfully' give up his life, with two little squares marked 'Yes', 'No', which the candidates had to tick. Presumably those candidates who answered 'Yes' were then given a further quizzing. Admiral Zumwalt, when he was on the staff of the Secretary of the Navy in the rank of Commander, and who later became the CNO, was a candidate for the captaincy of the nuclear-powered cruiser, *Long Beach*. He made a written record of his Rickover interview. After being seen separately by three senior members of Rickover's staff, he was kept waiting for weeks before he was abruptly summoned to appear in the Admiral's office, where Rickover began what can only be described as an abusive interrogation, interrupting Zumwalt's answers every now and then by warning him not to try to conduct the interview, and making all too clear his dislike of naval officers who had served as 'aides'. Rickover kept sending him out of the room to reconsider some answer he had just given before finally telling him to return to the Pentagon. When Zumwalt was offered the post, he rejected it.

Before I knew about the nature of these interviews, I was lunching with Rickover in his office one Saturday during the period of the Vietnam war, and asked if it was true that he saw all candidates who wanted to join the nuclear navy. He yelled to one of his secretaries in the adjacent big office, asking whether 'any of those guys' were still around. 'If there are any, send one in.' A few minutes later a man in his early thirties came in. 'Sit down,' said Rick (by this time that was the name by which I knew and addressed him). 'Now you interview him.' The man did not have the slightest idea who I was, and I did not know how to begin. 'Ask his name and rank,' said Rick. I did. He was a lieutenant-commander. 'What was your last posting?' I asked. He had been in command of a 6,000-ton supply ship in the Pacific. I then stopped. 'Hell,' said Rick, 'you don't know how to interview.' Taking over, he started asking all manner of questions, leaving the officer, who had been through it all before, thoroughly confused. Rick ended by asking: 'Did you work hard this past year, all days of the week?' 'Yes' came the reply. 'Harder than at any other time in my life.' 'Supposing you had had a year like that at the start of your career, what then?' asked Rick. 'Oh,' the man answered, 'I would probably have resigned from the Navy.'

Rick motioned to him to go, and he left, still obviously puzzled by what had happened. I felt that Rick had been given the answer that he deserved, but I was none the less amused to have seen him behaving true to form.

He placed his own men in the submarine construction yards, as he did in Westinghouse and GEC, as well as in those AEC laboratories which were co-operating in different parts of the work. He was determined to create his own intelligence service in order to know about everything that was going on in his empire. He made it a rule to read carbon copies on pink paper of all letters and memoranda that went out from his office: '. . . he had learned over the years to question everything he read, no matter who wrote it'.[4] I once asked how he found time for such reading. He passed me a heap of 'pinks' from his desk. They happened to be the weekly reports that he demanded from the commanders of all nuclear submarines. They had to report specifically on anything, however trivial, that had gone wrong in their ships during the week, and to outline

4. Hewlett and Duncan, op. cit.

whatever action they had taken to rectify the fault. Rick did not want to know that all had gone well. There had to be something that had gone wrong. The reports ended with a standard sentence stating that the commanders formally accepted responsibility for whatever action they had taken to repair the fault.

Rick treated his contractors in the same way. They may have been working to his plans, and the responsibility for the quality of the work was theirs. But Rick questioned everything they did. There was nothing rigid about the way that his organization worked, except that there had to be absolute discipline, and no departure from what he himself had authorized. Without this regimen he could not discharge what he told me was his personal responsibility to the American people: the safe operation of ships that were nuclear powered.

In March 1953, little more than two years after Westinghouse had begun its work, the prototype pressurized water reactor went 'critical'. Against the advice of the officer who was in charge of the project, Rick immediately ordered that it should be kept running at full power for as many hours as it would take a nuclear-powered submerged submarine to cross the Atlantic. Nothing untoward happened. Rick had made his point. Some years later he told me about an experiment he had laid on to determine whether a nuclear-powered submarine could withstand a specified level of shock resulting from the explosion of an underwater mine. When he arrived at Key West in Florida to board the submarine, he was told that the head of the Navy in Washington had banned the experiment. It was after midnight, but Rick insisted on being put through to the CNO. 'I asked him', Rick told me, 'whether what I had just been given to understand was true. The answer was yes. I then told the CNO that unless he countermanded his order, I would be on to the papers straight away to tell them that the CNO had refused to allow a test to be made to help determine a level of danger to which American boys might well be exposed when in action. The order was withdrawn, and I went on board, took charge, and the experiment went off without incident.'

The story was typical of Rick. He never shilly-shallied in reaching a decision, and was fearless in its execution. He had a clear appreciation of the risks involved with nuclear propulsion plants. The only changes he allowed in reactor design or operation were those that he had authorized himself. Although I had neither authority in these matters nor any engineering knowledge, he warned me, as the chief scientific adviser to the British Minister of Defence, never to allow the Royal Navy to make any changes in the specifications of their nuclear propulsion units, the first of which were based on one of his own designs. In the end this conservatism was to make him appear to many as an opponent of technological change.

The prototype PWR having proved successful, work went on speedily to complete the *Nautilus*, of which Rick, in khaki and without insignia, took command in its sea trials, as he did of the scores of nuclear submarines that followed before his retirement. When the time came to commission the *Nautilus*, he insisted that his nominee should be given command of the vessel. That also became future practice.

The ceremonial launching of the *Nautilus*, in January 1954, attracted great publicity, as did the launch of the *Seawolf*, the only American vessel that put to sea powered by a sodium-cooled reactor, a design which Rick then abandoned.

The Controversial Admiral

Rickover was now in his mid-fifties, and suddenly the unpopular loner of naval circles had become a public figure – the idol of congressional committees and the man who knew how to tame the atom. Against much opposition, he was given the responsibility for the building of the first US civilian nuclear power station, whose reactor had started life as a possible power source for an aircraft-carrier. This, the now-silent Shippingport pressurized water reactor in Philadelphia, was built by Westinghouse, and went critical in 1957, a few months after Calder Hall, the first British civilian nuclear reactor, had started to feed power into the national grid. What with the Shippingport plant and *Nautilus*'s 1958 passage through northern seas and under the Arctic ice, Rick had become a national hero. The way he successfully overrode the Navy's decision to retire him, and to pass him over for promotion, added to the public's interest.

Rick's name had first come up for promotion from Captain to Rear-Admiral in 1951, at a time, so it has been said, when he was under the impression that he would be selected to succeed Mills as the head of the whole Bureau of Ships. He was passed over. In 1952 the promotion board again decided that the Navy did not want Rick as an admiral. As a captain with some thirty years of service behind him, and who had twice failed to be promoted, this meant that he would have to retire from the service the following year. Rick and his friends went to work. Clay Blair Jr, a *Time-Life* reporter who had already published a laudatory piece about Rick, organized a highly effective press campaign to make the public understand that Rick, although the greatest naval innovator of his age, was the victim of prejudice, the impression being created that it was anti-Semitic in nature, in contrast to a hierarchical prejudice in the Navy against EDOs as opposed to line officers. According to Polmar and Allen, Blair was helped in writing his book both by his subject and by Mrs Rickover. Support for

Rick was canvassed in those congressional circles where he had friends. The Senate Armed Services Committee called for an inquiry into the way the Navy's selection boards operated. The Navy capitulated, and in 1953 awarded Rick the promotion that had twice been denied him.

He was then fifty-three (or fifty-five, according to his school record), and the way his victory had been achieved made him even less liked in naval circles than he already was. But this meant little to him. He knew how to get Congress and the Senate to back him against either the Secretary of Defense or the Navy chiefs. Congress indicated its confidence in him even more than it had already done by awarding him in 1958 a gold Congressional Medal of Honor for his 'signal achievement in the practical use of Atomic Energy'. At the same time they saw to it that in 1958 he was promoted to the rank of Vice-Admiral. Rick became a full Admiral in 1973, and was the recipient of a second congressional gold medal in 1982.

Rick always realized that nuclear-powered vessels were very much more expensive than their conventional counterparts, but he none the less argued that the additional cost was justified on operational grounds. As he put it to me, those fools in the Pentagon could not see that, cost what it may, nuclear power in the end was cheaper than oil, given the possibility that a battle at sea might go on for days or weeks. How can you put a price on the ability to go on fighting without the need for refuelling? Vast nuclear carriers, and nuclear escorts, surface and submarine – yes, of course they are more costly; of course they are vulnerable to nuclear attack. But costly or no, vulnerable or no, they are the most significant way of projecting power across the globe. And anyhow, isn't everything else vulnerable in the nuclear age?

He wanted the aircraft-carrier USS *John F. Kennedy* to be nuclear powered. Robert McNamara, then the Defense Secretary, was opposed to the idea both on technical grounds and because what Rick wanted was so costly that it would affect other priorities in the defence budget. The case was debated in congressional hearings, Rick feeding his political friends questions with which to oppose McNamara. When the decision went in the latter's favour, it did so at the cost of an undertaking that the three giant carriers which would follow the *John F. Kennedy* would be nuclear powered. That was the way Rick worked.

His freedom to oppose the Secretary of Defense derived from his appointment as an official of the Atomic Energy Commission. As an admiral in BuShips, it would not have been possible for him to behave as he did. Assured of powerful congressional support, he also engaged in a fierce battle with the Defense Department in promoting the SSN 688 class of fast nuclear submarines. The department was opposed both because there was not enough money to pay for the new vessels, and because there was reason to doubt that Rick's design of a more powerful and therefore heavier reactor – which would call for a larger submarine – was the best way to meet the operational requirements of speed and reduced noise at depth. The Defense Secretary's staff had therefore launched their own enquiries to find a better solution to the problem.

Rick would have none of it. It so happened that the CNO of the day was ready to back him against the Defense Secretary, and with the concurrence of the relevant congressional committees, a commission of seven submarine commanders – all of them, as it turned out, loyal members of the 'Rickover navy' – was set up to consider the arguments. The only way they could see of putting the heavy reactor to use was by 'shaving' the thickness of the hull and by making other changes that reduced weight. The commission's design, using Rickover's new reactor, won the day. But the Navy paid a critical penalty for Rick's victory. The depth at which the new submarine could cruise could no longer meet the operational requirement of 1,000 feet plus. Rick's victory also led to other penalties – delays in construction and vast 'cost overruns'.

On paper, Rick was technically responsible only for reactor design and reactor safety. He saw to it, however, that the consideration of safety dominated every other aspect of submarine design. As a consequence of his successful crusade for costly nuclear-powered vessels, the Navy's shipbuilding programme not surprisingly became distorted in ways that the Navy chiefs found highly undesirable. But with Rick's hold on Congress, there was little that they could do. He had become a one-man national institution. They could neither retire him nor fail to promote him.

A Stormy Retirement

But there had to be an end. By the time Rick reached his eighties, there were worries that while mentally as alert and pugnacious as ever, he was not physically up to the job of putting new submarines through their sea trials. Not only the Navy but also congressional leaders were tiring of his battle to stop cost-overruns being settled in the way they were. John Lehman, the man who was appointed Navy Secretary when Ronald Reagan became President in 1981, and who had previously been in the arms-consultancy business, made the task of getting rid of Rick almost his first priority, as it also was for the White House. Rick had become a danger to the Navy. Since many of his powerful congressional supporters had departed the scene, the time was also now ripe to retire him. Over the years, Rick, so Lehman charged, had accepted and even solicited gifts from his contractors to the tune of some $80,000, an average of nearly

$3,000 a year. The gifts, as spelt out, were mostly trivial items such as the special fruits and fresh fish that Rick demanded should be ready for him when he put a new submarine through its sea trials. The list, which especially detailed some items of ladies' jewellery, also included the not very attractive pieces of cheap silver or silver plate that commemorated keel-laying and launching ceremonies. The pieces he sent me of the latter became quite a collection. Rick received a 'public censure' and was informed that he was being retired from the service.

The final scene was truly remarkable. To soften the blow of his dismissal, the Navy Secretary arranged that President Reagan would say some nice things to Rick on his retirement. When on the appointed day Lehman arrived at the reception-room in the White House, he went up to Rick and offered his hand. According to the verbatim account he wrote immediately after the meeting, Rick said, 'What the hell are you doing here' and then 'launched into a stream of vituperation' in front of a number of people who were also waiting their turn to see the President.[5]

When the two entered the Oval Office, the President had with him Caspar Weinberger, the Defense Secretary, and Jim Baker, the President's Chief of Staff (later President Bush's Secretary of State), as well as the President's national security adviser. Formal photographs having been taken, the President, in accordance with his brief, began to compliment Rick on his great achievements. Rick suddenly interrupted, asking: 'Well, if that is so, then why are you firing me?' When the President replied that the Pentagon had recommended that it was 'time for a transition', Rick pointed to Weinberger and Lehman, saying: 'Then they are lying; they told me that you ordered me fired.' Lehman immediately interrupted by saying, 'Mr President, that is absolutely not true', whereupon Rick embarked upon a fierce tirade against Lehman, beginning by calling him a 'piss-ant'. When the President tried to calm him, Rick turned on him and shouted: 'Are you a man? Can't you make decisions yourself? What do you know about this problem? These people are lying to you. You won't get away with this. You won't get away without this hurting you. Don't you think that people aren't already using this against you? They say you are too old, and that you're not up to the job either.'

The President again tried to calm Rick, who then presented him with some papers, saying: 'Mr President, I want you to read these papers. They are on a number of subjects, and this one here is on how to run the presidency. I have given this paper to President Nixon and he liked it very much, and I gave it to President Carter and he liked it very much.'

Rick then resumed his tirade against Weinberger and Lehman, and this

5. John F. Lehman Jr, *Command of the Seas* (New York: Scribner's, 1988).

time, when the President put in some conciliatory words, Rick stopped him with the words, 'Aw cut the crap'. The others in the room then tried to bring the meeting to an end, but Rick again turned on the President, saying: 'Are you a man or not? I thought this was to be a meeting between you and me. I want to speak to you alone.' The President motioned the others to leave, and allowed Rick a further fifteen minutes. Lehman says that the President later told Weinberger that Rick had continued along the same lines as before, breaking off only when Jim Baker went in to remind the President about his next engagement.

Lehman also says that Rick came out of the Oval Office smiling, and went up to him to offer him a lift back to the Pentagon. Overwhelmed by the disastrous turn his initiative had taken, it is not surprising that the Navy Secretary declined the invitation.

The Chip on the Shoulder

When I read this account of Rick's final appearance in the White House – he must have been there many times before – I felt that I understood his extraordinary behaviour. Humiliated for years at the start of his career, he now felt he was being humiliated at its end. I kept wondering whether the grand dinner given in his honour a few weeks later, and attended by ex-Presidents Nixon, Ford and Carter, made up for what he must have felt in the Oval Office. I should have loved to have seen his face on that occasion but, although he had seen to it that I was invited, I could not be there.

Anti-Semitism, as John Lehman writes, was rife in the US in the twenties and thirties – not only in the services, but in the universities, industry and commerce. Many hotels and holiday resorts were out of bounds to Jews. Golf and other clubs were closed to them. Unlike Rabi who had been unaffected by the anti-Semitism he had taken for granted, the highly sensitive Rick was deeply bruised when he became prey to it in Annapolis. The experience had scarred him. It is easy now to understand that he stored up resentment as he went along, until the moment came when he was given command of the *Finch*. That was his first opportunity to let it all burst out. Ever after, it went on doing so.

Ruth Masters, his first wife, appreciated his great qualities, and she too undoubtedly shared the resentment and humiliation he felt because of the hostility he had engendered. It would have been the correct thing for her to be asked to 'sponsor' one of his ships – in all he was responsible for the building of some 150 nuclear-powered vessels. Time after time she was passed over, and when an invitation finally came towards the end of her life, she and Rick decided that it should be declined. To accept it would have been another humiliation. Her belief in him was unbounded. I felt that she always saw him standing head and shoulders above other men both in intelligence and in the ability to get things done. On the first occasion that Rick arranged a dinner party for me, the other guests were Gerard Smith and his wife, and a Supreme Court judge with his. Before sitting down to the table, we were having drinks in the apartment adjacent to the one in which they lived, and in which the Rickovers kept their library. On one wall was an enlarged photograph of the nuclear aircraft-carrier *Enterprise* with the ratings lined up on the deck in the form of the equation $E = mc^2$. When the judge's wife asked me what it meant, I replied that it was Einstein's famous equation, a foundation stone of nuclear physics, and that without it there would have been no nuclear navy. I was unaware that Mrs Rickover, a tall, strongly built woman, was standing just behind me. She tapped me on the shoulder, saying: 'And what about my husband.' I felt that in her eyes Rick's brain was at least the equal of Einstein's.

After the *Finch* it was BuShips electrical division that gave him a yet bigger opportunity to humiliate people who worked under him. Consciously or unconsciously, he sought to get even with those who had made him suffer, and at the same time to show that, when it came to getting things done, no one was his equal. At congressional hearings he was often inclined to wave the flag somewhat ostentatiously, but I also feel that he was truly animated by a deep patriotism, and that on such occasions he genuinely wanted to show that a first-generation American could be as devoted to his country as any native-born citizen. He threw his weight around more and more as his confidence grew. He started to overdo things, to regard himself as infallible, to make aggression a habit, and to be contemptuous of the views of those who stood in his way. Backed by the high regard in which he was held by congressional committees, mostly comprising men whose professional life was politics, not science or engineering or education, he began to overreach himself.

It was not only the presidency that he knew how to run. On my retirement in 1971 from my full-time appointment as chief scientific adviser to the British Government, Edward Heath, the Prime Minister, gave a dinner in my honour. I had nothing to do with the choice of guests, and when I arrived at Downing Street I was delighted to see Rick and two of my other American friends in the company. When we rose from the table, Rick came up and said to me: 'I'm now going to tell Heath how to govern your country.' And within a few minutes, there he was, earnestly pouring words into the Prime Minister's ear.

The Spartan offices in which Rick worked did not worry him, and I think it gave him pleasure that they showed up the relative splendour which surrounded the naval hierarchy in the Pentagon. When I first met him, his office was in one of the First World War temporary huts that lined part of Constitution Avenue in Washington. It was small and, apart from his desk, the only furniture was a deal table and a small, crammed bookcase. A second door in the room opened into a small store-room lined with shelves full of odds and ends, such as the boxes of presentation cigars that were handed out to mark the launching of a ship. On the wall of his office was a plaque that bore the words *Battles are won in the engine room*, beneath which was the name of the author, the First World War British admiral, Lord Jellicoe, the victor of Jutland. The linoleum that covered the floor was patched, and some patches were themselves patched. On my many visits to Washington, and until President Nixon ordered the demolition of the 'temporary' huts, I almost always lunched with Rick in this office on the meagre fare that a secretary would bring in. There was no question of choice. I can remember only bread, soup and an apple cut into thin slices. At the end of my visit, he would always ask whether I needed anything, and before I could say no, he would go into his store-room and say, take this, and this, and this, gifts which he would then get one of the girls in his large outer office to mail to me.

Looking at the volumes on history and military affairs crowded into his bookcase, and remembering his library at home, I wondered when he could ever have time to read, and then I recalled that Mrs Rickover was always there in the background. She must have been his second pair of eyes and hands. Our conversations would range widely, with Rick generalizing on a host of subjects, but never about the arts. Pictures, music, novels, the theatre seemed to be outside his field of intellectual interest, as they mostly were outside Mountbatten's. Maybe he had no time to spare for them. His talk often included the condemnation of somebody or other by whom he was being frustrated or who was leading the world astray. Once when he was dilating on the stupidity of those who did not recognize the value of nuclear propulsion, I asked whether he really believed in the possibility of an East/West nuclear conflict now that the price could be a Soviet ICBM onslaught that devastated the US. 'No, I don't,' he replied. 'That's why I agree with what you have been saying about Nato policy all these years. Nothing would make me happier than to think that all our nuclear boats were lying in the deepest crevice in the floor of the Atlantic.' I used to wonder whether he ever expressed the same sentiment to others.

Sometimes Rick allowed his aggressiveness to slip unnecessarily into extraordinary bad manners with strangers. The first time he visited me in England was when I still held a chair in Birmingham University and had a house in the city. The second was in Norfolk, where we had a summer home. When I picked him up at a big RAF airfield some 15 miles from where we lived, he stepped out of the small aircraft that had brought him from Holy Loch, with the station commander, a group captain, together with two of his officers, standing to attention nearby. As they saluted smartly with their white-gloved hands, Rick waved to them disdainfully, saying: 'We can't afford that kind of crap in the States. Where's your car?' He would not even allow me to present the officers to him. The small village in which I live happens to be the birthplace of Horatio Nelson, the victor of Trafalgar. As we entered the village, I pointed to the site of the rectory where Nelson was born. Rick merely glanced at it and went on talking. Perhaps our national hero did not fit into his hall of fame.

He had started talking about the British nuclear submarine programme from the moment we got into my car. The subject always interested him because it had its definitive start when the British Government bought an entire Skipjack propulsion plant from the United States. Because of his consuming fear of the danger of American secrets falling into foreign hands, Rick could have prevented the purchase. In fact, in 1955 he himself had suggested to the British admiral who was then in charge of submarines that the US could provide the know-how which could overcome many of the development difficulties with which the Royal Navy was at the time contending.

The exchange of information about defence matters, including nuclear propulsion, had been made legal under agreements between the US and the UK that were concluded in 1954. These, and a US/UK military atomic co-operation agreement the following year, had made it possible for Rickover to allow a team of UK engineers and scientists to visit the US in 1957 and to be shown what his organization was doing. Dickie Mountbatten, as First Sea Lord, must have been informed about and authorized the visit although, as I have explained, it is difficult to reconcile the stories of his relations with Rickover with the facts. The team was led by a Rear-Admiral Wilson, and one of its members was the physicist B.T. ('Terry') Price, who later became a close colleague of mine. His description of what happened on the visit shows Rickover at his most eccentric. Wilson was asked to give an outline of the British nuclear propulsion programme, and had not spoken for more than ten minutes before Rickover brought his fist down on to the table, saying: 'Wilson, you have the valour of ignorance.' From that moment he could not have been more helpful. He arranged a tour of the main establishments where his programme of work was being carried out, and wherever they went the UK team were told everything they wanted to know. Realizing that the British team were travelling on a very meagre allowance, Rickover wherever possible arranged cheap accommodation for them.

But it was the last day of the tour that must have been the most memorable. The team had assembled in Rickover's hutted headquarters on Constitution Avenue, and after spending some time in final talks with members of his staff, all sat down for a frugal lunch at tables arranged in the form of a U. From this point, I cannot do better than quote verbatim the account with which Terry Price later provided me.

Promptly at noon Rickover returned. 'Gentlemen, will you please stand.' In came his attractive secretary, Sally Higgins, who clasped her hands demurely and sang, without accompaniment. 'The Star-Spangled Banner' and 'God Save the Queen'. We sat down. The British looked at each other, and thought, 'How nice'.

The girls brought in fried chicken in cardboard boxes and soft drinks, and we settled down to a no-trimmings meal. We were nearing the end when Rickover came back into the long room in which we had met, and said, 'Sally, sing them your State song.' Sally sang 'Song of Georgia'. She had an excellent soprano voice, and once again the British looked pleased. Before long Rickover said: 'Sing them some songs of England.' Sally sang 'D'you ken John Peel', and 'Drink to me only with thine eyes'. After another few minutes Rickover made a fresh request: 'Sing them that thing about the Lord is my Shepherd.' Sally sang a metrical paraphrase of the twenty-third psalm.

By now the British were, so to speak, sitting to attention on the edge of their chairs, hardly daring to move a muscle lest offence might be caused. Then followed a memorable closing exchange.

Rickover (to us all): 'Sally's a good girl, aren't you Sally?'
'Yes sir.'
'And you go to church, don't you Sally?'
'Yes sir.'
'Do you pray?'
'Yes sir.'
'Whom do you pray for?'
'My father and mother, sir.'
'Don't you pray for me?'
'No sir.' After a moment's thought she added, with great emphasis: 'but in future I shall.'

The tension broke. We laughed. The meeting was quickly concluded, and we left, with feelings of extraordinary gratitude to our eccentric host.

The following year Rickover spoke out strongly in support of what is known as the 1958 amendment to the Atomic Energy Act of 1954, an amendment that made the sale of the Skipjack propulsion plant to the UK legally possible. Later, in the early sixties, he again provided help when the Royal Navy got into trouble after it had made changes in the pressure-tubing and valves of the design it had bought. I was sent over to persuade him to provide the necessary materials to make good the damage. He agreed, somewhat reluctantly, saying that it wasn't his business to run the Royal Navy. He had enough on his hands with the American. But he kept his word.

A few years later, the then British Navy Minister, Lord Jellicoe, the son of the Jellicoe whose words were on the plaque in Rick's office, paid him a courtesy visit, accompanied by a small party that included two British admirals. Rick was at his surliest, and conversation soon faded away. To break the silence one of the visiting admirals asked whether Rick thought there was a future for nuclear propulsion in merchant vessels. Rick asked whether the officer knew what he was talking about. 'No', came the honest answer. 'Then don't ask stupid questions,' said Rick. When I next saw him, I told him that I had been given an account of the visit, and asked, pointing to the plaque on his wall, why he had been so rude. It turned out that he had known all the time that the Jellicoe who had visited him was the son of the hero of Jutland. 'What do you want?' Rick asked. 'Do you want me to apologize?' And we passed on to another subject.

On another occasion he was unnecessarily rude to a senior British admiral. Admiral Sir Michael Le Fanu, a delightful man who was soon to be Chief of Naval Staff, was visiting the Pentagon. He also wanted to see Rick, but was kept waiting for an appointment for a full week. When one Saturday afternoon he was ushered into Rick's office, Rick began by saying that he was authorized by the US Government to negotiate with Le Fanu on such matters as he wished to raise. 'Have you the authority of the British Government?' Le Fanu replied that he was no plenipotentiary. He was soon shown the door.

Lastly, in 1966, there was an unfortunate meeting with Chrisopher Mayhew, the then British Navy Secretary, about radioactive levels in the Holy Loch – a sensitive political matter in the UK. Rick had spent the previous night with me, and I had had to arrange the get-together for a Sunday afternoon. It was a stormy meeting. Rick had never met Mayhew before and tried to take charge of the meeting and berate the minister who, however, wasted no time in letting Rick know that it was he who was in charge. We broke up inconclusively, Rick having said to Mayhew: 'Call yourself a politician? You know nothing about politics. We'll show you.'

Not surprisingly, the Royal Navy developed a dislike of Rick that all but equalled that of the US Navy. Secretly this must have irked him. He made it quite plain to me that he was dismayed when the British Government awarded Admiral Levering Smith an honorary knighthood for the help he had given the UK in implementing its Polaris programme. He reminded me that in 1955 it was he who had suggested that the US could save the UK a lot of money and time by providing know-how about nuclear propulsion. He sent me a copy of his favourable testimony to the congressional hearing that led to the amendment of the Atomic Energy Act without which it would have been illegal for the US to pass information about nuclear propulsion to the UK. He also reminded me that unless he had said 'Yes', the British Government would never have been allowed to purchase the Skipjack unit that formed the prototype of the UK's nuclear propulsion plants. He clearly felt that he should be honoured as Levering Smith had been.

But neither my advocacy, powerfully reinforced by that of Dickie Mountbatten, a man whom Rick greatly admired, nor that of the then UK ambassador in Washington, succeeded in getting the support of the Royal Navy. They were not going to see Rick made an honorary knight. It was enough that he had been among those in BuShips who, for help that they had given the UK during the Second World War, had been awarded the lower honorary rank of Commander.

So far as I can discover, Rick was not awarded any major US honour until he was nearing sixty. From then on honours were showered on him, the most prestigious of which, after his two congressional gold medals, being the Fermi Award for contributions to nuclear technology. Previous recipients had in the main been distinguished nuclear physicists, among whom he had few, if any, friends. When honours started flowing, one can only assume that, like his promotion to Rear-Admiral, he treated them as another sign that he had won against those who had stood in his way in the first half of his career.

The Private Man

The welcome he customarily received from congressional committees must also have been balm to his soul. Most of his many appearances concerned nuclear matters, budget appropriations and the economics of defence policy and procurement. Another main topic was education, a subject about which he was always eloquent as he complained about the inadequacies of American school education as compared with the Swiss and British systems, particularly the Swiss, about which he wrote a book. His appearances seem to have been always looked forward to by the committees, and after what was usually a somewhat obsequious beginning, his testimony was always delivered with eloquence, erudition and sparks of wit. The Congressmen and senators must have been amazed by his many allusions to classical and modern literature, for Rick had a fabulous memory, and while he may not have studied the works to which he so often referred, he certainly remembered various apt quotations. It was clearly Ruth Masters, his first wife, who had enlarged his knowledge of literature, and who helped, if not ghosted, some of his general writings. He acknowledged this in the dedication of his book *Eminent Americans: Namesakes of the Polaris Submarine Fleet*, which was published by the US Congress in 1972, the year after her death. It reads: 'This book is a memorial to my wife, Ruth Masters Rickover, who gave me immeasurable assistance in preparing the text. She was at once the most human and intelligent person I ever knew, the greatest influence on my life and work. To borrow from Tibullus: *Tu mihi curarum requies, tu nocte vel atra lumen, et in solis tu mihi turba locis.*'

I do not know when it was that Rick began the practice, but after returning from the first sea trials of his ships he started to send to a number of people an abbreviated version of the chapters that make up the book. I have a few, as well as of cards commemorating the keel-laying and launching of his ships, and also of invitations to attend the associated ceremonies – which, alas, I was never able to do. Until the practice was quickly stopped, he also sent to his commanders in the nuclear navy his own political and military appreciations of the way the Vietnam war was progressing.

Rick also sent me some of the many addresses he gave to various institutions, and these, although stamped with his fervour, also bear the mark of his wife's interests. One, entitled 'Liberty, Science and Law', begins by declaring that the US no longer has men of the quality of the Founding Fathers. Each generation, he declared, has to defend liberty against new perils. Society must not allow itself to be crushed by bureaucratic power, and so on. Another address is devoted solely to the topic of 'Democracy and Bureaucracy'. I arranged for him to give two addresses in the UK. The first, not a very profound one, was on the occasion when in 1965 he was awarded the honorary degree of D.Sc. by Birmingham University, of which I was still a professor. It was entitled 'The Meaning of a University', and one of its sentences seems to sum up Rick's picture of himself: 'Being born bright is pure luck, but to complete the long and tough course of studies that brings this special gift to fruition is a personal achievement – the kind of victory in which everyone can rejoice, for it is won on individual resources alone, with no aid from social, material or technical props.' The second, delivered in the same year in the Guildhall of the City of London, had the title 'A Humanistic Technology'. It was later published in the journal *Nature*. Rereading these pieces I am impressed by their lucidity, but have to confess that none conveys ideas that are truly original. What they do is display Rick's ethic: relentless duty to society, hard work and integrity.

I also find it odd that nowhere do they reflect the subtlety of his mind, and the lightness of touch of which he was capable. Rick's sense of humour may have been brutal when he interviewed candidates for his navy, but there was another side to it, as his farewell to the visiting British team in 1957 demonstrated. I could cite many examples that came my way, but one stands out in particular. At the time of one of his visits to me in Norfolk, I was trying to set a weather-vane – wind-vane to sailors – on the roof of my house, and had been reading an article which among other things explained the difference between true north and magnetic north. When I told him that I was trying to set the vane to true north, he asked what difference did it make either way. Was I intending to set sail in my house to some distant land? I laughed, and we started to talk of other matters. Months later a big wooden crate was delivered to the house. It contained an old ship's compass, obviously from some ancient sailing vessel, with a note saying that it was sent with Admiral Rickover's compliments.

He never laughed out loud when he told his funnier stories. Sometimes he told them with a wistful smile. There was one that related to an inspection he paid to a US naval base in the Pacific. He had arrived in the early hours of the morning and was formally met at the airfield by a line of officers all smartly dressed in white, and whom he waved aside. When he got to the supply ship where he was to spend the rest of the night, he was shown to his quarters without, however, being greeted by a single officer. He started dialling one number after another on the telephone in his cabin, until a sleepy voice came from the ship's blacksmith. When the man identified himself, Rick ordered him to bring a sledge-hammer to his cabin. Surprised by the demand, the man brought the hammer and watched Rick as he banged on the nearest bulkhead until the whole ship's company had been awakened. Rick kept the hammer, suitably mounted, in his office.

I always thought that Rick saw me as a fellow-Jew who had been welcomed into, and become part of the British 'establishment', whereas he had had to create one for himself. But I cannot believe that I was the only one to whom he exposed his gentler as well as his rough side. I may well have been the only academic scientist whom he counted as a trusted friend, but there must have been some among his loyal staff to whom he revealed himself as he did to me. Probably he also counted as personal friends a few of his congressional admirers, and no doubt he had correspondents other than myself to whom he wrote as frequently as he did to me. When, after his death, I scanned through his many letters, it made me realize, as I always did when I was with him, just how wide his interests were.

Most were brief notes that covered a document which dealt with matters relating to nuclear propulsion. But there are several others, and the strange thing is that he never followed up a topic once I had replied to a letter in which it had been raised. For example, one letter covered an article about the nature of British universities. It was faulty in many respects, and I answered at length. That was the end of the matter. There was no further comment from him. There was another that covered a report he had had from a naval medical officer about the prevalence of the killing African helminthic disease, schistosomiasis. His letter ended: 'Since schistosomiasis is the leading chronic infectious disease in the world our ignorance concerning it serves as a good example of how American medicine is not keeping up with the rest of our society in assuming a position of helpful leadership.' The subject was one that had already interested me, and I replied at some length. Again, no follow-up. He wrote making observations about the ritual of Christmas, and I enlarged on the topic by referring to the festivals that are associated world-wide with the solstices and equinoxes and the seasons, pointing out that, so far as I knew, there had been no festival associated with the northern winter solstice among the peoples of South Africa until the advent of the white man. The same thing – no further comment.

Another letter in my files is a copy of one sent him by John Freeman, when he was UK Ambassador in Washington. Freeman sent it to me knowing of my close relationship with Rick. The two had lunched together and Rick had raised the matter of the textual origins of the Lord's Prayer, focusing particularly on the possible source and date of the 'inscription' which usually appears at its end in the Anglican liturgy. Freeman made several enquiries and sent Rick a lengthy letter in which he retailed his somewhat inconclusive researches. I never received any further letter about the question. Perhaps it was another of those inconsequent interests which had captured Rick's attention for a brief moment.

It was as though Rick picked up a subject that had caught his attention, turned it over for a moment, and then found himself asking questions about some new topic. In 1974 he read a newspaper article that reopened the question whether the sinking of the US battleship *Maine* in Havana harbour in 1898 – one of the triggers of the Spanish-American War – was due to a Spanish mine or to an internal explosion. Two years later he published a book[6] in which he meticulously examined all the evidence that

6. *How the Battleship Maine Was Destroyed* (Washington, DC: Department of the Navy, Naval History Division, 1976).

had been considered by two official naval enquiries which had concluded that a mine was responsible. The book is part technical, part historical, and I imagine that when Rick embarked on his research the former was his dominant interest. But the conclusion to which his enquiry led him reinforced his constant cry for technical competence and understanding. Had the courts of enquiry decided, as he had, that the *Maine* did not sink as a result of the explosion of an enemy mine, war with Spain might have been avoided. 'In the modern technological age,' he concluded,

the battle cry 'Remember the *Maine*' should have a special meaning for us. With almost instantaneous communications that can command weapons of unprecedented power, we can no longer approach technical problems with the casualness and confidence held by Americans in 1898. The *Maine* should impress us that technical problems must be examined by competent and qualified people; and that the results of their investigation must be fully and fairly presented to their fellow citizens.

Rick always delved deeply into subjects that were related to his professional concerns. But none the less he was not an intellectual in any academic sense, a calling which he would castigate as made up of people who could develop theories without ever having the responsibility of testing them in practice. He was an engineer concerned with practical matters.

Nor was Rick a religious man in any accepted sense of the term. He did not attend religious services. He swore, he cursed, and with few exceptions seems to have expected that his staff should follow his example and, regardless of their own religious habits, work on Saturdays and Sundays. He discussed religion in 1974 during one of his appearances before a congressional committee. Among his many statements, he remarked that it makes little difference what particular religion a man follows. What religion does is provide 'for a feeling of belonging in the broadest sense'.

At least for the first half of his life his peers had made him feel that he did not belong. He married Ruth Masters in a church ceremony and, according to Polmar and Allen, simply wrote to his parents saying that he was renouncing Judaism. From then on he described himself as an Episcopalian, although there appears to be no record that he was ever formally received into the Church by baptism. But his marriage did not make him 'belong' any more than he had before. Ruth Masters simply had to share his concerns. Rick's second wife, and widow, is a Catholic, and that being so, their marriage took place in accordance with Catholic ritual. But Rick never did forget that he was a Jew, and experience must have taught him that whatever religion he chose to espouse, that was the way he was regarded in the world in which he moved.

The county of Norfolk where I live is famous for its hundreds of magnificent medieval parish churches, and one autumn afternoon when Rick was staying with us I took him for a short drive, stopping at one point at a small eleventh century, round-towered church which, before the silting of estuaries on the coast, had looked out directly on to the North Sea. For some years during the second half of the eighteenth century Horatio Nelson's father had been its rector. There was no one else in the church and Rick walked around silently, spending some time in front of the church's famous fifteenth-century painted pulpit. There was a look of awe and reverence on his face, and after we drove away it was many minutes before he said a word. I wondered whether he was thinking of those thousands of people who over the centuries had worshipped there and had belonged?

When he died in 1986, he was given a private burial in Arlington National Cemetery, and a few days later a memorial service was held at the National Cathedral. It followed traditional lines, including a eulogy delivered by an admiral who was one of Rick's few naval admirers. I wonder whether, if Rick had been looking down from above, he would have felt that at last he really did belong.

After his retirement in 1982, Rick invited me to join the board of trustees of a charitable foundation he had set up under his own name, and partly with his own money, for the purpose of furthering both 'excellence and integrity in business, science and education' and the preservation of world peace. It was almost a parallel to Dickie Mountbatten's World Colleges. I continued to see him, but two years later he suffered a serious stroke, though one that did not impair his mental faculties. Then one day I received a letter from Admiral Inman, an ex-deputy director of Central Intelligence who had been appointed vice-chairman of Rickover's board of trustees, saying that Rickover had decided that his name should be removed from the foundation he had set up. The letter covered a copy of a formal deposition, which Rick had signed with a cross, with a lawyer's note attesting that the 'signature' was genuine. A few months later he was dead. Admiral Inman never replied to a letter in which I asked whether, now that Rick had gone, there was any reason why the trustees should not restore his name to the foundation. I still wonder why Rick wanted to disappear as anonymously from the public scene as he had entered it, but which his presence had enlivened for so many years.

If there had been no Rick, the United States would still have built a nuclear navy. Yet if Rick had been allowed to 'belong' when he was at Annapolis, his career might never have touched the fringes of nuclear power. But Rick did not belong, and so became the man he was. Fortune moved him on to the nuclear path. His determination, his genius as an engineer and manager, the pugnacity that was fuelled by resentment, together provided the US with a fleet of nuclear-powered ships which without him it would never have had in the time before he died – four nuclear-propelled aircraft-carriers, nine missile cruisers, and some 130 nuclear-powered submarines.

A senior British admiral once wrote to me that Rick was 'conceited, arrogant, self-centred and impossibly rude'. All this was true. But inside Rick there also lurked a sensitive man who nourished a hurt which success never assuaged, and whose differences from other mortals made him unique in the society in which he spent his life, and which he did so much to change.

Index

* * *

Bold figures denote main entries

Acheson, Dean, 15, 27, 46, 47
Anderson, Sir John, 26
André, Gérard, 165
anti-Semitism, 40, 41, 172, 181, 185
Antrim, Earl of, 137
Appleton, E.V., 21
Ardennes offensive, 87–8, 92, 119
Arnold, General H.H., 101, 102, 110,
   111, 115, 116, 118, 119, 121–3
Atomic Energy Acts (US), 46, 151,
   189–91
Atomic Energy Commission (US), 46,
   48, 50, 124, 175–9
Atoms for Peace, 29, 37, 39, 49–50
Attlee, Clement, 26, 30, 32, 33, 92, 93,
   142, 143, 152

Barlow, Sir Alan, 30, 31
Baruch, Bernard, 27, 47, 49
Benn, Tony, 35, 36
Bernal, J.D., 23, 24, 136, 138–42
Bhabha, Homi, 36–7, 50
Blackett, Constanza, 14, 18, 26
Blackett, Lord, 13–38, 39, 47, 66n., 132,
   163–4
Blair, Clay, jr, 181
bombing policies, 23–4, 27, 79–92, 95,
   101–4, 108–20
bombing surveys, 78, 85, 88–91, 95,
   108, 127
Borden, William, 177
Bottomley, AM Sir Norman, 91n, 118,
   119
Boyle, ACM Sir Dermot, 145–6
Bradley, General Omar, 100, 117n.
Brereton, General Lewis, 74, 107, 108,
   123
Broadhurst, Air Comdr Harry, 103
Bureau of Ships (US), 173–6, 181, 182,
   186, 191

Burke, Admiral Arleigh, 151
Bush, Vannevar, 46
Byrnes, James, 46

Cabell, General C.P., 114
Carter, President, 184, 185
cavity magnetron, 22, 43–5
CERN, 29, 39, 49
Cherwell, Lord, 13, 19–25, 58, 69, 138
Churchill, Winston, 13, 19, 21, 23, 24,
   26, 58, 69, 71, 72, 73, 75, 82, 83, 90,
   92, 102, 110–11, 114, 120, 134–5, 138,
   139, 152, 154, 167, 168
Clutterbuck, General W.E., 104, 105
CND, 29, 163
Cockcroft, Sir John, 43
Combined Operations, 134–42
Coningham, AM Sir Arthur, 70–2, 74,
   75, 81, 107, 117n.
Cousins, Frank, 34–5
Crossman, Richard, 34
Cuban missile crisis, 157
Cudlipp, Hugh, 161–2
Curtis, General Edward P., 104, 105,
   120, 126

defence organization (UK), 97–8, 145,
   152–4
Defence Research Policy Committee,
   19n., 31, 153
Dieppe raid, 140
Doolittle, General J.H., 74, 120, 123
Douglas, ACM Sir Sholto, 75, 77, 168
Dresden raid, 120
Dulles, John Foster, 50

Eaker, General Ira, 101, 102, 104, 109,
   110, 115, 126
Economic Objectives Unit (US), 80, 83,
   91

198

Eden, Anthony, 134, 143–4
Eisenhower, General D.D., 25, 39,
    49–51, 56, 57, 59, 65, 66, 74–7, 79,
    81–4, 86, 87, 90–2, 100, 102, 104,
    106–8, 111, 112, 116, 118, 127, 151,
    165, 168
Elworthy, ACM Sir Charles, 151–2, 156

Fermi, Enrico, 47, 60
Festing, General Sir Francis, 146, 147,
    152, 156
Franck, James, 16, 17n.
Freeman, John, 194
Frisch, Otto, 25

Goodeve, Sir Charles, 138
Groves, General Leslie, 121–2, 174
Gunn, Ross, 174

Habbakuk, 137–9, 141
Hafstad, Lawrence, 176
Harding, General Lord, 146
Harris, ACM Sir Arthur, 65, 80–1, 83,
    84, 102, 110–20
Hasler, Major H.G., 140
Healey, Denis, 144n., 148, 154–6
Heath, Edward, 186
Hill, A.V., 18, 19, 21, 22, 42
Hopkins, Admiral Sir Frank, 155
Hull, General Sir Richard, 153, 156
Hussey, Capt. T.A., 135–7

Inman, Admiral B.R., 196
International Atomic Energy Agency,
    50

Jackson, Derek, 54–5
Jellicoe, Earl of, 190
Jenkins, Roy, 158
John, Admiral Sir Caspar, 146, 152,
    156

Kahn, Herman, 57
Kennan, George, 29
Kennedy, President, 57, 151, 157
Kenney, General George, 121, 122, 127
Killian, James, 51, 56
King, Cecil, 160–2
Kistiakowsky, George, 56, 57
Koepfli, Joe, 52

Lambe, Admiral Sir Charles, 145, 146
Le Fanu, Sir Michael, 190
Lehman, John, 183–4, 185
Leigh-Mallory, ACM Sir Trafford,
    79–83, 107, 111, 113–17
LeMay, General Curtis, 109, 124
Lilienthal, David, 15, 27, 46, 47
Longmore, Sir Arthur, 69, 70, 72
Lovell, Sir Bernard, 15, 17, 27–8, 34,
    37, 45
Lovett, Robert, 106
Luce, Admiral Sir David, 155

MacArthur, General Douglas, 121, 122,
    ' 127, 165
McMahon, Brien, 177
Macmillan, Harold, 144, 147, 149, 153,
    154, 157, 166, 167
McNamara, Robert, 182
Manhattan Project, 15, 17n., 26, 45, 48,
    121–2
Mayhew, Christopher, 155, 190
Mediterranean and Middle East
    campaigns, 70–80, 103–6, 108, 141–2
Melville, Sir Ronald, 147
Mills, Vice-Admiral, 175, 176, 181
Montgomery, General Sir Bernard, 73,
    79, 82, 84, 92, 94–5, 98, 117n., 127
Mountbatten, Edwina, 133, 134, 142,
    145, 146–7, 158
Mountbatten, Lord, 16, 17, 70, 71, 76,
    77, 96n., 103, 126–7, **131–68**, 187,
    188, 191, 196
Mulberry, 135, 137, 164
Mumma, Capt. A.G., 175, 176
Murphy, Peter, 132, 135

National Electronics Research Council,
    158–60
Nato Science Committee, 39, 52–6
Nehru, Jawaharlal, 36–7, 96n.
Nicholson, E.M., 31, 32
Nimitz, Admiral Chester, 121, 122,
    127, 175
Norstad, General Lauris, 54, 103–5,
    122
nuclear weapons/warfare, 15, 17n.,
    25–30, 32, 42, 46–50, 55–7, 93–4, 97,
    99, 121–7, 143–4, 148–51, 156–7,
    162–3, 187

Oliphant, Mark, 25, 44
Oppenheimer, J. Robert, 15, 27, 28, 41, 45–8, 52, 56, 176–7
Ormsby-Gore, David, 157
Overlord, 25, 76n., 79–92, 110–18

Peierls, Rudolf, 25, 41
Pelly, AVM Sir Claude, 95
Perutz, Max, 138–9
Pike, ACM Sir Thomas, 146, 149, 152
Pile, General Sir Frederick, 22
Piore, Emanuel, 59
Playfair, Sir Edward, 153
Polaris, 149, 151, 191
Portal, ACM Sir Charles, 69, 72, 73, 75, 76n., 78, 81–2, 87, 89–90, 92, 102, 110–12
Potsdam Conference, 50, 127, 164–6
President's Science Advisory Committee, 51, 52, 53, 55–7, 59, 156
Price, B.T., 188
Pyke, Geoffrey, 135–9, 167

Quesada, General E.R., 109

Rabi, Helen, 41
Rabi, Isidor I., 13, 15, 17, 27, 29, 34, 37, **39–62**, 177, 185
radar, 18–21, 43–5, 69
Ramsey, Norman, 46, 52
Randall, John, 44
Reagan, President, 60, 183, 184, 185
Rickover, Admiral H.G., 41, 131, 133, 150, 151, 155, 167–8, **169–97**
Rickover, Ruth, 172–3, 181, 185–7, 192, 195
Robb, AM Sir James, 86, 103, 104, 107, 141
Robertson, H.P., 39, 54
Roosevelt, President, 42, 75, 83, 114, 121, 134

Sabath, Adolph, 171
Sandys, Duncan, 144, 145, 148, 150, 153, 154
Scarman, Wing Comdr Leslie, 86, 98
science policy (UK), 30–7, 58–9
science policy (US), 46
Scott, Sir Robert, 153, 154, 157, 170
Skybolt, 149, 151
Slessor, ACM Sir John, 24, 25, 110

Smith, Gerard, 170, 186
Smith, Admiral Levering, 191
Snow, C.P., 18, 21n., 30, 58
Spaatz, General Carl, 65, 66, 68, 75–8, 80–2, 84, 93, 98, **99–127**, 141, 142, 165, 166
Spaatz, Ruth, 100, 104, 122, 123
Stephen, Adrian and Karin, 14
Stimson, Henry, 122
Strauss, Lewis, 48
submarines (and ships), nuclear powered, 150–1, 165, 174–83, 185–6, 188, 190–1, 196–7
Suez crisis, 97, 143–4, 164

Technology, Ministry of, 34–6, 158
Tedder, Lord, 19, 25, 50n., **65–98**, 102, 104, 106, 107, 108, 110–13, 115–19, 124, 125, 127, 134, 141, 142, 166–8
Tedder, Rosalinde, 67, 68, 73
Tedder, 'Toppy', 65, 78, 96, 98
Teller, Edward, 13, 41, 47–9, 177
Templer, General Sir Gerald, 144–6, 150, 153
Thorneycroft, Peter, 148, 149, 153–5, 157
Tizard, Sir Henry, 18–25, 31, 32, 42–4, 58, 69
Tots and Quots, 14, 32
Trenchard, ACM Lord, 27, 68, 101, 104
Truman, President, 46–9, 51, 95, 178

United World Colleges, 159–60, 196

Vandenberg, General Hoyt, 113–14, 122

Watkinson, Harold, 145, 148, 149, 152, 155
Watson-Watt, Sir Robert, 19, 21, 43
Wavell, General Sir Archibald, 72, 143, 166
Weinberger, Caspar, 184, 185
Welsh, AM Sir William, 74
Wernher, Sir Harold, 135, 138
Whitney, John Hay, 105, 160
Wiesner, Jerome B., 57, 149
Wigner, Eugene, 41, 49
Wilson, Harold, 28, 34–6, 147, 155, 160–1
Wimperis, H.E., 18–19, 43

Zumwalt, Admiral E.R., 178–9